THE BIG 50: PHILADELPHIA EAGLES

THE MEN AND MOMENTS THAT MADE THE PHILADELPHIA EAGLES

Mark Eckel

This book is available in quantity at special discounts for your group or organization. For further information, contact:

Triumph Books LLC
814 North Franklin Street
Chicago, Illinois 60610
(312) 337-0747
www.triumphbooks.com
Printed in USA.

ISBN: 978-1-62937-261-7

Design by Andy Hansen
Page production by Nord Compo
All photos are courtesy of AP Images.

This is for all the die-hard Eagles fans who have waited not-so-patiently for that elusive Super Bowl.

CONTENTS

1

FROM BOOS TO LOVE

It began when he was drafted to a serenade of boos and ended when the Eagles honored him at a retirement ceremony and he referred to himself in the "third number." Before or since, there has not been a more misunderstood or unappreciated athlete in Philadelphia than Donovan McNabb.

McNabb, who quarterbacked the Eagles from 1999 to 2009, owns franchise marks for most completions (2,801), passing yards (32,873), and touchdown passes (216); he also guided the team through its most successful run in the NFL's Super Bowl Era.

With McNabb the starter at quarterback, the Eagles made the playoffs eight of his 10 seasons—he didn't start as a rookie—and in one of the years they missed, 2005, he was hurt for nearly half of the season.

Of the franchise's 19 playoff wins, McNabb quarterbacked nine of them. Think about that for a minute. In 11 years McNabb won 10 playoff games. In the Eagles' other 72 years, as of 2016, they won 10 playoff games.

Still, the boos—which began when a radio station act that supported drafting Texas running back Ricky Williams on his 1999 Draft day and chorused all the way to the end, mocking his retirement speech in which he concluded, "No. 5 will always love you"—have been as much a part of his Eagles career as all of his successes. Maybe more. Simply because McNabb couldn't achieve what no other Eagles quarterback has done: win a Super Bowl.

"Primarily it's because we as a team didn't fulfill our potential and the quarterback is the one who gets the criticism," former Eagles linebacker Ike Reese, now a radio host in the city, said. "Those championship game losses weighed heavy on him. And the more we lost, the more of an issue it became.

"From the fan's side it was Donovan's fault, and that couldn't be further from the truth. And then when that blame got placed on him, he became resentful and felt unappreciated. So he needed to remind you [in his retirement speech] of what he did, and that didn't sit well with the fan base either."

Fans ranged from the typical blue-collar guy sitting in the upper deck of Veterans Stadium and later Lincoln Financial Field to heavyweight boxing champion and Philadelphia native Bernard Hopkins, who openly criticized McNabb. In 2007, Hopkins questioned McNabb's heart; the following year he questioned whether he had sacrificed enough to win, saying that he "lacked a killer instinct."

McNabb, in his 10 years as the Eagles starter, took the team to five NFC Championship Games, yet the team went 1–4 in those games, losing two at home where they were heavy favorites. And the one Super Bowl they did reach, Super Bowl XXXIX, they lost as well.

"It bothered me early [on]," McNabb said. "When you're young, you're first of all just trying to fit in. You want to be appreciated. Everything that you put yourself through during the off-season, during the year, you're winning games, making the playoffs and it's not good enough. Then it became, 'They lost because of Donovan.' So you're trying to find the reason why, when you go year in and year out winning games and you're not appreciated. I did a lot of things in the community, but I would hear that I never did anything. By my fourth year or so, I just didn't care what people thought. I felt like winning is everything, so let's just win. I reached out to kids and helped in the community, but I didn't make a big deal of it, because I just didn't care what anyone else thought anymore."

Others would say that McNabb always cared too much, and those boos on Draft day in 1999 were never forgotten. "That was my greatest moment, to hear my name called, walk across that stage and shake hands with Paul Tagliabue," McNabb says to this day. "And that's all I say."

And then the boos came. The radio station and most of the 30 members of the group that formed the chorus apologized to the quarterback as time passed. Still, the hurt lingered.

"He came in and wanted to be accepted," former Eagles cornerback and now NFL director of football operations Troy Vincent said. "He reminded everyone that this was the new era of Randall Cunningham in Philadelphia. There was a lot of pressure on him just from that. He was the missing piece, the quarterback that the team needed. Keep in mind, back then all the leaders on the team were on the defensive side of the ball. The offense was still trying to find its way. This was a defensive-dominated team both in play and in personality. That was difficult in what had become a quarterback-driven league. And it was on Donovan [to change that]."

McNabb took over quarterback duties from future Eagles head coach Doug Pederson at the end of that 1999 season. He became the full-time starter in 2000 and turned a 5–11 team into an 11–5 playoff team.

"You saw him mature as a player and a person," Vincent said of McNabb. "From the way he wore his hair—the cornrows were gone—to the way he dressed—his suits actually fit. It was all a

DONOVAN AND RUSH

It was September 28, 2003. The Eagles were about to get their first win of the season, at Buffalo, after an 0–2 start.

ESPN's *Sunday NFL Countdown*, featuring political analyst Rush Limbaugh that season, dropped a bombshell on the Eagles and quarterback Donovan McNabb. Limbaugh during the broadcast uttered the now infamous line when the conversation turned to the Eagles, their quarterback, and their 0–2 start to the season: "Sorry to say this, I don't think he's been that good from the get-go," Limbaugh began. "I think what we've had here is a little social concern in the NFL. The media has been very desirous that a black quarterback do well. There is a little hope invested in McNabb, and he got a lot of credit for the performance of this team that he didn't deserve. The defense carried this team."

McNabb didn't say much after the game, because he hadn't heard the comments himself. Then before that Wednesday's practice, the next time the team was together, he did. "It's somewhat shocking to hear that on national TV from him," McNabb said of Limbaugh's statement. "It's not something that I can sit here and say won't bother me."

It also bothered him that none of the other panelists at the time had his back. "I'm not pointing at anyone, but someone should have said something," McNabb said. "I wouldn't have cared if it was the cameraman."

Limbaugh, who resigned from the program the next day, apologized, but McNabb didn't want any part of it. "You can say you're sorry all you want. It doesn't matter," McNabb commented. "It's been said."

maturation process. And then we, as a team, rallied behind him, because as your quarterback goes, you go. Now, all of a sudden we're winning games. He's scoring late for us to win games, bringing us back to win games. We started to say to each other, just keep it close and No. 5 will lead us."

"No doubt about it," Reese said. "That's how we all felt as defensive players. If we could keep the game close, in the fourth quarter he'll find a way to make a play or two and we'll win. In his heyday, say from 2000 to 2005, he was one of the top quarterbacks in the NFL, right behind Tom Brady and Peyton Manning."

From 2001 to 2004 the team went to four straight NFC Championship Games, finally winning one in 2004 and then losing the Super Bowl. "Quarterbacks are always measured by Super Bowl wins," McNabb said. "Tom Brady has four. John Elway lost two, then came back and won two at the end. But I say quarterbacks should be measured by total wins and losses. Not every quarterback can take [his] team to a Super Bowl. It's not just one person. You need all the guys on the same page.

"I look at my career, it was a fun time for me. It was a dream come true for me to play in the NFL. I played the game because I loved it. And when you look back at a lot of our careers, for a decade we were probably the second- or third-best team in terms of winning percentage, and that's over an entire decade. There were a lot of teams that had one great year, maybe even won a Super Bowl, but then missed the playoffs the next few years. If we would have won a Super Bowl or two, we might be talking about a dynasty. Every year it was the Philadelphia Eagles as one of the best teams in the NFC."

Coming close, being good, but not good enough never sat well with an Eagles fan base that hadn't seen a championship since 1960. They would have easily traded a decade of success for that one Super Bowl trophy, or at least that's what they say.

"I would have loved to win the Super Bowl too," McNabb said. "Who wouldn't? But the way I handled things, on and off the field, I think it's helped make me who I am as a person, as a man. I wouldn't have done things any differently. The ups and down, the highs and lows, overcoming a lot of adversity, and to let it waver, I wouldn't have changed any of that."

The one thing he would have changed?

"If I could I probably would have hired a quarterbacks coach to work with me away from the facility to refine my game and to work on certain parts that needed it," he said. "We had great coaches, but it would have been good to have that other set of eyes [from someone] who was not getting paid by the organization."

After the Super Bowl season of 2004, McNabb and the Eagles got back to the NFC Championship Game in 2008, despite just a 9–6–1 regular-season mark, but lost to the Arizona Cardinals. Also, the team had drafted quarterback Kevin Kolb in the second round of the 2007 draft.

When the Eagles made the playoffs as a wild-card team in 2009 and lost to the Dallas Cowboys in the first round, that was finally it for the franchise's all-time quarterback. On Easter Sunday night in 2010, he was traded to the Washington Redskins. And as of 2016, the Eagles still haven't won a playoff game without McNabb at quarterback.

"As a player, it really affected me [in 2008]," McNabb said. "There was no communication when I was benched [at halftime] in the Baltimore game. There was no real communication all season.

"There [were] conversations even before that about Kevin Kolb getting some time. Then when I was benched, and with those conversations I never really knew what was happening. I came back and played the following Thursday night [against Arizona] and we won.

"I said then, I'm going to sit down with everyone—[head coach] Andy [Reid], [team president] Joe Banner—and see what's going on.

This had been building up, and I had seen it with other players. I had two years left on my deal, so a decision had to be made. They were either going to give me a new deal or trade me. Then the rumors started that if we didn't get to the second round, I was gone. Now, when you hear those rumors and they're out there—well, someone was putting them out there. And it wasn't by the players; I knew who it was. So going into the Dallas game the rumors picked up, and we lost.

DID HE GET SICK?

Just days after the Eagles lost Super Bowl XXXIX to the New England Patriots, former Eagles center Hank Fraley, on a radio show mentioned that quarterback Donovan McNabb threw up during the team's late-fourth-quarter drive (which, by the way, ended in a McNabb touchdown pass).

Wide receiver Freddie Mitchell, never a fan of his quarterback, backed up Fraley's claim in even more disparaging words, and a year later wide receiver Terrell Owens made it famous. "I wasn't the one who got sick in the Super Bowl," Owens said when asking for a new contract.

So *did* McNabb get sick? "People always focus on me supposedly throwing up," McNabb said. "[Patriots defensive end] Richard Seymour got me pretty good. I got hit in the face and my helmet went backwards and I had stuff in my face. I'm trying to catch my breath and get my vision back. I wasn't tired. I was getting killed."

And most everyone saw it.

"When you watch that game and you see the shots Donovan took," then–Eagles special teams coach and now Baltimore Ravens head coach John Harbaugh said. "It's incredible what he was able to do."

"Donovan was getting hit [on] every play and he just hung in there and hung in there and hung in there," guard Artis Hicks said. "It was crazy."

"I went home after that game and told my wife, 'This is it. I've seen this story before.' But what hurt was there was never any communication. They were calling other teams [for a trade] but not telling me about it. They reached out to both Buffalo and Oakland. What they didn't know was the Raiders' [offensive coordinator] at the time was Hue Jackson, and he's my cousin. He told me. And then I'm talking to Joe [Banner] and [team owner] Jeffrey [Lurie] and they're telling me, 'Don't worry about it.'"

The trade went through, and suddenly McNabb was wearing a different jersey. And when he came back to Veterans Stadium with the Redskins in 2010, he helped beat the Eagles 17–12.

He distanced himself from the organization until they retired his No. 5 jersey early during the 2013 season. "I said after I was traded [that] I would never step back in that building again," McNabb said. "I never wanted to step back there again. The only reason I came back, and I was still pissed off, was because of Brian Dawkins. He and I talked about it. I came back for Dawk."

2

THE LAST TITLE

Maybe only Chuck Bednarik can change the current Eagles' fortunes the way he once did back in 1960. Though this time it will have to be divine intervention.

Bednarik, before he passed away in 2015, less than two months shy of his 90th birthday, reflected on the fact that no Eagles team has won a NFL title since his team did so with a 17–13 win over Vince Lombardi's Green Bay Packers on December 26, 1960. "I am kind of surprised they haven't won again," Bednarik said. "When I die, I'll be up in heaven, and I'll do what I can to see they win one again."

Bednarik, along with quarterback Norm Van Brocklin and receivers Pete Retzlaff and Tommy McDonald, saw to it the Eagles won it in 1960. Head coach Buck Shaw had entered his third and final year as Eagles head coach in 1960, and Van Brocklin had been with him all three years. After a 2–9–1 campaign in 1958 there had been improvement by way of a 7–5 mark in '59. Hopes were high in 1960 for a team that had once gone back to back as champions in 1948 and 1949.

"There was just something about that [1960] team," McDonald remembered. "We lost our opener [to Cleveland], but then we got on a really good roll and you could just sense that something special was happening."

The Eagles lost at home at Franklin Field to Cleveland, 41–24. Jimmy Brown ran for 153 yards for the Browns—and he wasn't even the leading rusher. Bobby Mitchell ran for 156 yards and scored three touchdowns. Van Brocklin's three interceptions didn't help the Eagles' cause either.

Then Philadelphia didn't lose again for more than two months. It started with a 27–25 win at Dallas in Week 2 and the

Eagles rolled off nine straight wins, including a 31–29 revenge win over the Browns in Cleveland.

"They were a good team that had everything break its way," longtime Philadelphia sportswriter and Eagles historian Ray Didinger said. "They weren't the most talented team in the league, but they were good."

Van Brocklin passed for 2,471 yards and 24 touchdowns to make up for a running game that averaged just 3.2 yards per carry. Retzlaff caught a team-high 46 passes for a team-high 826 yards. McDonald (39 receptions for 801 yards) averaged 20.5 yards per catch and scored an amazing 13 touchdowns. And a defense that allowed an alarming 183.3 yards rushing per game and 4.9 yards per carry saved itself by forcing an incredible 45 turnovers (30 interceptions and 15 fumble recoveries) in just 12 games.

"They didn't run the ball well at all and the defense gave up a ton of yards," Didinger said. "But they had a great quarterback and a great passing game. And defensively, while they gave up a ton of yards, they took the ball away. And it was always at a time when they really needed it."

That nine-game winning streak, in which five games were decided by a touchdown or less, allowed the Eagles to pull away from the second-place Browns (8–3–1) in the Eastern Conference. When the Eagles ended the season with a 38–28 win over the Washington Redskins—a game in which Retzlaff, McDonald, and rookie Timmy Brown all had more than 100 yards receiving—all that was left to determine was who their opponent in the title game would be. Would it be the upstart Packers, under Lombardi in his second year as head coach, or a veteran Detroit Lions team that had won the title in 1957?

Green Bay's win against the Los Angeles Rams sealed the Western Conference title and set the stage for the NFL Championship Game for the day after Christmas in Philadelphia.

"It was one of those seesaw games," Bednarik said. "We led at halftime by a couple points [10–6]. They came back to take the lead, then we came back again. But with all the great players they had then—Bart Starr, Jimmy Taylor—we knew they weren't done."

Starr's seven-yard touchdown pass to Max McGee early in the fourth quarter gave Green Bay a 13–10 lead. Rookie Ted Dean, who had not scored a rushing touchdown on 113 carries during the entire regular season, scored on a five-yard run to put the Eagles back in front, 17–13, with five minutes to play. Dean's touchdown came on a play that Van Brocklin changed at the line of scrimmage.

"I knew Billy Barnes was going to get the ball," Dean said. "Everybody did. He was a good runner. I was just a rookie. And

LONG DROUGHTS

Where does the Eagles title drought rank among other NFL teams, or teams from the other three major team sports?

Heading into the 2016 season, only two NFL teams have gone longer between titles. The Cardinals last won one in 1947, when they were based in Chicago; the Detroit Lions last won in 1957.

Only two Major League Baseball teams have gone longer without a title: the Cleveland Indians (1948) and, of course, the long-suffering Chicago Cubs (1908). And only two NBA teams have gone longer: the Sacramento Kings (1951), when they were the Rochester Royals, and the Atlanta Hawks (1958).

No NHL team has gone longer than 1960 without a title.

that's what [Van Brocklin] called in the huddle. Now, we're walking up to the line and he yelled out 'Switch!' and changed the play. I can't speculate why he did it and I never asked him. He just had faith in me. I had fumbled earlier in the game and he knew I was hot about that because I rarely fumbled. Maybe that's why he gave me the ball."

Dean scored and the Eagles led, but the Packers didn't go down without a fight. Behind future Hall of Famers Starr and Taylor, Green Bay drove inside the Eagles red zone with precious seconds ticking off the clock. There was time for only one or maybe two plays. Starr dropped back and looked into the end zone where McGee, his primary receiver, was covered. He dumped it off to Taylor and let his star back try to do the rest. He almost did. He got to the 8-yard line, where he met Bednarik.

"Taylor caught the swing pass, put his head down, and started running," Bednarik said. "A couple of our guys tried to tackle him, but he was a big guy, tough to bring down. I had to make a play there or we would lose the game. I was the only one left between him and the end zone. I gave him a big bear-hug tackle up high and wrestled him to the ground."

And time expired.

"I'm on the ground, but I could see the time ticking away," Bednarik said. "Four, three, two, one, zero."

The Eagles were champions. As it turns out, they were also the only team ever to beat Lombardi, or Starr, in a playoff game. And the last Eagles team to win a title as of 2016.

Some Eagles fans call it the "Lombardi Curse"—that beating Lombardi meant never winning a Lombardi. "They've knocked on the door a lot of times," McDonald said. "They've gotten it about halfway open a few times, but they just haven't been able to get all the way through and win that Super Bowl. They have had their share of great players, and that's where it starts. But to win a championship, the right things have to happen. You have to be healthy. You have to get some breaks. You have to have the ball bounce your way, not the other guy's way. There is a lot that goes into winning it all."

Shaw retired as head coach after that 1960 title game and Van Brocklin retired as a player.

"I think it's the only time in history that a team won a championship and the head coach and quarterback both retired," Didinger said. "Coaches have retired after championships and quarterbacks have retired after championships, but I don't think there's ever been both."

They took the Eagles' last NFL title with them.

3

THE MINISTER OF DEFENSE

Here's all you need to know to understand just what kind of dominant player Reggie White was for the Philadelphia Eagles. It was a story, an actual story in the newspapers, when White did not get a sack in a game.

Whether the Eagles won or lost was inconsequential at that point. If White, the league's all-time sack leader when he retired, did not get a sack, the offensive lineman or linemen who blocked him would be interviewed. Meanwhile, White would have to answer questions such as, "What happened, Reggie?"

It didn't happen very often. In 121 games as an Eagle, White recorded 124 sacks. During the strike year of 1987, when he played in just 12 games, he had 21 sacks. That was just one shy of the record at the time held by the New York Jets' Mark Gastineau and just 1.5 off the current record of 21.5 achieved by the New York Giants' Michael Strahan in 2001. And he missed four games because of the strike.

"To see a man that big, that fast, that powerful, he made good offensive linemen look like they didn't belong in the league," former Eagles linebacker and teammate Garry Cobb said. "He would just totally dominate them, humiliate them. There were times where he just could not be blocked. Double-team, triple-team, it didn't matter, he was getting to the quarterback. I've never seen a guy like that before or after."

Twelve times in his first 14 years he had 10 sacks or more in a season, including 16 for the Green Bay Packers in 1998—when he was 37 years old. There really wasn't anyone else like him in the history of the game.

"When you have a guy who is six foot five, 290-something pounds and he runs like a linebacker, that is just a special person," former Eagles linebacker Seth Joyner said. "When I first got to the Eagles I really didn't know who Reggie was. I had heard his name from college but I didn't know him. But it's pretty evident when you get to a team who the great players are. Then you read up on him and learned about him. Reggie was certainly someone special. Then to actually be on the field with him and see how dominant he was, it was 'wow.' To see a guy with his speed and that power, those type of athletes are generational."

What White did, like a great point guard in basketball, was make the players around him better. The Eagles had their share of talented players on defense during that Buddy Ryan Era, and they may have been good even without White, but they were great with him.

"The first thing you could tell about Reggie, what stood out to me, was how he could run really well for a guy his size," former Eagles linebacker Mike Reichenbach said. "But not until we put the pads on could you tell how strong he was. And he wasn't a guy who spent a lot of time, or much time at all, in the weight room. He was just naturally blessed to play football. And he had that ability to change a game. He made the guys around him better. The offense had to double-team him every play. You could never let him go one on one. You would get killed."

So no team ever did. "When you play against great players and when you play with great players, it inspires you to be great, to be the best you can be," Joyner said. "Reggie was just a natural specimen. But his work ethic and his desire to be the best was infectious and rubbed off on everyone. It was especially true with us. Because as Buddy began to build the football team, from the talent level we had very talented players. When you have guys like Reggie and Clyde [Simmons] and Jerome [Brown] and Mike Pitts and Mike Golic, there was a healthy competition among all of us. When Reggie got a sack, Clyde wanted two; then Jerome wanted three. On football teams that healthy competition within the competition can be good, just as long

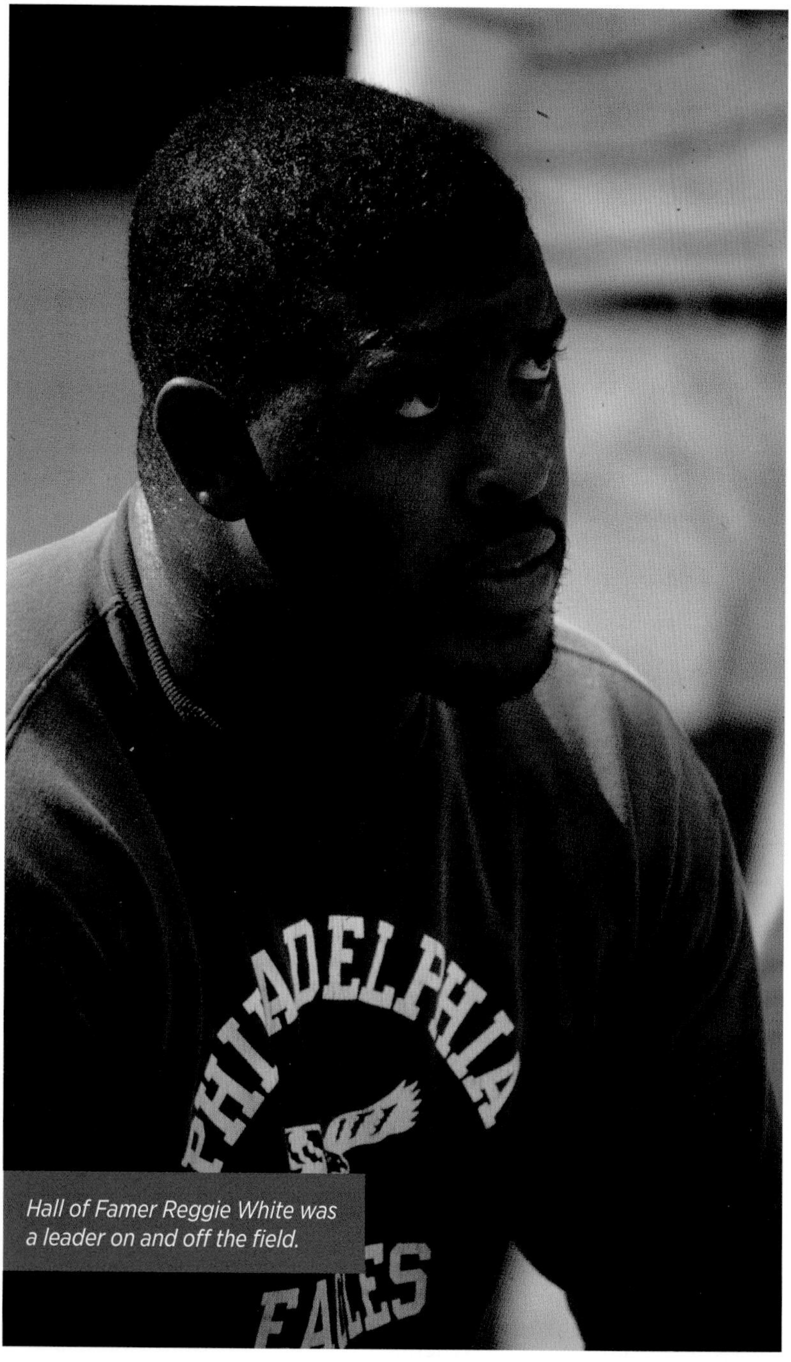

Hall of Famer Reggie White was a leader on and off the field.

as there's no animosity among teammates. I've seen that happen on other teams, where there was jealousy. We didn't have that at all. Not at all. On that rare occasion when I got two sacks and Reggie only had one, that was motivation for me, and Reggie was happy for me too. But you knew next week he wanted two."

White dominating an offensive lineman, taking over a game, and making plays became so commonplace that his teammates just expected it. And, like the writers who covered the team, they were shocked when it didn't happen. In the Eagles' playoff win over the New Orleans Saints, White's last win as an Eagle, he sacked quarterback Bobby Hebert for a safety that turned the game around and led to a 36–20 victory.

"I made sure to go over and say. 'Great play, Reg,' because with Reggie. whenever he made a big play, nobody ever said anything. We all just expected it," former Eagles cornerback Eric Allen said.

"I remember in 1988, my rookie year, he made a great play and I jumped on him, celebrating. After the game, he said, 'E.A., you're the first guy who's ever expressed his excitement about a play I made.' It wasn't that the guys didn't appreciate him. We were just used to it."

Yet White was appreciated, both on the field for his dominance and off the field for his Christian leadership. An ordained minister, White was there to help the younger players when they needed it. "Being an ordained minister, that was more of his calling, believe it or not, than football," Joyner said. "I always believed that. Football was his platform for his ministry. To be honest, it was tough at the beginning. He wanted to have that spiritual effect on us right from the start, and here you have a bunch of young 20-year-old guys who now have a little bit of money in their pocket for the first time in their life. That's not what they wanted to hear. Then Reggie got to a place where it was like, 'OK, guys, I'm here. Whenever you're ready for that part of your life and need some direction, I'm here,' instead of trying to cram it down our throats. And that was better for everyone. But there was no doubt about it he was the spiritual leader of our team."

Quarterback Randall Cunningham was one of those young players. He came in with Jheri curls, "dressed like Michael Jackson, when Michael was on stage," as Cobb remembered, and had a good-time, carefree attitude. "Playing with Reggie you got more than you bargained for," Cunningham said. "You're playing with the greatest defensive player in the history of the league, but then you've got a friend. Reggie was a guy who was more concerned about your soul than playing a football game. I think God used him as an instrument to get me out of where I was. I was bright-eyed, bushy-tailed, and lost. I was trying to figure out [myself], and Reggie pointed me to God. And that allowed me to become what they first called an enigma. But where I am today [Cunningham is a pastor and has his own church in Las Vegas], Reggie planted that seed. I owe a lot to Reggie."

White left the Eagles as one of the league's first big-name free agents after the 1992 season signing a then–exorbitant $17 million deal with the Green Bay Packers. Combined with the acquisition of quarterback Brett Favre, the Packers went on to win Super Bowl XXXI, their first Super Bowl since Vince Lombardi won Super Bowls I and II.

"I think I can speak for most of us when I say that everyone was happy for Reggie when the Packers won that Super Bowl," Cunningham said. "If anyone ever deserved it, it was him."

4

CONCRETE CHARLIE

Chances are if you're reading this book, you never actually saw Chuck Bednarik play for the Eagles, you just heard about his many accomplishments on the football field. And some of what you heard probably wasn't true. But what is a fact is that he was one of the greatest, if not the greatest, player to ever play for the Eagles.

"I think he's the greatest player to ever play for the franchise," longtime Philadelphia sportswriter Ray Didinger said. "There were guys who played both ways back then and that's pretty good in its own right. What set Bednarik apart from any other player was he didn't just play both ways; he was the best player at two positions. He was the best center in the league and the best linebacker in the league."

The myths are out there, though. Let's start with his classic nickname, "Concrete Charlie," the perfect moniker for a guy who was as tough as Bednarik and played the game the way it was played before the rules stopped you from playing that way. You don't hear nicknames like that anymore. Except Chuck's nickname had nothing to do with the way he played the game. "Let them think what they want," Bednarik said with a chuckle before he passed away in March 2015.

Truth is that the nickname came from an off-season jobs Bednarik had—football players held off-season jobs back in the '50s and '60s—selling concrete. Once one of his teammates found out about the job he became "Concrete Charlie." Had he been a liquor salesman, as some players were, he might have been "Whiskey Charlie," or had he been a mechanic he might have been "Lug Nut Charlie." But he sold concrete, so the name stuck—and it also fit pretty well.

"Charles was a football player," said Tom Brookshier, another former Eagles great, before he passed away in 2010. "Some men are born to be poets or astronauts or teachers. He was born to hit people."

Two of Bednarik's famous hits—the one that knocked out the New York Giants' Frank Gifford and cost him a year of football and the one on the Green Bay Packers' Jim Taylor that won the 1960 Championship Game, also bear some urban lore that just isn't 100 percent true. Chuck did not taunt an unconscious Gifford and he didn't sit on Taylor until the clock ran out.

On the Gifford hit, which occurred during the Eagles' 1960 championship season, Giants quarterback George Shaw found his primary target open at the Eagles 35-yard line for a first down. Gifford then attempted to cut back behind Bednarik, who was circling in coverage. Bad idea.

Bednarik belted the Giants receiver with a high, hard, blindside hit so ferocious that it sent him crashing to the frozen Yankee Stadium turf and left him unconscious. The football came loose, Gifford stayed down, and the Eagles recovered, sealing a 17–10 win over their rival.

"It was a clean hit, clean all the way," Bednarik said as recently as 2010. "I just hit him high in the chest about as hard as I could. His head snapped and he went flying one way and the ball went the other way. I was trying to follow the ball, so I really didn't know what happened to Gifford. When I saw our other linebacker, Chuck Weber, got the ball, I raised my hand in the air because I knew we had just won the game. I really didn't know Gifford was lying there on the ground. I had no idea. I wasn't taunting him or any of that. I would never do that. I was just celebrating because I knew we had just won the game."

As the years went on, "The Hit" would never go away, and Bednarik was linked to Gifford the way Muhammad Ali was linked to Joe Frazier. "I would do autograph shows and someone always comes up with a picture [of him standing over Gifford] for me to sign,"

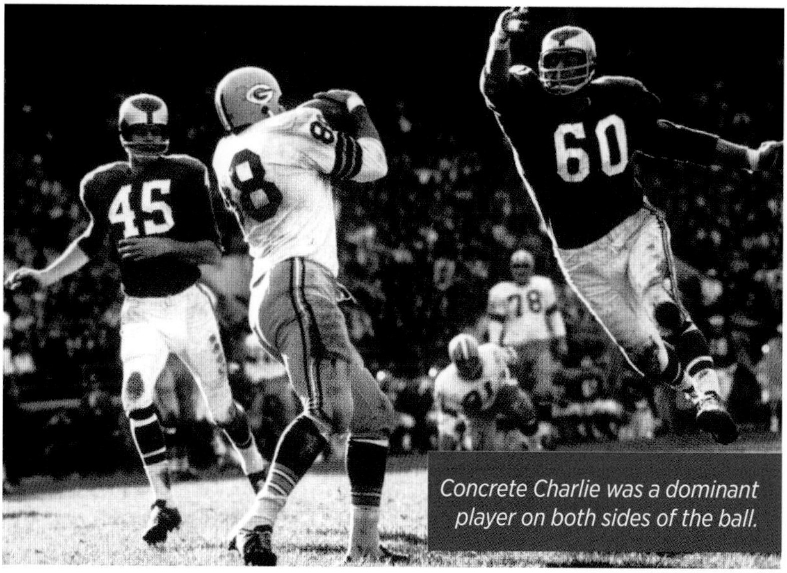
Concrete Charlie was a dominant player on both sides of the ball.

Bednarik said. "One time a guy asked me, 'Mr. Bednarik, what were you saying there?' I told him I said, 'This f——ing game is over.' So that's how they want me to sign the photo."

At a charity roast for Gifford in the early 1990s, Bednarik was invited as one of the roasters. He told this story to *Sports Illustrated* in 1993. "Before the roast starts, I ask the manager of this place if he'll do me a favor," Chuck said. "Then, when it's my turn to talk, the lights go down and it's dark for five or six seconds. Nobody knows what the hell is going on until I tell them, 'Now you know how Frank Gifford felt when I hit him.'"

Bednarik's tackle of Taylor on the final play of the 1960 Championship Game also comes with the lore that he wouldn't let the future Packers Hall of Famer back up until the clock ran out. The reality is that he made the game-saving tackle at the Eagles' 8-yard line, and time ran out before Green Bay could run another play. "On the ground,

I could see the clock tick away, four, three, two, one, zero," Bednarik said. "Then I got up and I said the same thing I said when I hit Gifford, 'This f——ng game is over.'"

A native of Bethlehem, Pennsylvania, and a decorated B-24 crewman during World War II, Bednarik never left his home state during his football career. He was a two-time All-American at the University of Pennsylvania before becoming the first-round draft pick of the Eagles in 1949.

With the Eagles he was a part of two of the franchise's three championships, the 1949 title in his rookie year and the 1960 title, when he came out of retirement.

"He just had enough," longtime Philadelphia sportswriter Ray Didinger said of retirement. "The Eagles had a Chuck Bednarik Day the last game of 1959 and honored him. That was it. He was done."

Until his wife Emma became pregnant during the off-season. "We were having an addition to the family, so I decided I had better keep working," Bednarik quipped.

Eight times he was named All-Pro and he was selected to eight Pro Bowls. He was named to the NFL's All-Time Team in 1994. And college football's top defensive prize is named in his honor.

He was by all counts a dominating player. And his big-time hits didn't just come at the expense of the opposition either. "He did it at times in practice," former teammate and Hall of Famer Pete Retzlaff said. "I remember when Chuck was leading us in jumping jacks and Jesse Richardson said, 'Awww, Chuck, we don't want to do these damn things.' Chuck walked over to him and, *whap*, gave him a right hand. And then we went back to doing jumping jacks."

Maxie Baughan, a rookie on the 1960 team who would go to five Pro Bowls himself as an Eagle, learned right away who was the player on the team to watch.

"He was a mean son of a gun but with a great big heart, and everybody loved him," Baughan said. "He never minded knocking your block off, and that attitude rubbed off on everybody. He set the tone for the entire team."

Even the guys on the offensive side of the ball. "Old No. 60, there will never be another one like him," Eagles Hall of Fame wide receiver Tommy McDonald said. "There was only one Chuck Bednarik. Nobody could ever fill his shoes."

Nobody would ever try. "As time goes on, legends grow," Didinger said. "You know 400-foot home runs become 600-foot home runs, or they say a guy broke 20 tackles and you watch the play and he broke two or three. With Chuck the legend doesn't even describe how good he was."

Still, there are the myths, like he was a 60-minute man. Bednarik himself disputed that one with a grin. "Really, I was a 58 and-a-half minute man," he said. "I didn't play on the punt or the kickoff team."

5

WEAPON X

How did an undersized safety out of Clemson who wasn't even heavily recruited out of high school and selected at the bottom of the second round during the 1996 Draft, become the most revered athlete in Philadelphia history?

"If football players could be labeled saints for a city, that would be Dawk," former Eagles safety Quintin Mikell says of former teammate Brian Dawkins. "He's the epitome of the city of Philadelphia. He's a blue-collar guy, fights through everything, brought it every single Sunday. He just epitomized what Philadelphia Eagles football is all about. That's why he's revered so much."

Philadelphia is a tough sports city. It loves its teams but doesn't always love its stars. Mike Schmidt, perhaps the greatest third baseman in Major League Baseball history, wasn't adored by the fans. Donovan McNabb, the greatest quarterback in Eagles' history, isn't even liked all that much.

And then there's Brian Dawkins. Go to an Eagles game at Lincoln Financial Field in 2016 and you'll still see more DAWKINS 20 jerseys in the stands than any other. And he hasn't played for the team since 2008. When Dawkins came back as a member of the Denver Broncos for a game in 2009, the stadium was filled with Dawkins' Broncos jerseys as well.

"Here's the thing," Dawkins said. "I am what I am. I know that's Popeye, but that's me. I'm a hardworking guy. I'm a blue-collar guy. Throughout my sports existence, my football career, I've never been given anything. Seriously, I had to earn. I had to push. I had to work harder than everyone around me. And that's how I was when I came to Philadelphia. Every contract I got, I felt I had to work even harder. I had to earn it. I had to scrape to get my contracts. It was never a time I felt anything was given to me. Sure, you go to Pro Bowls and make All-Pro teams, but I never stopped feeling that I had to outwork everybody as soon as I stepped on the field. That was ingrained in me from the time I played Little League.

"So, I think that was one thing that the Philadelphia fans felt and saw in me. And when I hurt, I hurt. I showed my emotions. Them knowing that I was that way and that I played that way, they appreciated that. As I began to hear the stories of the Philadelphia fans and how hard it was for them. How they grew up, and there wasn't a lot of love some times, but they had football. That's how it was with me, the game of football never loved me. Go back to my recruiting days. You have five-star guys and four-star guys, I didn't have any stars next to my name. I wasn't a star. Clemson wanted my [high school] teammate. So to get him, they took me."

The Eagles took Dawkins with the final pick of the second round of that 1996 Draft, the 61st pick overall, a supplemental pick the league gave the Eagles for their overall loss of free agents in 1994. He was the 11th defensive back selected.

"I always tell people I was a third-round pick because they took me with a supplemental pick. So you could say I was the last pick of the second round, but I was really the first pick of the third round," Dawkins said.

That was always his mentality. Even after becoming one of the best safeties to ever play the game, he still felt he was the underdog. Just like the fans who still wear his jersey.

"People were always telling me I couldn't do something," he said. "I wasn't big enough coming out of college to be an every-down safety. I'd have to move to nickel or just be a package player. So I gained more muscle so I could absorb the pounding and give out the pounding. I had to earn. I had to *earn* everything. I lifted with the linebackers instead of the DBs, sometimes the linemen. Just because I wanted to prove something."

THE SAD ENDING

If any player should have played their entire career with one team it was Brian Dawkins for the Philadelphia Eagles.

Unfortunately, that's just not how the Eagles operated during the presidency of Joe Banner and the Andy Reid coaching days. There's a reason the last player to play a minimum of 10 years all for the Eagles was Jerry Sisemore, who retired in 1984. Although in 2016, with a new contract, tight end Brent Celek has a chance to do it.

When Dawkins' contract came up at the end of the 2008 season the team let him hit the free-agent market, and he signed with the Denver Broncos.

The contract negotiations between him and his agent and the Eagles got nasty. The Eagles' best offer to one of the best players in the team's history was a one-year deal for $3.75 million. He had made $3 million the year before.

"After all I did, that was the raise they were giving me?" Dawkins said. "And that was their final offer."

Denver had offered $7 million for the first year in a three-year deal and then before he got on the flight, upped it to $7.5 million, twice as much as the Eagles offer.

"The franchise tag for a safety was $5 million," Dawkins said. "I would have taken that to stay. Then Denver gave me a great offer and then a better offer."

It hurt him then, and it still hurts years later. "It didn't hurt a little bit. It hurt a lot," Dawkins said seven years after he left. "I tell people that was my time of mourning. It hurt that much. Mentally and emotionally I was hurting for months. I had to get over it because I had to be who I needed to be for my new teammates [in Denver]. But it hurt. It still does.

"When it gets to me the most is when I see guys who get to retire and be in that one spot where they started. Ray Lewis in Baltimore, that got to me. That should have been me. It's a shame. I did so much [more] for that team than just play football. I didn't want to leave. My plan was to play two more years, retire, then hang around and be a part of the team... however they wanted to use me."

It didn't happen that way. Instead Dawkins went to Denver. He played three years for the Broncos, made two more Pro Bowls, and now makes his home there as well.

In Dawkins early years with the Eagles he played the game and played it well. In the Ray Rhodes / Emmitt Thomas defensive scheme he was used more in coverage, both as a deep safety and at times as the nickel corner in the slot. Off the field he was friendly but quiet. He went about his business just as it was, as a business.

"Brian came in and he was quiet," Eagles cornerback Troy Vincent and one of Dawkins' closest friends during their years with the team, said. "The coaches, Ray and Emmitt, allowed him to be unique. He was the kid who went straight home from school. Now, on the field he could play. I remember Emmitt telling me right after I signed as a free agent, 'We have our eye on this safety from Clemson. We think he can be special.' He had that quick twitch and that explosiveness. He was fearless.

"It must have been around year five, maybe year six. He'd become more mature. [Defensive coordinator] Jim [Johnson] called him a 'special agent.' He was doing things at his position that other players didn't do, especially at his size. You just watched him mature. He really didn't change deep down. He did what most people dream about doing, and that's enjoying all 60 minutes of the game. You can't teach that.

"Then you would see the transformation in the locker room too. The equipment guy, Angelo, would come in and say '10 minutes' and you would see him transform right before your eyes."

That's how Brian Dawkins, undersized safety from Clemson turned into "Dawk," or "Weapon X." In the Eagles locker room at the NovaCare Complex, where the team practiced every day, there were even two locker stalls. One bore the nameplate DAWKINS 20 and the other that read WEAPON X.

"Weapon X came about because he was a weapon as a safety," Eagles linebacker Ike Reese said. "That hadn't really been seen before. I saw the transformation. We knew him when he was Brian Dawkins. He was 'Scooter.' Those early impressions were great as well. He was a catlike, quick defender. I never saw anyone as quick as a safety as he was. During those early years, he was quiet. Then, under Jim, he became something special to watch. I mean when your peers, the players in the league, the good players in the league talk about you, that's a special player. And with that he grew from a relatively quiet guy to a vocal leader."

Dawkins laughs a little when he hears what his former teammates have to say about that transformation. But he agrees with their summation. "It started when Jim began to use me all over the field, adding blitz packages for me and not just me blitzing but covering for the guy who did blitz," he said. "Weapon X came into existence from him using me in so many different ways. It was because of Jim Johnson and using me the way no safety had been used before.

"I would watch guys like Troy and Willie T. [linebacker William Thomas] and see how they went about their business. As they left, I sort of felt the need to become more of a spokesman. I needed to say more. And that was a challenge, too, because I wasn't always comfortable doing that."

Dawkins also became a mentor to younger players like Mikell, whom he watched grow from an undrafted free agent to a top special teams player to the starting safety next to him. "I remember watching him when I was in high school, and then to play in the same secondary with him, that was something," Mikell said. "I mean, he was the guy you wanted to be just like. He had a tremendous impact on me as a player, watching him, and then him teaching me. He took me under his wing, so to speak. He helped me become a much better player."

6

THE VET

Every year, almost without fail, it was voted the worst football stadium in the league.

The field itself, a kind of green concrete, had taken years off player's careers and completely ended Chicago Bears wide receiver Wendell Davis' when he tore the ACL in both of his knees—without being hit—in a 1993 game against the Eagles.

Head coach Brian Billick took his Baltimore Ravens home before a preseason game in 2001 because of surface problems with the field. Just went home. The game was canceled. "Where else would a game get canceled like that?" onetime Eagles cornerback Troy Vincent, now the NFL's vice president of operations, said.

Veterans Stadium was one of the 1970s multipurpose, cookie-cutter stadiums. Unlike Pittsburgh's Three Rivers Stadium or Cincinnati's Riverfront Stadium, which looked almost exactly the same as the Vet, the Vet was different. Oh was it different.

"I loved it," Vincent said. "Oakland has the Black Hole. Cleveland has the Dawg Pound. We had the Vet."

For one thing, "the Hole" and "the Pound" were just sections of the stadium; the Vet was the entire stadium, the playing field, the catlike—or were they rat-like?—creatures that ran amok under the tunnels. It was something completely different.

The Eagles shared the Vet with their baseball counterparts, the Phillies, and also used it to practice until the NovaCare Complex was built down the street in 2001. All of the team offices were there as well.

"I was the only one in the building," former Eagles assistant coach John Harbaugh remembered. "I'm in my office, and, all of a sudden, I hear this scratching sound above me. I thought somebody was trying to break into the place. I didn't know what it was. It was dark. It was cold. OK, what's going on? Just then, a dead bird falls onto my desk."

It could have been worse.

"You haven't lived until you've experienced the mutant cats at the Vet," Jon Gruden, now the voice of *Monday Night Football*, but at one time an Eagles assistant coach, said. "I remember one time when our running backs coach Dick Jamieson got to work in the morning. He unlocked his door and these two cats—who were shaped like wolves, really—darted out of his office. He screamed, a really loud scream, and I went running down there. Evidently, they had fallen through his ceiling the night before. I just love the Vet."

Gruden tried to investigate, but kind of like looking into a mob hit, he was told to just leave it alone. "There was some old security guard upstairs," Gruden said. "One day, I was walking out and I see these two cats—I mean *cats*. These cats are like wolves. So I say, 'What's the deal with all these cats?' Guy says, 'The cats eat the rats. You want cats or rats?' Yup, that was the Vet."

But for the players who played there, it was home, a place like no other. "When I grew up I didn't have much. A lot of the places I lived weren't the best, but me and my brothers were always proud of where we lived," Eagles linebacker Ike Reese, now a radio host in Philadelphia, said. "It was the same with my teammates and the Vet. It's a dungeon. You would see rodents coming in as you came in or as you left, and they were the size of your house pet. But the bottom line is it was our place. And there was a fear factor from other teams coming in there.

"And we practiced there every day and that made us feel even closer. Those were the years [when] we became what we became. My fondest memories of playing for the Eagles were at the Vet. I'm happy I played at the Vet. I thought it was great. I enjoyed playing at the Vet. Part of it was the history. Now, the conditions, I don't think it's possible to exaggerate about the conditions at the Vet."

Or how much visiting players despised playing there. There are a lot of stadiums with distinct home-field advantages. None were like the Vet. "Veterans Stadium was like going into someone's neighborhood," another former Eagles linebacker, Garry Cobb, said. "It had that feel. There was just so much emotion and noise. It was always so loud. It was a ferocious place. There was a tremendous home-field advantage there. When I was with Dallas some of those guys were intimidated going [to the Vet]. The Philly fans were not very nice to the visiting team. It all went together. I mean, I'm talking about good players, guys that went on to win Super Bowls. They just didn't want to play there. They hated it."

One of those players was Cowboys Hall of Fame quarterback Troy Aikman. "It seemed like it was always cold and damp and dreary there," Aikman said. "I played in three Super Bowls, but when I think back, those games against the Eagles at the Vet, those are some of my most vivid memories. I always felt like if I could play at the Vet, I could play anywhere."

Aikman wasn't alone as a visitor coming to the Vet. "Let me tell you, when you came to the Vet, you saw guys looking for where the holes in the turf were. I knew where they were," Vincent said. "The seams for first base, second base, the pitcher's mound. We knew all of that; they didn't. People would say, 'I hate playing there.' 'It's nasty.' 'It's the worst stadium in the league.' I'd say, 'That's home.' They hated coming there and we embodied it."

Mike Quick, the legendary Eagles wide receiver, was one of the players whose career was cut short because of knee injuries courtesy of the Vet's unforgiving surface. But he never complained. "I'm sure it was bad for teams who came from nicer facilities," Quick said. "I didn't know any better, because it was all I knew. It was where we played. It's kind of like where you grow up. It might not

A JAIL AND A JUDGE

In 1997, the Eagles put a jail cell in the basement of Veterans Stadium. It is believed to be the first actual jail in a sports stadium. It also came complete with a municipal court judge.

Deep in the stadium bowels, in an old baseball maintenance room, was the courtroom of Judge Seamus McCaffery. On its first day in use, a game in which the Eagles beat the Pittsburgh Steelers 23–20, 20 defendants were brought to see the judge.

It was the Eagles Court dressed with purple curtains, a blue carpet, and United States and Pennsylvania flags placed beside Judge McCaffery's bench. The city of Philadelphia, the municipal judges and the Eagles set up the courtroom and jail after an incident during a Monday night game against the San Francisco 49ers in which a fan set off a flare gun in the stands.

Now any unruly conduct in the stands would be handled as if it had been done on the streets.

"In general, we felt it was a huge success," Eagles owner Jeffrey Lurie said after the first day of court, Eagles style. "The key was the evaluation of fan behavior."

be good, but you don't see it that way. It's home. That's what the Vet was: home.

"And we certainly had a home-field advantage there too. The fan base was great and that helped the advantage. When you're warming up before the game and you see the other team looking for where the seams were and how bad the turf was, yeah, I think that helped."

If the players think it helped them, it helped them. And in most cases it really did. "You see guys during the off-season, or even before or after the game," Reese said. "How do you guys play on this stuff? They just wanted to get out of there without any injuries. You couldn't ask for a better home-field advantage than that."

7

A REAL THOROUGHBRED

If there was one thing Steve Van Buren liked more than football, it was horse racing. The greatest running back in Philadelphia Eagles history, and one of the greatest in NFL history, was a regular at Belmont Park and Aqueduct in New York as well as closer to his home, what was then called Philadelphia Park and is now Parx Racing.

That really shouldn't come as much of a surprise since Van Buren was himself a thoroughbred on the football field. "He loved the track," said David Boyce, a former basketball player at St. Joseph's under Dr. Jack Ramsey who became Van Buren's close friend in his post-NFL days. "I don't know if this is true, but Steve told me when he signed his first contract with the Eagles, he asked [head coach] Greasy Neale if he could have $200 of his contract in cash. And he took it right to the track.

"We would go every day. We would go up to New York most times. He loved the New York racing. One time we're up there and we're walking through the parking lot and I tell him, 'You'll get a break today. Nobody up here is going to ask for your autograph.' He says, 'Wanna bet?' He signed seven autographs in the parking lot and I had to give him $20.

"I loved it too. Somebody asked us once, 'Which one of you guys like the track more?' It was a dead heat."

There was no doubt who the best running back of his era was. Van Buren was an All-Pro selection for seven straight years from 1944 to 1950. In his eight years in the NFL, all with the Eagles, he ran for 5,860 yards and 69 touchdowns in just 83 games.

Those 69 rushing touchdowns are still the most by any Eagle, and 24 more than second-place Wilbert Montgomery, who played in 17 more games. Van Buren's 77 total touchdowns are second on the

Eagles' all-time list just two short of wide receiver Harold Carmichael, who played in more than twice as many games.

Van Buren took the Eagles to three straight NFL title games, winning back-to-back titles in 1948 and 1949 after losing to the Chicago Cardinals 28–21 in the 1947 game.

In 1947, Van Buren put up his first 1,000-yard rushing season, with a then–league record 1,008 yards. Two years later, as the Eagles were about to win their second title, he broke his record with 1,146 rushing yards and became the first player in NFL history to lead the league in rushing in three straight seasons.

Only three other backs since—Cleveland's Jimmy Brown, who won five straight from 1957 to 1961 and three more from '63 to '65, Houston's Earl Campbell (1978–80) and Dallas' Emmitt Smith (1991–93)—have accomplished the feat.

"Red Grange had the same ability to sidestep," Neale once said of Van Buren. "But he never had Van Buren's power to go with it. He was better than Grange because Grange needed a blocker. Van Buren didn't. He could run away from tacklers like Grange, or over them like Bronko Nagurski."

Van Buren scored the only touchdown in the Eagles' 7–0 1948 Championship Game, played in the snow. He also ran for a then–playoff game record 196 yards in the 1949 Championship Game, when the Eagles beat the Los Angeles Rams 14–0 in the rain.

Guess you could say Van Buren was a pretty good mudder.

What he also was, according to those who saw him, was underrated. Perhaps that was part of his own doing, because he was also so humble. People didn't appreciate how good he was, what he did as a player," Allie Sherman, a teammate of Van Buren and later the head coach of the New York Giants, said. "He was the Jimmy Brown of his time."

When Van Buren retired after the 1951 season, he held the NFL record for career rushing yards (5,860) and rushing touchdowns (69). Both records were eventually broken by Brown.

"A lot of guys, they have records and they don't want to see them broken. Steve wasn't like that," Boyce said. "He would cheer for guys to break his records. Just a real humble guy. He'd always say things like those guys are better than me, they deserve the record. But they weren't better than him. Nobody was."

The Eagles drafted Van Buren with the fifth pick of the 1944 NFL Draft out of LSU, where he began his career as a blocking back for Alvin Dark, who would later go on to become a Major League Baseball All-Star and longtime manager.

When Dark graduated, Van Buren took over as the Tigers' featured back. In his senior year he led the nation in scoring with 98 points and finished second in the nation in rushing with 847 yards.

"He probably was the greatest running back in Southeastern Conference history," LSU coach Bernie Moore said then, "and I used him as a blocking back until his last year. The folks in Baton Rouge never let me forget that."

In LSU's 19–14 Orange Bowl win over Texas A&M that season, Van Buren ran for 160 yards, ran for a touchdown and threw a touchdown pass. "You think people love him here," Boyce said, "go down to LSU and ask about him. To this day he's still loved down there."

Boyce didn't meet Van Buren until the late '60s, long after his playing days were over. The two hit it off immediately and became such good friends that Van Buren was Boyce's best man at his wedding.

"I met him on a hotel elevator," Boyce said. "He walked on and I said 'I know who you are. You're No. 15.' He laughed. I asked him if he'd like a drink, that we had some vodka in our room. He said he'd be there in five minutes."

One of Boyce's favorite stories about Van Buren doesn't involve football or horse racing, but boxing and the great heavyweight champion, Joe Louis.

"Steve was going to fight Joe Louis," Boyce says. "It was a few years after he was finished playing. He was getting $25,000 to fight Louis. The most he ever made playing football was $15,000 and he's getting $25,000 for one fight. So he goes up to Hershey, [Pennsylvania] where Louis was training. He sees Louis warming up in the ring and yells out to him, 'Hey, Joe, let's have a drink tonight and talk about this fight.' Louis yells back 'Meet me at seven at the bar.'

"As the story goes, they talk that night. Steve says, 'Joe, you're not going to hurt me in the ring are you?' Joe says, "Steve I might hurt you, yeah." Steve called off the fight. He told me he didn't want the Eagles fans to see him get hurt."

Another story involves a job Van Buren had with the Eagles, as a scout, watching the top college players. "It was kind of an easy job," Boyce said. "But they were paying him pretty good to do it. One year he's watching players, or he's supposed to be watching players, and I think it was Lynn Swann. Steve asks some guy, who knows who it was, it was probably the janitor, or somebody, 'What do you think of this Lynn Swann?' The guy talks him off, says you don't want to take him. So Steve tells the Eagles not to take him. When Swann became as good as he was, Steve quit. He felt he messed up, and that's how it was with him."

Van Buren also had a little bit of a friendly rivalry with fellow Eagles great Chuck Bednarik, with whom his career overlapped for a few years. Through the years there was always the debate of who was the greatest Eagles player ever.

"He and Chuck loved each other," Boyce said. "But they had that rivalry going too. Chuck would always say he was the greatest Eagle. But Chuck told me once, 'Your buddy was the greatest, and the greatest running back the NFL has ever seen, the best to ever lace them up.'"

8

JEROME DIES

Tragic news is always remembered. Where, how, when, it all comes back—even years later. Any baby boomer can tell you where they were November 22, 1963, when President John F. Kennedy was assassinated. Younger people will never forget September 11, 2001.

For Eagles' players and fans that indelible date is June 25, 1992. That was the day Jerome Brown lost his life in a car accident in his hometown of Brooksville, Florida.

"It's a day I'll never forget," Eagles linebacker and Brown's good friend Seth Joyner said years later. "June 25 is always on my mind."

Joyner was in California filming a television show when he heard the news. Reggie White was at Veterans Stadium, where he and Brown had dominated offenses for the previous five years, to speak at a Billy Graham rally. Garry Cobb, who was keeping an eye on Brown's New Jersey house, was on the radio doing his sports-talk show. None will ever forget.

"It was tough," Joyner said. "I was out in California. I was actually competing in *American Gladiators*, if you can believe that. They didn't know if they should tell me or not. I was going into the final competition against [All-Pro running back] Charles White. The producers came up to me and said, 'We have some bad news.' I said, 'What?' I had no idea what they were going to tell me. They said, 'Your teammate Jerome Brown was killed in a car accident.' I was done. I needed to see it on ESPN or something, for validation. They found a monitor for me and I saw it for myself. I was heartbroken. I didn't know what to do or what to say at that point."

White, who would tragically die young himself, announced his friend's passing in front of a packed house before the Graham rally. It was as an emotional of a speech as you'll ever hear. Tears ran down White's face as he broke the news to a pin-drop-quiet crowd.

Cobb remembers it all. "Just a horrible, horrible day," he said. "I was on the air, doing my show, when the word broke. Of course, I couldn't believe it. Not Jerome. There was no way. Somebody must have something wrong. This was Jerome Brown. He was so big, so strong, a mountain of a man. How could he be killed in a car accident?

"I did the show, and of course that's all anyone wanted to talk about that night. Nothing else, at that point, mattered from a sports sense. Sure, it was difficult, but I actually think doing the show was kind of therapeutic for me. I grieved with the rest of the city."

Quarterback Randall Cunningham, now a pastor, still has a difficult time when Brown's death is mentioned. "It was a terrible, terrible day," Cunningham said. "So sad. That's something I can't even talk about now."

Mike Golic, who lined up next to Brown on the Eagles defensive line in that "Gang Green" Era, remembered his friend on his national radio show years later. "I got the call that Jerome Brown was killed in a car accident," Golic said. "That's horrible in and of itself, but then to make it even worse, in the car was his 12-year-old nephew, who was also dead. Jerome Brown was a friend to me more than a teammate. He was so many people's friend on that team. He lived a fast life. He had a good time. He lived fast and he lived hard. We talked about that in the locker room. We laughed and joked about it. You kind of held your breath with Jerome. He lived fast. He lived hard. Could this come to a bad end? You thought, down the road. Of course, you never think this as a young, professional athlete—it can happen to you. You think you are invincible. Nothing can touch you. And then I got the call."

Said cornerback Eric Allen, "When Jerome passed away, you just felt like, 'Wow, we're not invincible.' You really can't predict what our futures are going to be. It's life and death. It took us a long

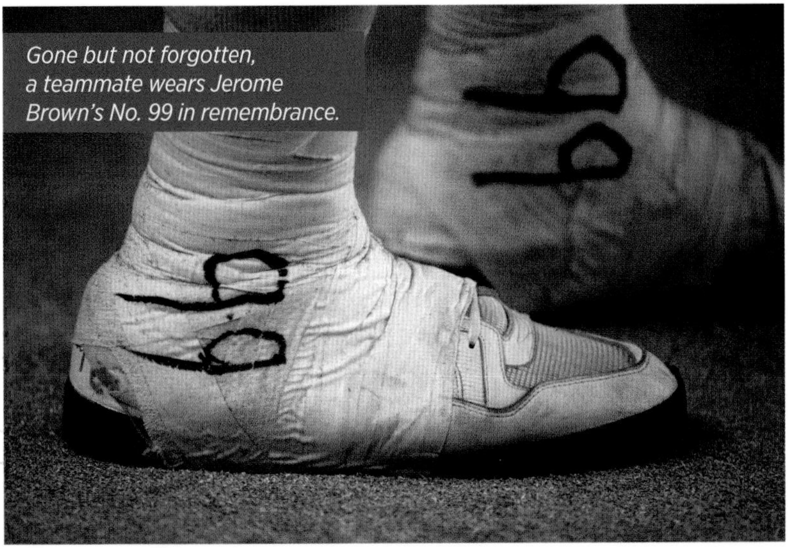

Gone but not forgotten, a teammate wears Jerome Brown's No. 99 in remembrance.

time to understand how to come back and try to fill that friendship void. That was like a brother, not a teammate. It was very difficult for us. Because we were so tight, we tried to keep his great sense of humor alive."

If White was the Eagles' spiritual leader and Joyner was the team's emotional leader, then Brown was the comic relief. The big man always had a big smile and would bring one to his teammates' faces as well.

"Jerome, he definitely lived life to the fullest in every shape, fashion, and form." Joyner said.

You couldn't find a player on the late '80s Eagles to disagree.

"Jerome's persona was bigger than life, but he was bigger than life," former Eagles linebacker Britt Hager said. "When that guy got into the room, the atmosphere changed."

Mostly for the better. And Brown, after five seasons with the Eagles, was starting to realize what it took to be great. He had gone to the Pro Bowl in his last two seasons and wanted more. "He

JEROME'S LOCKER

Jerome Brown was gone, taken way too soon in an automobile crash in the summer of 1992. Yet his teammates wouldn't just let him go away. They kept a piece of him with them throughout that '92 season.

Brown's locker at Veterans Stadium remained intact. It wasn't so much a shrine as it was a remembrance. And it gave them extra motivation—to win for him.

"Because we were so tight, we tried to keep his great sense of humor alive," Eagles cornerback Eric Allen said. "Whenever we traveled, we took his locker, his jersey with us. We tried everything we could do to get to the big game for him."

The Eagles made it to the playoffs that year as a wild-card team and brought Brown's locker with them on the road to New Orleans, where they won their first playoff game since 1980. They would lose the following week, however, in Dallas to the Cowboys.

"But what it came down to [was] we needed him," Allen said. "He was a huge piece of our success. Jerome was the glue that held us together."

was getting into a different place. He was evolving, maturing as a human being and a player," Joyner said. "I used to talk to him all the time about training. I wanted him to come out to El Paso with me and train. And he was turning the corner. He started to work out. I remember just before [the car crash] he was working out and he sent the video to [trainer] Otho Davis. He wanted everyone to know he was trying.

"I saw him turning that corner from just using his athletic ability to enhancing what he had and becoming a complete player by working out and getting in great shape, and then understanding what we were doing defensively. It was the craziest thing you ever saw, because he was just so fast, so quick, so powerful. He was a load to move. I never saw anything like him. There was not a guard in the league who could block him one on one.

"Talent-wise, you never had a defensive tackle back then who could do it all. You were either a pass rusher like a Keith Millard, or a run stopper. Jerome could do it all. And he knew he couldn't be blocked. There were times he would turn to me and say, 'Cover me, I'm going in.' I'd say, 'Going where?' I got my spot covered. But I would back up a yard and cover him, and more times than not he would go get the sack, or a tackle for a loss."

Brown was already one of the best defensive tackles in the NFL when he died. How good might he have become? "Hall of Fame talent, for sure," Cobb said. "He was the guy who stirred it up, he stirred the pot. He made sure everyone around him came to play. Reggie was great, the greatest, but Reggie was the guy who was the emotional leader. Jerome led in different ways."

Cunningham made the comparison to another University of Miami talent who became an NFL star. "He was such a great player. He would have been a Hall of Fame player for sure," Cunningham said. "He was Warren Sapp before Warren Sapp."

9

THE ULTIMATE WEAPON

Randall Cunningham has no regrets. Sure, he would have loved to have won a Super Bowl, or even gotten to one—especially as a Philadelphia Eagle. The former quarterback, now a pastor, has no bitterness.

Cunningham did amazing things in his NFL career with the Eagles and later the Minnesota Vikings and Baltimore Ravens. He just never had quite enough to get where every player wants to go. With the Eagles it was the lack of a running game to complement his passing skills. With the Vikings, it was a missed field goal.

"Listen, I can't complain about anything." Cunningham said years later. "I played in the NFL for a long time and had a great time doing it."

From 1987, his first year as a starter, to 1993, Cunningham threw 122 touchdown passes and just 72 interceptions, passed for more than 17,000 yards, rushed for more than 3,000 yards, went to three Pro Bowls, won two Most Valuable Player Awards and one Comeback Player of the Year Award.

"As just a pure football player, he may have been the greatest ever," former teammate Garry Cobb said. "He's certainly the greatest I've ever played with or against... He could throw the ball as far as any quarterback. He had a great arm, a tremendous thrower. He could have been a Pro Bowl punt returner, because in the open field you couldn't get him down. He was as fast as most wide receivers. And of course he could have been a Pro Bowl punter. So he was a Pro Bowl quarterback, and he could have been a Pro Bowl player at any number of positions. We're talking about one guy. He had all those skills. That's what was so amazing about him. You saw when he went to Minnesota and became a pocket passer with Randy Moss and Cris Carter. He showed what he could do as just a passer.

"When he came to Philadelphia he was a young guy coming out of UNLV. He's the Eagles quarterback and all of a sudden he's a superstar. That's not easy."

Cunningham tried to make it look that way, because he understood what it meant to be the quarterback of the Philadelphia Eagles—or at least he does now. In a city where football is held so high above anything else, the quarterback can be a polarizing figure. And Cunningham embodied both ends of that spectrum.

"The way I looked at it was, only one person gets that position in that town. Being the quarterback for the Philadelphia Eagles is like being the mayor of the city," Cunningham said. "It's not a position to be taken lightly. You have to enjoy every minute of it, the good and the bad. And there's going to be good and bad. [When] we lost those playoff games, it was tough. It was bad. But you have to deal with it. Then, when we finally went down and beat New Orleans. It wasn't the Super Bowl, it was a playoff game, but it just felt so good. How could you not be happy about that? And then we came home and people are waiting for us at the airport. It was a great feeling."

Cunningham enjoyed playing as much as fans enjoyed watching him play for the Eagles, from 1985 to 1995. He was as much entertainer as he was football star. From his gold-tipped shoelaces to his personalized baseball caps to his weekly television show, he was way ahead of his time on and off the field.

Sports Illustrated called him "the Ultimate Weapon." Morley Candy Company gave him his own candy bar, the Randall Bar, which consisted of chocolate, peanuts, and caramel "scrambled" together. He was a 22-year-old from Southern California, who had lost both of his parents as a teenager, loving life in the ultra-glare of Philadelphia.

"I was a young guy and I ate up all that stuff. I really did," Cunningham said recently. "Because, hey, you're only as good as your last game. And you never know when it's going to end."

Unfortunately, it didn't end well for Cunningham as an Eagle. He never seemed to fit the mold new head coach Ray Rhodes and offensive coordinator Jon Gruden wanted from their quarterback in 1995 and was actually benched during the season in favor of Rodney Peete. When Peete was injured in the team's playoff loss to the Dallas Cowboys, Cunningham came in but did not play well.

That off-season he wasn't re-signed and actually took a year away from football. He resurfaced with the Vikings in 1997 as Jeff George's backup, became the starter in 1998, and led the team to 13 wins in the final 14 games and all the way to the NFC Championship Game, where they lost in overtime to the Atlanta Falcons.

Still, Cunningham says he'll always be remembered as an Eagle. "The thing I remember most is the support system I always had there," Cunningham said. "And the great fan base we had too. The crazy thing for me was when I would go places, out of the country even, and see people wearing my Eagles jersey. I still see it today sometimes. And then whether it was Will Smith [on *The Fresh Prince of Bel Air*] or Kadeem Hardison [on *A Different World*] wearing it on TV, that was just crazy.

"And the fans in Philadelphia, they take ownership of the team. It's amazing. We live in time now where people are so wishy-washy. Eagles fans aren't like that. They talk about you all day, they root for you on Sunday, and then they start talking about you again on Monday.

"I loved the rivalries we had, like with the Giants. The Giants fans don't like the Eagles. But it's a sport, and you have to keep it in perspective. I'd come out of the tunnel up at the Meadowlands and these guys sitting in the one end zone would start yelling at me, 'Hey,

THE PUNT

Those who were fortunate enough to have watched the Eagles practice, either at training camp at West Chester University or during the season at Veterans Stadium in the late 1980s, got to see Randall Cunningham do things that were hard to believe. Not with his rocketlike arm, and not using his mercurial speed, either, but with his foot. On any given day, Cunningham would mess around and kick 60-yard field goals, or send off 70-yard punts without much of an effort.

On a wind-swept day in 1989 at Giants Stadium, he did it for real. Eagles punter John Teltschik was on injured reserve and his replacement, Max Runager, was struggling. So with the Eagles backed up at their 3-yard line and the score tied in the fourth quarter, Buddy Ryan left his quarterback on the field to punt.

"You know, he did it in practice all the time," Ryan said in 2009. "He said he could do it. So I said, 'Go ahead, punt it.' And when he kicked it, I thought he knocked it out of the damn stadium."

Cunningham's punt went 91 yards, still the longest in Eagles history and as of 2016, the third longest in NFL history. It also set up the Eagles' winning touchdown after a Giants turnover.

"That day I told Buddy I could punt if he needed me," Cunningham said. "The wind was really swirling, like it always did at the Meadowlands, but I knew if I got a hold of one it would go."

Cunningham, we're going to smash you.' I'd be like, 'C'mon guys, you're starting already? I just came out of the tunnel. Can I get warmed up first?' And then I'd hear them at halftime, and then after the game. When we would win, they'd say, 'Good game, Cunningham. But we're gonna smash you next time.' And that's what's great about the game. You have your fans, the trash talk. It's great for the game. It was fun for me. And I would see those same guys in that same spot every year. I actually formed a relationship with them. It was love/hate. They hated me before the game, then after they would show me some love. I actually looked forward to seeing them. I came back years later with Minnesota and those same guys were there. 'Hey, Cunningham, we're gonna smash you.' I can still hear it now."

There were the ups and down for Cunningham the Eagle. He took a lot of the heat for the team's three consecutive playoff losses from 1988 to 1990, and there are still those who claim he got head coach Buddy Ryan fired after that third playoff loss. It's a claim he denied then and still does today. "I loved Buddy," he said. "Buddy was like a father figure to a lot of us back then. I'll always love Buddy."

Cunningham loved the game, too. He loved being the Philadelphia Eagles quarterback. He loved his life. "When you're a little kid and you're watching *Monday Night Football* and you hear Howard Cosell, 'Welcome to Monday Night Football,'" Cunningham said in his best Cosell impersonation. "And that becomes your dream and your aspiration to get there. Now, when you do get there, how can you not enjoy it? How can you get upset over things? You're in the NFL. I was a kid in the candy store.

"Now you're in a game and you look across the line of scrimmage and you see [Bears linebacker] Mike Singletary across from you and you look into those eyes, those same eyes you've seen on TV all those times. Man, now you know you're in the NFL. You might get a little nervous, a little water might run down your leg, but that's OK. Either you are going to fail or you are going to enjoy it. So you better enjoy it."

Nobody enjoyed it quite like Randall Cunningham.

10

MIRACLE OF THE MEADOWLANDS

The game was over, and with it any momentum that had been built during the majority of the season.

The Eagles had fought back from a two-score deficit to trail the underdog New York Giants, 17–12, late in the fourth quarter and had the ball deep in Giants territory. Giants' rookie cornerback Odis McKinney, however, intercepted a Ron Jaworski pass in the end zone to give his team the ball, and presumably the win. The Eagles had no timeouts and about the same amount of hope.

"Ron throws the interception and it looks like it's over," Eagles tackle Stan Walters remembered. "I'm not even watching from the bench. I never saw Herm score. I hear this noise from the crowd, kind of a loud groan. I said, 'What happened?' Sise [Jerry Sisemore] says, 'We scored.' I'm thinking, 'How the hell did we score?'"

With 31 seconds on the clock, the Giants called a play, 65 Power-Up, that lives in infamy for both teams. Instead of taking a knee and letting the clock run out, quarterback Joe Pisarcik handed off to running back Larry Csonka. Or at least he attempted to hand off to Csonka.

There's a little behind the scenes take on the call. Giants offensive coordinator Bob Gibson, who called the plays, hated having his quarterback take a knee. And actually, in 1978, quarterbacks didn't take a knee the way they do in today's game. Instead, they kind of went to the ground and got sacked. As such, Gibson didn't want his young quarterback to get injured by an overly aggressive Eagles defense.

Csonka, the former Dolphins great and future Hall of Famer, didn't want the ball and made that clear in the huddle. But Pisarcik, who had been chastised by his coaches during the season for changing plays, didn't want to go against his bosses with a win

MIRACLE 2

Ten-year anniversary remembrances of "the Miracle of the Meadowlands" dominated the headlines as the Eagles traveled to play the Giants 10 years and a day after Herman Edwards' famed fumble recovery.

And it happened again, sort of. This one might have been even crazier, if that's possible. Tied, 17–17, in overtime, the Eagles lined up for what would be a chip-shot 31-yard field goal attempt by Luis Zendejas to win the game.

Giants great Lawrence Taylor rushed from the right side, got through just enough, and blocked Zedejas' kick. What happened next is the miracle.

"You know the sound when a kick gets blocked," Eagles defensive end Clyde Simmons, on the field goal protection team, said. "I'd heard it before. So I kind of knew where to look for the ball." Simmons didn't have to look very far. "It bounced right to me," he said.

And he rambled 15 yards to the end zone for the winning touchdown in a 23–17 win. "I just spun around, grabbed it and ran," Simmons said. "I was going to do whatever it took to get it in there. The funny thing about that play is everyone told me it was partially my fault the kick got blocked. It came from my side. I thought I did my job, but everyone else said it was on me."

The win moved the Eagles ahead of the Giants into first place in the NFC East to stay, ultimately claiming their first division title in eight years.

just 31 seconds away. So they ran the play, 65 Power-Up. Csonka never secured the ball and it popped loose. It glanced off Pisarcik's hands, hit the ground, and took a bounce right into the hands of Eagles cornerback Herman Edwards.

Twenty-six yards later, Edwards was in the end zone and the Eagles had the most improbable 19–17 win in franchise history. "I really didn't know what happened," said Edwards, who later became the head coach of both the Kansas City Chiefs and New York Jets. "All I

MIRACLE 3

The Eagles had gained a total of 135 yards of offense all day; just 24 of it after halftime. They trailed the Giants, 10–7, with 1:34 to play, and forced a punt from near midfield.

Sure they only needed a field goal to tie, but they hadn't moved the ball all day. Why would they now? And then Jeff Feagles punted and Brian Westbrook did the rest.

"That's one of my most memorable plays," said Westbrook, who was put into the Eagles Honor Roll in 2015. "Mainly because of the magnitude that it had in the game. If it had happened in the first quarter, it wouldn't have been the same. When it happened and how it happened magnified it."

Westbrook fielded Feagles' punt on a bounce at the 16-yard line, picked up a block from Pro Bowl special teams player Ike Reese on the Giants' David Tyree (who would perform his own miracle in a Super Bowl years later), turned up the left sideline right past the Giants' bench and into the end zone, giving the Eagles a 14–10 lead.

"We really never got anything going on offense all day," Westbrook said. "Now we have one last chance. I was just hoping for a returnable punt, to get an opportunity to do something."

What Westbrook did didn't just win a game, it saved a season. With a loss the Eagles would have dropped to 2–4 in the 2003 season. Instead they went on a nine-game winning streak that earned them home-field advantage in the playoffs and a third straight trip to the NFC Championship Game.

saw was the ball. I wanted to make something happen because I felt I owed the team one."

Edwards, in his second year with the Eagles, had blown coverage on a 30-yard touchdown pass from Pisarcik to Johnny Perkins earlier in the game.

Eagles linebacker Bill Bergey, who was on the field for the play, still shakes his head about it, almost 40 years later. "One of their linemen yelled out, 'Joe just take a knee,'" Bergey remembered. "And Joe says, 'No, we better run the play they told us to run.' We just looked at each other. We knew there wasn't much hope. It was going to take, well, a miracle. But as long as there was time left on the clock, we were going to play hard. If they were going to actually run a play, then we were going to blitz. I turned to [Frank] LeMaster and said, 'Let's both hit the same gap.' That's what we did."

Eagles head coach Dick Vermeil was probably already thinking about the following week's game in St. Louis against the Cardinals and how to get his team back on track after a tough loss. Then Edwards scooped up the ball and went 26 yards for the touchdown. "They were running out the clock," Vermeil said. "And the next thing you know there's jubilation on our sideline and everybody is jumping up and down celebrating. I was just stunned that something like that could happen."

What happened turned around both franchises. "I felt it was a secure play," Giants head coach John McVay said after the game. "How much more secure can you get [than] giving the ball to [Csonka] and running it? I've been in this game 25 years. And that's the most horrifying end to a game I've ever seen."

The Giants, who were trying to get to .500 that day, didn't recover from the play. They fired Gibson the next day and went on to miss the playoffs for the 15th straight season. McVay was fired at the

MIRACLE 4

All of a 21-point fourth-quarter deficit had been erased in the span of eight minutes. If that wasn't miraculous enough, what happened next surely was.

There were 14 seconds left in what was now a 31–31 tie between the Giants and Eagles at the "New Meadowlands," later named MetLife Stadium in 2010. The Eagles sent DeSean Jackson back to field Matt Dodge's punt. Jackson had been the NFL's best punt returner in 2009, with a 15.2 yard average and two returns for touchdowns. In 2010, with an increased role in the offense and a nagging foot injury, he didn't return quite as often, but he was still a threat.

"He whistled and I looked up, because you know that whistle is from Coach [Andy] Reid," Jackson said. "He said, 'Get your butt back there.' So I go back there and he keeps whistling at me. He's whistling and whistling. I look over and he's yelling, 'Look it in, look it in, make sure you're good.' I'm like 'Coach, I got this.' But to be honest I never thought they were going to kick it to me. I thought they were going to kick it out of bounds and that would be that. We would go to overtime."

That was the plan.

"I was definitely looking to kick it out of bounds," Dodge said. "Everyone kept telling me that. They didn't have to tell me. It wasn't rocket science not to kick it to him. Sometimes you just don't execute as well as you would like. It was a bad time to get off a line drive."

Jackson bobbled the ball, but it bounced right back to him at the 35-yard line. He high-stepped past one defender, got a block from wide receiver Jason Avant, and he was gone. He actually ran along the goal line to make sure there was 0:00 on the clock when he scored.

It was the first walk-off punt return in NFL history.

end of the season, which led to the hiring of Ray Perkins as Giants head coach, which led to the addition of Bill Parcells as defensive coordinator, which eventually led to two Super Bowl titles with Parcells as head coach.

For the Eagles, the win made them 7–5 on the season and propelled them to a 9–7 season, their first winning season since 1966 and a wild-card playoff appearance. From there they would make the playoffs in four straight years, including their Super Bowl run in 1980.

"You know I grew up in North Jersey, right near the Meadowlands," Walters said. "A friend of mine owned a restaurant near the stadium, and every year we played them he had a party for me there after the game. We had won [at the Meadowlands] all of my first three years with the Eagles, so it was always a good time. Now, I'm sitting there, as we're losing, and I'm thinking [sarcastically], 'This is going be a real good party.' Then Herm makes that play and we win the game. It was stunning."

Edwards' play didn't just turn around that game, or even that season. It gave an Eagles team that had been down for a long time a reason to believe. "I've always said this," Walters said. "That 'Miracle of the Meadowlands' play might have turned it all around for us. Who knows what might have been if that never happened?"

11

BACK TO BACK

What the Philadelphia Eagles did in 1948 and 1949 had never been done before and has never been done since. Not only did those Eagles, under head coach Earl "Greasy" Neale, win back-to-back NFL titles, but they won both championship games with shutouts.

In 1948 the Eagles beat the Chicago Cardinals 7–0 at home to win their first-ever title; then they came back the following season to beat the Los Angeles Rams 14–0 in Los Angeles.

Consider the Eagles won two titles in two years and have won just one more since. And that the back-to-back shutouts are the only time it's happened in NFL history.

"That Eagles team of the postwar era is one of the greatest teams ever," longtime Philadelphia sportswriter and coauthor of *The Eagles Encyclopedia* Ray Didinger said. "Think about back-to-back shutouts in the NFL Championship Games. The Cardinals team they beat was 11–1. The Rams team had two Hall of Fame quarterbacks and two Hall of Fame receivers. And they shut out both of them."

As most Eagles fans know, that 1948 game against Chicago was played in a snowstorm that blanketed the field and almost canceled the game.

"You know the story about Steve, right?" David Boyce, a close friend of the late Steve Van Buren, said. "He wasn't going to go to the game. He thought it was off. He thought there was no way they were going to play the game," Boyce says now with a chuckle. As legend has it and no one has ever denied it, Van Buren woke up the morning of December 19, 1948, looked out his window, saw all the snow, and went back to bed.

Most of the rest of that Eagles team that had gone 9–2–1 during the season had made it to Shibe Park, the Eagles' home in

1948. Van Buren, the star running back who rushed for 945 yards and 10 touchdowns, was MIA.

Neale gave Van Buren a call suggesting he might want to find a way to the game. The player lived in Haverford, a Philadelphia suburb. He couldn't drive his car through the snow, and it was plowed in anyway. So he took a bus to 69th Street, then took the Market-Frankford-El to City Hall. From there he transferred to the Broad Street Subway, which he took to Lehigh Ave. He walked the final six blocks to Shibe Park, which sat at the corner of Lehigh and 21st Streets.

Imagine the greatest player in the game at the time and one of the greatest of all time doing any of those things, never mind all of them in one day, in order to get to a game.

Van Buren actually arrived in plenty of time, since the start of the game had been delayed almost an hour. Players from both teams turned into grounds-crew members to help clear the field as

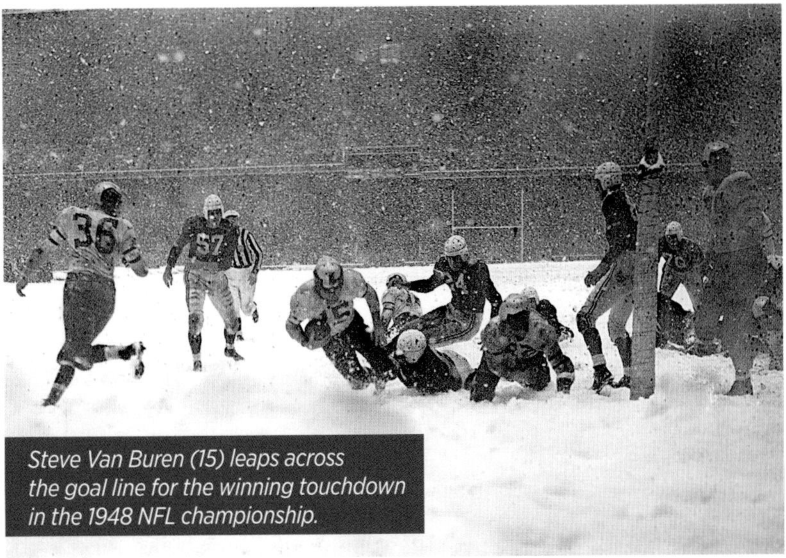

Steve Van Buren (15) leaps across the goal line for the winning touchdown in the 1948 NFL championship.

much as they could. “It was quite a sight to see,” Eagles lineman Al Wistert said. “And the snow kept coming down.”

The ’48 Eagles had a prolific offense for its time. Not only was there Van Buren at running back, but quarterback Tommy Thompson had thrown 25 touchdown passes in the 12-game season. Five times that season the Eagles scored 42 points or more; seven times they had scored 34 or more. On this day the snow provided the best defense they had seen all season and through three quarters it was a scoreless game.

“I was starting to think nobody is going to score,” Wistert said in 2010. “I thought, ‘We’re going to be out here all night.’”

Then late in the third quarter, Cardinals’ quaterback Ray Mallouf fumbled. The Eagles’ Bucko Kilroy recovered at the Chicago 17-yard line.

The Eagles moved to a first-and-goal from the Cardinals 5-yard line as the fourth quarter began. Van Buren got the call and ran behind Wistert on a cut to the left and into the end zone. It was the only touchdown of the game in what remains the lowest scoring championship game in NFL history.

“Nobody even touched him,” Wistert said.

Nobody could touch the Eagles in 1949, either. They won their first three games of the season, including a 28–3 win over the Cardinals, before losing for the first and only time all season, 38–21 to the Bears in Chicago. The Eagles finished the season with an eight-game winning streak, winning by an average of almost 26 points per game. The closest game they played down the stretch was the regular-season finale against the New York Giants which they won 17–3.

Van Buren was again the star of the team, setting a league record with 1,146 yards rushing and 11 touchdowns. Thompson’s numbers were down from ’48, but he still threw 16 touchdown passes.

The defense, which held six opponents to seven points or less during the season, also intercepted 29 passes and recovered 14 fumbles in the 12-game season. Dick Humpert, playing in his final season, had seven interceptions, as did Frank Reagan, from the University of Pennsylvania. Pat McHugh had six.

They stood to face the Rams in the first-ever NFL Championship Game played on the West Coast. Neale didn't like to fly, so the Eagles took a three-day train trip across the country, with a stop in Albuquerque, New Mexico, to practice. When they arrived in Southern California they were greeted with heavy rains that turned the Los Angeles Coliseum field to slop.

The Eagles scored just before the half on a 31-yard touchdown pass from Thompson—one of just five passes he would complete on the day—to Pete Pihos.

It stayed that way until late in the third quarter, when the Rams were forced to punt. Future Hall of Fame quarterback Bob Waterfield was also the Rams' punter, and he barely fielded a high snap from center. Eagles rookie Don Skladany broke through, blocked Waterfield's punt, and scored the game's final touchdown.

"He almost got one earlier in the game," Wistert said. "He came close. But that time he came full bore and by golly, he got that punt."

Van Buren was the star of the day with a playoff-record 196 rushing yards, and the Eagles defense held the Rams to a total of just 119 yards.

The rookie Skladany, who passed away in 2003, played in just seven NFL games in his career and started just one. His blocked punt and touchdown play, however, remains one of the biggest in Eagles history.

During those two championship seasons the Eagles went 22–3–1, counting the two NFL Championship Game wins and outscored their

ALMOST A THIRD

The only team ever to win three straight NFL Championships were Vince Lombardi's Green Bay Packers from 1965 to 1967. But the Eagles came oh so close.

Before winning back-to-back titles in 1948 and 1949, they lost the 1947 NFL Championship Game to the Chicago Cardinals by a single touchdown. And just like the snowstorm in the '48 game and the driving rains in '49, weather played a factor in the '47 game. Comiskey Park, host to its only NFL title game, was frozen, which led to tough conditions.

The Cardinals jumped out to an early 14–0 lead, and while the Eagles closed to within seven points three times, they could never get any closer. Tommy Thompson passed for 297 yards that day but threw three interceptions. And Steve Van Buren could manage just 26 yards rushing on the slick turf.

opponents by an average score of 29–11. From those teams, Van Buren, Pihos, Alex Wojciechowicz, and Chuck Bednarik are all enshrined in the Pro Football Hall of Fame, as is Neale.

"It was great knowing that everybody was trying to defeat the defending champions," Van Buren said after the '49 game. "And no matter how hard they tried, they couldn't knock us off our perch."

12

THE FOG BOWL

December 30, 1988, was unseasonably warm for Chicago, where wintertime temperatures could and usually did hit single digits. That was far from the strangest weather of the weekend. Because of the warm air mass that drifted in off Lake Michigan combined with cooler air over Chicago, New Year's Eve day turned from a sunny 25-degree morning into a compete fog as the Philadelphia Eagles and Chicago Bears met at Soldier Field in the NFC playoffs.

"It's just before halftime and we're standing on the sideline and all of a sudden it was thick billows coming over the wall," Eagles linebacker Mike Reichenbach remembered. "We thought it was a fire. I really thought there was a fire somewhere in the stadium. It was so thick you could see it rolling down the steps. It was like one of those horror films, step by step by step."

Perhaps fittingly, it turned into a horror show for the Eagles, who eventually lost to the Bears 20–12 after falling behind, 17–9 before the fog rolled in and took over Soldier Field.

"It wasn't just the fog," Reichenbach said. "We had chances early and didn't score. We had two touchdowns called back. Keith [Jackson], who played a great game, dropped a touchdown pass. When you're in playoff games and you're kicking field goals, you're in trouble."

The Eagles had their chances in that first half while the sun was still out. They drove into Chicago territory seven times—six times inside the 30 and three times inside the 15—and never scored a touchdown. Instead they settled for three Luis Zendejas field goals, which just wasn't enough, fog or not.

"No excuses, because we should've scored more early and had the lead," linebacker Seth Joyner said. "But it was almost like the minute the Bears took the lead, then the fog rolled in. And I remember when it started to roll in I said, 'Whoever has the lead is going to win.' And the Bears had the lead. Some people thought they might delay the game. But they were not going to delay the game."

Both teams went in at halftime and by the time they returned the fog had become so thick that the league actually allowed the writers in the press box to go onto the field to "watch" the game. I can tell you that in the press box it seemed as if someone had painted the glass white; unfortunately, being on the field wasn't all that much better.

"It just kept getting thicker and thicker," Reichenbach said. "We come back out at halftime and it's so thick you can't see. You really can't see. The ref was Jim Tunney. I see him standing near the end zone, Buddy [Ryan, the Eagles head coach] tells me to go find out what he's going to do. I go over and he says, 'If we can see the other goal post, we're playing.' I don't know how he could see it, because I couldn't see it."

Nobody could.

"It was the strangest game ever," Eagles wide receiver Mike Quick said. "You really couldn't see anything."

Not from the field, or high above it. Eagles play-by-play man Merrill Reese, who began his 40th year doing Eagles games in 2016, never experienced anything like it. "Stan [Walters, his color analyst] said it looked like someone set off a smoke bomb," Reese remembered. "By halftime you couldn't see anything. I tried to keep it going by saying funny things. I said, 'Randall Cunningham just broke the huddle led by a German Shepherd.'"

But how did he continue to broadcast the game? "They had a public address announcer I couldn't see, who was on the sideline with a microphone," Reese said. "He would say what happened and

I just tried to string together what I heard him say. It was the only game I ever did that I didn't actually see."

Reese wasn't alone. Eagles quarterback Randall Cunningham, who threw for 407 yards but was intercepted three times, couldn't see either. "It was horrible," Cunningham said. "Realistically, when Mike Quick and the other receivers went to line up, I couldn't see them. I saw [Chicago middle linebacker] Mike Singletary across the line, but if he dropped back I couldn't see him either. The refs couldn't have known what was going on. They couldn't see anything either. It was impossible to tell what was going on out there. The game was over at that point."

It was as tough for the Eagles defense as it was for the offense. "Reichenbach had to run to the numbers to get the signals

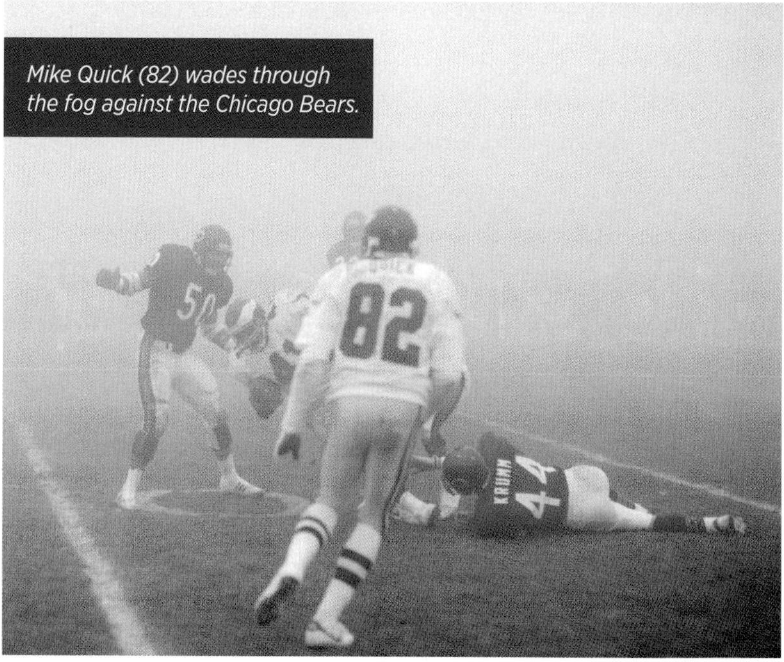

Mike Quick (82) wades through the fog against the Chicago Bears.

because you couldn't see the other side of the field," Joyner said. "That's how bad it was."

"We made our calls from the sideline," Reichenbach explained. "Buddy is trying to give me hand signals, like he always did, and I can't see him. I had to run over to the sideline to get the signals, or at least to the hash mark. Now I have to find out where everybody is going and then get our guys matched up. But it was hard to see where their guys were. Luckily they were wearing dark jerseys. If they were wearing white we would have really been in trouble.

"I never played in any game like that. The hardest part was when we dropped back in pass coverage, you couldn't see who had the ball. You were just grabbing guys in your area. And it got brutal, because you couldn't see anything and the refs couldn't see anything. There was all kinds of stuff going on out there. It was like the WWF."

The fog, which cleared about an hour after the end of the game, ended the Eagles' season. It denied them a spot in the NFC Championship Game against the San Francisco 49ers. It also

ON THIS DATE

Playing on New Year's Eve was never kind to Buddy Ryan's Eagles. The year after that foggy loss in Chicago, they hosted the Los Angeles Rams on December 31 and lost 21–7 in the wild-card round of the playoffs.
The curse lifted on New Year's Eve 2000, when the Eagles finally got a New Year's Eve win. In Andy Reid's first playoff game as head coach, the Eagles hosted and beat the Tampa Bay Buccaneers 21–3 in a wild-card game.

diminished the matchup of Ryan against Bears head coach Mike Ditka, a heated rivalry that stemmed from the two working together during the Bears' Super Bowl XX victory.

"This was a big game for Buddy," Joyner said. "Everyone knew that Bears team won because of Buddy's defense, and I'm sure he thought he should have been the head coach of that team. And then there was the fact that he and Ditka didn't get along. So, yeah, it was a big game for him."

It was a big game for an Eagles team that would never get closer to a Super Bowl under Ryan nor under anyone else until 2001.

"I believe that was the Eagles' best team of the Buddy Ryan years and it could have gone far," Reese said. "But to Buddy's credit, he never made the fog an excuse."

Quick thought so too, though he blamed the fog himself. "During my entire career, that was the one legitimate opportunity I had to go to a Super Bowl," he said. "And to this day I believe the main reason we didn't go was because of the fog. I really believe that was our year."

CIRCLING THE FIELD

Buddy Ryan said he was going to do it. And almost 30 years later, nobody believed he actually did it.

When the Eagles won the NFC East in 1988 and learned a week later they would travel to Chicago to play the Bears in the second round of the playoffs, Ryan was thrilled. It was a chance to go back to Soldier Field and to face his archrival, Mike Ditka, with an Eagles team that could give the favored Bears trouble.

Ryan and Ditka had coached together and built the Bears into a world champion that rolled through the 1985 season on the way to an easy Super Bowl XX win against New England.

Now Ryan had a chance to go back with his Eagles team and face most of that same Bears team he helped build. "We can't wait," Ryan said early in the week. "We're not going to sneak into town either. We're going in with the lights on and the horns blowing. We're going to let them know the Eagles are in town."

Ryan wasn't speaking in metaphors. That's exactly what they did. After the Eagles plane landed at O'Hare Airport the team bus took a detour to their downtown hotel, riding by Soldier Field with, yes, its lights on and the horn blowing.

"I still can't believe he did it," Jeff Fisher, Ryan's defensive coordinator at the time and later the head coach of the Tennessee Titans and St. Louis / Los Angeles Rams, said. "I mean, we thought he was kidding."

He wasn't.

"We leave the airport and we're actually going to drive around the stadium," middle linebacker Mike Reichenbach said. "We drove around and there wasn't anyone around. The only ones who heard the horns beeping were us."

Still, not everyone was surprised. "Nothing Buddy did surprised me," linebacker Seth Joyner quipped.

13

A RETURN FOR THE AGES

What turned out to be the greatest interception return in Philadelphia Eagles history, maybe NFL history, almost never happened.

"I was just going to run out of bounds," Eagles cornerback Eric Allen said many years after his incredible touchdown return against the Jets in 1993. Instead Allen ran everywhere—except out of bounds. All you need to know is that he picked off the pass at the Eagles 6-yard line in front of the Jets sideline and when he scored he ran past the Eagles sideline.

"I really wasn't thinking about a big return when it happened," Allen said. "But I began to see some of their offensive linemen walking toward the sideline. So, now I'm thinking, 'OK, I'll just get as many yards as I can.' But I still didn't think I was going to go all the way. I went to the Pop Warner days, 'There's an opening here, an opening there.' If it was a big guy, I ran around him. If there was a small guy, I ran through him."

Allen ran and ran and ran some more. It went down in the box score as a 94-yard return, which at the time was tied for the second longest in Eagles history. In reality, Allen ran close to 150 yards on the play.

"You think it was 150?" Eagles linebacker Seth Joyner asked. "I thought it was closer to 200." However many yards it covered, it ended in the end zone and gave the Eagles a 35–30 comeback win over the Jets at the Meadowlands.

"It seemed like every hole I ran through was about to close, but I got through it just before it did," Allen said. "Then I picked up some blocks and started going. I remember [cornerback] Ben Smith running with me and yelling for me to pitch it to him. Pitch it? Are you kidding me?"

This was the scene. The Eagles, who trailed at one point 21–0 and had lost quarterback Randall Cunningham to a broken leg, had fought

BILL BRADLEY

Before Eric Allen or Troy Vincent or even Brian Dawkins, all star defensive backs for the Eagles, there was Bill Bradley.

From his rookie year in 1969 to the time he left in 1976, Bradley was as good a safety as the Eagles, or the NFL, had seen. The problem was, not too many people saw it.

In Bradley's day the NFL wasn't anything like what it is today. And the Eagles were at the bottom of the pecking order when it came to being televised or getting any national exposure.

Bradley's Eagles team never had a winning record, reaching .500 just once in his nine seasons for a combined record of 41–81–6. That didn't stop the safety from Texas from making plays.

Forty years after his last game as an Eagle, Bradley still shares the franchise lead in career interceptions (34) with Allen and Dawkins. His 11 interceptions in 1971 is still the most by an Eagle in any one season, and his nine interceptions in 1972, is tied for second.

"I've gotten to know Eric over the years," Bradley said. "And we've talked about sharing the record. But shoot, that record has been around since 1977. That might be as long as a record has lasted."

The interception he'll never forget is his first, on his first NFL play from scrimmage. It came against the Cowboys, when he picked off a Roger Staubach pass intended for Mike Ditka and had Bob Hayes chase him to the end zone.

"Yeah, three Hall of Famers and me," Bradley said. "Roger checked off and threw where he thought Ditka was going to be. But Mike ran straight ahead and I ran to the spot where he was supposed to be. Now I'm running to the end zone with the ball in one hand and I'm showing the Cowboys my IQ with my other hand. Now, keep in my mind I wasn't all that fast, and all of a sudden Hayes is chasing me. He hits me just as I got to the end zone."

back to make it 30–28 in the fourth quarter. The Jets, however, were driving, with a chance to put the game away. On second down Jets quarterback Boomer Esiason, who had been shaken up earlier in the drive on a late hit by defensive tackle Keith Millard, looked down the left sideline for receiver Chris Burkett. Millard again pressured Esiason on the play, perhaps making him throw it a little sooner than he would have liked. The pass hung in the air just long enough for Allen to get in front of Burnett and make the interception. Then the fun began.

"He was zigzagging all over the field," Eagles defensive tackle Andy Harmon remembered. "I'm out there trying to help him. I want to block somebody, but I didn't know who to block because I didn't know which way he was going to go next."

It was one of just many great plays Allen made in his career with the Eagles, New Orleans Saints, and Oakland Raiders—a career that included 54 interceptions, eight returned for touchdowns, over the span of 14 years. He shares the franchise's all-time mark of 34 interceptions with safeties Brian Dawkins and Bill Bradley.

"Eric was just a phenomenal athlete," Joyner said. "Any time he got his hands on the ball he could take it to the end zone. He was a true playmaker in every sense of the word."

What's more, the play against the Jets in 1993 wasn't over when Allen crossed the goal line. The cornerback saw Cunningham standing, on crutches, just outside of the tunnel that led to the field. He ran over—what was a few more yards at that point?—and handed him the ball.

"That's the kind of team we had back then," Cunningham said. "That was what Buddy [Ryan] built: guys who were unified. I mean, here he just made that great play—and it was a great, great play—and that ball is his. He could have done anything with that ball. And he comes over and hands it to me. To me it was like saying, 'OK, man, here's the ball. Start your way back.'

"I'm just standing there when it happens. And I had just gotten the X-rays back on my leg and I'm feeling down. I'm going to be out for the rest of the season. Then I heard [wide receiver] Fred Barnett broke his leg too. And we're losing the game. It was a bad day. Then Eric makes that play. It was incredible. I started to jump up and down—and then I remembered I was on crutches.

"Then he comes over and hands me the ball. It turned everything around. I was standing there feeling so bad, feeling sorry for myself. I mean, I was helpless. I thought we were going to lose the game too. Then all of a sudden we're winning and I'm holding the game ball."

When asked about the gesture, Allen said he saw Cunningham as he entered the end zone and just felt it was the right thing to do. "We were such a close team," Allen said. "And it hit me right there that his season was over. After all the ups and downs we had been through, now he's hurt for the second time in three years and is going to miss the season. Reggie [White] had left [as a free agent]. Randall was our leader and his season was over. I wanted to make sure he realized and that everybody recognized what a big part of our team he still was. I wanted him to feel at that point that he wasn't alone. You're not by yourself, you're still a part of this team."

Allen would play just one more season for the Eagles before leaving as a free agent for the Saints. He ended his career with the Raiders, his final game a 2001 playoff loss to the New England Patriots in the infamous "tuck rule" game.

"I loved my time in Philly because of all of those guys with me there," Allen said. "I love those guys and I loved that fan base, who didn't want anything less than your best. I had good times in New Orleans and Oakland, but I'll always be an Eagle."

14

FROM CHEERS TO TEARS

To understand the impact Dick Vermeil made on the Philadelphia Eagles you have to understand exactly what the coach walked into back in 1976.

"We were bad," wide receiver Harold Carmichael said. "There's no getting around that. We were a bad team. That's what for me, anyway, made winning so special: because I was there when we were so bad." From their 1960 NFL Championship team until Vermeil arrived from the campus of UCLA in 1976, the Eagles had posted just two winning seasons, in 1961 and 1966. Their combined record in those 15 years was 74–127–9. During that span they came in last place seven times.

"Dick just came in and instilled that discipline that was lacking on the team," Pro Bowl linebacker Bill Bergey said. "I tried to help him along at times. I remember there was one guy on the team, a real dog. He came up with a fake injury during the preseason. And I'm thinking. 'He's going to make the team now, because he says he's hurt.' I went to Dick, told him what I saw, and he said, 'Don't worry about it.' He knew what was going on, and that guy didn't make the team. You just saw things like that from Dick."

Not right away they didn't. Bergey, Carmichael, and left tackle Stan Walters were three of the best, if not the three best, players Vermeil inherited and all three of them weren't so sure about this hotshot college coach from the other coast.

"No, I didn't see it at first," Bergey said. "I remember one night early on, I'm in my room and I say to my roommate, Frank LeMaster, 'Are you hurting?' He said, 'Yeah, I'm hurting.' I said, 'I'm glad, because I am too and I thought it was just me.' This guy really worked us, and we weren't used to that. And it bothered you a little bit to have this coach from UCLA, who wasn't much older than me, and he's telling me I have to keep my chinstrap buckled and I couldn't take a knee and he would tell us when we could have water. This has to be the most Harry High School coach I've ever played for. This wasn't going to work. I'm an All-Pro. I know what it takes. I made All-Pro both of my first two years here. What's this guy done? But, you know what, I said to myself I'm going to buy into his way. I'm not going to drop out until I see how it goes."

Walters, like Bergey, came via trade from the Cincinnati Bengals. He arrived a year before Vermeil and suffered through Mike McCormack's final year as head coach. His story is similar. "My first reaction when Vermeil got there was 'This guy is kind of young.' I had been used to Paul Brown and Tiger Johnson, and then McCormack," Walters said. "This guy wasn't much older than me and he looked younger than me. I remember telling my wife, 'I don't know about this guy. I never played for a coach this young.'

"Then that first training camp was really, really tough. And you have to give him credit: he started at the bottom. I mean the very bottom. He brought the UCLA track coach out with him, and he taught us how to run. I mean, talk about starting at the bottom—he was teaching us how to run. That's pretty basic, about as basic as it gets. And it was tough. He has us running and telling us how to run. We're offensive linemen, we're not sprinters. We don't want to run. But we did. Every day.

"In Cincinnati with Paul Brown's camps, and that's all I know, we went an hour and a half in the morning and an hour in the afternoon and with very little contact. We went with 25 plays, and when that 25th play was over we were finished. That was it. Now we have Dick, who wants to coach everyone up. Paul protected his players. He didn't want to kill us. [In Philadelphia] we had 90 guys and 45 of them would be in the training room. Dick killed us. He had us out there two and a half, three hours some times."

It wasn't just the offensive linemen, the wide receivers worked just as hard. "The problem, it wasn't a problem, but none of us—and I'm speaking for the wide receivers—had ever worked that hard in practice before," Carmichael said. "He ran us all day, every day. I mean wide receivers used to be able to take some plays off and stand around and watch. Not anymore. He had us down on the other side of the field, and if he ever saw any of us standing around, he would jog down and talk to [receivers coach] Dick Coury and he would make us run some more. Yeah, when he first got here, it was tough to buy in at first. But after a while we went all in on him. We saw what he was building and thought it just might work. We felt we were becoming a winning team."

It took time. The Eagles went 4–10 in Vermeil's first season and were beaten soundly in eight of those 10 losses. They improved a game to 5–9 in 1977, but only two of the nine losses were by more than one score.

"You started to see something going on," Walters said. "And then you really saw the progress in the third year."

The Eagles made the playoffs as a 9–7 wild-card team in 1978, their first playoff appearance since the 1960 Championship Game, and posted their first winning record since 1966. When they failed to bring a place kicker to the playoff game against Atlanta (kicker Nick Mike-Mayer was hurt and they decided punter Mike Michel could handle it), they lost 14–13 on a missed extra point and a missed field goal.

In 1979 the team improved to 11–5 and won their first playoff game in 19 years with a 27–17 win over the Chicago Bears. They would lose in the second round at Tampa Bay, 24–17.

The fifth season, 1980, was the proverbial phoenix. Yes, the Eagles rolled to a 12–4 record during the regular season, won their first division title, beat the Minnesota Vikings 31–16 in the divisional round of the playoffs and the Dallas Cowboys 20–7 in the NFC Championship Game to advance to Super Bowl XV.

"Dick said it would be a five-year plan when he came in," longtime sportswriter and beat writer for the *Philadelphia Bulletin* Ray Didinger said. "The fifth year they got to the Super Bowl. Dick was everything you ever heard about him. He was fiercely driven and determined. He only knew one way to do things and that was 24/7. He was completely devoted to his football team."

And they to him.

"Go forward to our Super Bowl year," Bergey said. "There were only about eight or nine us left from when Vermeil first got there, and we still have the closest bond you could ever imagine. Those guys and Vermeil would do absolutely anything for each other. I mean that. In October [2015] I had a bunch of the guys over to the house. Vermeil and the guys with their wives or girlfriends. We were supposed to go from four to seven. Guys started getting there at three and the last

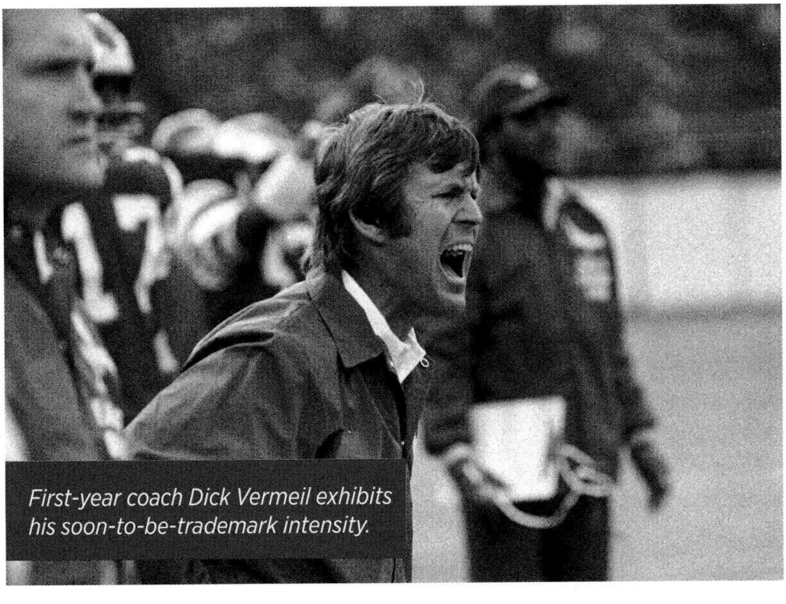

First-year coach Dick Vermeil exhibits his soon-to-be-trademark intensity.

ones didn't leave until two in the morning. Dick gave a speech and it was great. Everyone kids about him crying and all that, but we don't think about it. That's just the way he is."

After losing the Super Bowl to the Oakland Raiders, Vermeil took the Eagles back to the playoffs in 1981, but they were upset by the New York Giants, 27–21 in the first round. He coached the strike-shortened season of 1982 and made an impact on his first-round draft pick.

"I probably learned more football my rookie season in the NFL than I did any other time in my life, and that was because of Dick Vermeil," said wide receiver Mike Quick, the team's No. 1 pick in the 1982 Draft. "Training camp stuff and all of that, my head was swimming, but I learned so much: how to run stems on routes, and how to read coverages, the triangles to your side, the three defenders on your side. Things I didn't know anything about before. Dick was a great teacher."

And then he retired. In his tearful speech he talked of "burnout," and considering the way he worked it wasn't a surprise to anyone. Others around the team felt that the strike year took a lot out of him. Whatever his reasons, he was gone.

"*Charisma.* If you look up the word in the dictionary, Dick Vermeil's picture is there," Eagles longtime radio broadcaster Merrill Reese said. "I think he's the best Eagles coach of all time. To this day I think he's the single-most popular coach in Philadelphia history—any sport... Over 30 years after his final game here, he's still revered to the point where billboards still bear his picture. He can still take all the speaking engagements he can handle. He's just beloved in this city."

15

BUDDY

Buddy Ryan believed in coaches paying their dues, working their way up the coaching ladder and not being handed anything. That's why he got along better with, say, the New York Giants' Bill Parcells than he did at first with the Dallas Cowboys' Jimmy Johnson.

So why weren't Ryan and Don Shula, the NFL's winningest head coach, better friends? "I don't know," Ryan said. "I don't have anything against Don. He doesn't like me for some reason. After [the Jets, where Ryan was an assistant coach] beat him in Super Bowl III, I saw him at a function. I said, 'Hey, Don, thanks for the ring.' Ever since then he hasn't liked me."

That story that Ryan told me after he was finished coaching sums up the former Eagles head coach perfectly. He didn't care what he said, when he said it, or who heard him say it. He spoke his mind. He told the truth. That was true from his earliest days until he passed away on June 28, 2016.

In his first minicamp with the Eagles in March 1986, he took a look at the team's 1983 first-round draft pick, running back Michael Haddix, and commented, "He looks like a reject guard from the USFL." Dwayne Jiles, a starting linebacker, was "an old washer woman."

At a luncheon the day after his first game as head coach, a loss to the Washington Redskins (in a strange symmetrical way, his last game was also a loss to the Redskins), Ryan said of the way team president Harry Gamble had risen up the hierarchy, "He must be the owner's illegitimate son."

And Norman Braman was "the owner" or, when he wasn't around, which was a lot of the time, "the guy in France."

Things were going to be different.

Ryan became the Eagles head coach, the first hired by Braman, after he helped lead the Chicago Bears to Super Bowl XX. (And after deals with David Shula, Don's son, and Jim Mora fell through.)

To Philadelphia's gain, Eagles football hasn't been the same since. Writers who covered the team under Ryan still tell stories in 2016 to younger writers who can't believe what they're hearing.

This was a coach who, after beating Dallas once on the final play of the game said, "The Cowboys know we're going to beat them. They just don't know how." A coach who had the team bus drive around Soldier Field with the lights on and the horn blowing, the day before the 1988 playoff game because "we weren't going to sneak into town." The coach who had his quarterback fake a kneel-down and throw a deep pass in the final minute of a game that was already won. A coach who then said about Cowboys coach Tom Landry, "He opened the can of worms. I closed it."

A coach who was accused of placing a bounty on a kicker against those same Cowboys and asked, "Why would I want to hurt a kicker who can't make kicks?"

After that "Bounty Bowl," Johnson said he tried to talk to Ryan "but his fat ass ran off the field." To which Ryan replied, "I've been on that Slim Fast. I thought I lost weight. I thought I was looking good."

And when an opposing player referred to what Ryan said as "the pathetic ramblings of a senile old man," Ryan's response was "I'm not that old."

Oh, the Eagles were in for a change all right.

After their Super Bowl year of 1980, the Eagles had become just another NFL team. They weren't as bad, or good, as they were boring. That changed in a hurry under Ryan.

"The Eagles had kind of settled into a .500 attitude," said middle linebacker Mike Reichenbach, who was with the team for two years before Ryan arrived. "I remember I came in as a free agent and I worked and I trained and when I came to camp it wasn't anything that strenuous. I was shocked. The team had settled into that mentality. And they found ways to lose. It wasn't that way under Buddy."

That first summer of '86, as his players went through a camp like they had never seen before, Ryan grabbed a microphone and in front a packed house at West Chester University proclaimed his team, which had come in fourth place in the NFC East in 1985, would win its division and sweep its opponents. The crowd went wild. Then the Eagles went 5–10–1 and finished in fourth place in the NFC East.

"Buddy got it, that football was entertainment," linebacker Garry Cobb said. "It's why the game is so successful. Buddy played to the fans, and he played to the media. As a player, Buddy was fun to play for, especially if you were on defense. He cared about the players too. He didn't always want that side of him out there, but he really cared."

"Buddy was a lot deeper than he showed people. He was very intelligent. And he wore his emotion on his sleeve," Randall Cunningham said. "But he was a barroom brawler, a 'you weren't going to put anything over on me' kind of guy. And that's what I needed. I was laid back, from California. It was a change for me. That intensity level he gave us made us all better. He wanted us to be a little edgy. He wanted us to be a little different. Think about it, he allowed us to leave at halftime of a preseason game to go to Whitney [Houston]'s birthday party. What other coach would do that? But that's how much he cared about us. He said, 'I'll take it on the chin for you guys.' He was a father figure to a lot of us."

What did Cunningham have to do to allow the coach to let him leave? Not that much. "I showed him the invitation and I think he got a little overwhelmed," Cunningham said. "I think he was impressed. I think he wanted to go too. I told him I wanted to take some of the guys, but that we would have to leave at halftime. I remember him saying, 'You're not going to be playing after halftime anyway.'"

Linebacker Seth Joyner, one of Ryan's first draft choices, an eighth-rounder out of Texas–El Paso, who was originally cut and then re-signed, had him figured out better than most. Joyner played all five years Ryan was in Philadelphia and then both of his years as head coach of the Arizona Cardinals as well. "I played for some great coaches, some of the top defensive minds in the game: Buddy, Bud Carson, Fritz Shurmur. Buddy was something else with the way he handled players," Joyner said. "Fritz had a great personality, but there was a line between him and his players. Bud Carson, the same way. Buddy got close to his players, extremely close. That was the difference. We felt he was always 100 percent in our corner. Buddy played mind games, because he wanted to see who was tough enough to handle it. If you couldn't handle it, you wouldn't handle it when it got tough on the field. I figured him out. A lot of guys couldn't. With that said, every one of us would have run through a brick wall for him."

Once Ryan got rid of the players he didn't want, after his first cuts he said, "My wife could have cut those guys." And when asked about a specific player who had a decent camp, he said, "Check his record. He's been cut before." From that point on, the players became *his* players.

"When Buddy first got there, everyone is fighting for a job," Reichenbach said. "MAB Paints had this big team photo with every guy from the year before, as they got cut we would cut the guy out. There wasn't much left to that photo."

Once he got his guys, everything was different. "It was great playing for Buddy," Joyner said. "A lot of guys who came through Philly and Arizona, some didn't like Buddy. And a lot of people said with Buddy you either loved him or hated him, and I guess that was true. But the ones who hated him were the ones who couldn't play for him, because he was brutally honest with you. Once you became one of his guys, then there was a relationship there, a bond that was never broken.

"My first two years, I was known as 59. One day, out of the blue, he calls me by my name and I almost passed out. I knew right then and there I had won his approval. That's the way he was. Until you won his approval, you were just a number. I mean, I knew he knew my name. But he didn't give you that respect until he knew you were a guy he could go to war with. Now, once you won that approval it became a whole different relationship.

"I can remember when Clyde [Simmons] and I held out. We held out the entire training camp. We came in like the week before the regular season opener. But at the end of the prior season, Buddy came to me and said, 'I know your contract is up. Do what you got to do to get what you got to get. Now, you're probably going to have to hold out because they're not going to give you what you deserve from the start. Now, understand there are some things I'm going to have to say to the media or whatever, and you're going to hear some things. But that's what I have to say. You just do what you have to do.' How many coaches would tell a player that? Nobody.

"And then I heard it. 'This kid is playing great. Joyner better get his ass in here or he's going to lose his job.' Then I report that

Tuesday before the game and guess who's starting at practice Wednesday? How can you not love a coach who deals with you on that level?"

Reichenbach had the same kind of relationship with Ryan, and like Joyner he had to earn that respect. He did it by learning the calls for the 46 defense Ryan was installing. "When he first got there he called me into his office and told me he liked the way I played and that I was going to be his signal caller," Reichenbach said. "He hands me this thick playbook and says, 'Take this home and learn all the plays.' I'm sweating a little bit, but I go home and study the playbook. I come back the next day and he tests me on it. I got the calls right. Then he hands me another book and says, 'Now learn this one.' He did it for two weeks.

"Then after that he told me before our first camp started, 'You better come back in the best shape of your life because I'm going to kill these guys, and whoever falls is gone. I can't have you falling.' And he did try to kill us. But he changed our culture."

Ryan spent that first year, 1986, finding out who could play his way and who couldn't. The following year was the strike; and then his final three years with the Eagles the team went 31–17 and made the playoffs in all three years.

"We go to Detroit to practice that first year," Reichenbach said of scrimmages with the Lions before a preseason game. "We never showed them the 46. Then we would practice the 46 on our own. Now, we play the game and we line up in the 46 and we're blitzing from everywhere. It's the preseason. We killed them. We had like 10 sacks, but they never expected any of it. But Buddy was making a statement. He brought life back to the franchise."

And he brought great players to the Eagles. Yes, he inherited Cunningham and Reggie White, but his drafts added Pro Bowl players Joyner and Simmons, tight end Keith Jackson, defensive tackle Jerome Brown, and cornerback Eric Allen.

"Buddy's eye for talent was second to none," Cobb said. "His drafts were great. If he wanted to he would have been a great general manager."

Ryan had turned the Eagles into one of the top teams in the NFC. But three straight losses in the playoffs, two at home, combined with his disdain for the ownership, cost him his job after the 1990 season.

"Every coach has blind spots," Reichenbach said, "and Buddy just needed to surround himself with better people, more innovative people on offense, and I think it would have been different. He would have been there a long time and won a lot more games."

Reichenbach left the Eagles as a free agent before Ryan's final season and signed with the Miami Dolphins, where he played for Don Shula. "You know, Shula had a similar mentality [to] Buddy," Reichenbach said. "He wasn't as bold, but they were very similar in their approach."

Amazing that they didn't get along better.

16

THE DUTCHMAN

A promise that couldn't be kept led to a bitter ending to what should have been one of the greatest chapters in Philadelphia Eagles history. Maybe it's not the "Curse of Lombardi" that has kept the Eagles from winning a NFL title since 1960; perhaps it's the "Curse of Van Brocklin."

Let's go back to 1958, three seasons before the Eagles won the 1960 title with a 17–13 win engineered by quarterback Norm Van Brocklin against Vince Lombardi's Packers. It was the only playoff loss the great Lombardi ever suffered. Van Brocklin, frustrated in the offense run by Los Angeles Rams' head coach Sid Gillman, demanded a trade from the Western Conference team. It was a team with which he had won the 1951 Championship Game against the Cleveland Browns and gone to six Pro Bowls.

"He was exasperated with the Rams by 1957. He didn't get along with Sid Gillman. They were going to alternate quarterbacks [with Billy Wade] and he didn't want any part of it," longtime Eagles sportswriter and Eagles historian Ray Didinger said. "He went in and said, 'Trade me anywhere, just don't trade me to Pittsburgh or Philadelphia.'"

You know what happens next.

"So the Rams call him and say 'We traded you to the Eagles,'" Didinger continued. "He says 'Bulls——! I'm not going to the Eagles. I'll just retire.' He wanted no part of going to the Eagles."

Then came the promise. Bert Bell, former head coach of the Eagles from 1936 to 1940 and then NFL commissioner, wanted to make things right for both parties. He called Van Brocklin and convinced him to go along with the trade, with a big caveat: When he's finished playing, he would become the Eagles next head coach.

"Bert Bell called Van Brocklin," Didinger explained. "He tells him the head coach of the Eagles, Buck Shaw, is a little older and isn't going to coach much longer. 'You agree to the trade, go there, and in two, three years you'll be finished playing, Buck will step down as head coach, and I'll see to it that you'll be the head coach.'" It sounded like a good plan to Van Brocklin, who many called a coach on the field but who wanted to be a coach on the sideline sooner rather than later.

In between the trade and the unkept promise, Van Brocklin and Shaw turned the Eagles from a 2–9–1 team their first year together in 1958 to world champions in 1960. During that championship season, Van Brocklin threw for 2,471 yards and 24 touchdowns for a 10–2 regular-season finish.

"He was a great quarterback before he got to Philly," Eagles Hall of Fame wide receiver Tommy McDonald said of Van Brocklin. "He was great with the Rams. We were lucky to get him. I'll tell you one thing about Van Brocklin. He wasn't just a great quarterback; he was a great leader. He helped everyone on the team be better. We always knew if we had Van Brocklin we had a chance to win any game."

NO. 44

Norm Van Brocklin was the leader of the Eagles team that won the NFL title in 1960. No one doubts that. But Van Brocklin was helped at quarterback by having two great receivers in Tommy McDonald and Pete Retzlaff. In Van Brocklin's three years as Eagles quarterback, Retzlaff caught 136 passes for 2,187 yards. Acquired off waivers from the Detroit Lions in 1956, Retzlaff led the Eagles in receptions six times, made five Pro Bowls, and ultimately had his No. 44 retired by the Eagles organization.

"It's a great honor, it really is," Retzlaff said when his name and number went into the Eagles Honor Roll. "When you look at the names you're associated with, you can't help but be proud. It puts you in a very special category."

Said another Hall of Famer, Chuck Bednarik, about Van Brocklin: "We had a good team in '60, but we had a great quarterback. We would have never won without Van Brocklin."

The Eagles won, and Van Brocklin waited in the wings to take over coaching duties. In fact, both he and Shaw had announced their respective retirements going into the 1960 season.

"One of the reasons that team won in '60 was because they were afraid to let Van Brocklin down," Didinger said. "He had said before the season, 'This was it, and I want to go out on top.' His mission became their mission. They don't win the championship with any other quarterback."

Bell, the man who made the head coaching promise to Van Brocklin, died in 1959 of a heart attack suffered in the stands at Franklin Field during an Eagles game. And when Van Brocklin approached the Eagles about taking over as a head coach they were not only hesitant but they were poised to promote Shaw's assistant Nick Skorich. As irony would have it, Bell's replacement and the new commissioner of the NFL was Pete Rozelle, who had been the Rams general manager when Van Brocklin was traded to the Eagles.

Eagles radio broadcaster Merrill Reese, who calls Van Brocklin his "favorite player growing up. It's why I always wore No. 11," related the disappointment in the quarterback when he didn't land the head coaching job. "He was burned when he thought he was promised the coaching job," Reese said. "He thought the job was his, and instead they promoted Nick Skorich, who had been an assistant coach. It really hurt him."

Skorich's Eagles went 10–4 and were Eastern Conference runner-up his first year as head coach in 1961. Then fortunes quickly turned on the former assistant. The Eagles went 3–10–1 in 1962 and 2–10–2 in 1963. Scorich was replaced by Joe Kuharich in 1964.

Van Brocklin, spurned by the Eagles, was hired as head coach of the expansion Minnesota Vikings just a month after the Eagles won the 1960 NFL title. In seven years as the head coach of the Vikings, Van Brocklin compiled a 29–51–4 record, constantly battling with his quarterback, Fran Tarkenton, whom he preferred stay in the pocket as opposed to scrambling.

After Van Brocklin resigned from the Vikings in 1967, he spent two years as a broadcaster before he went back to coaching as head coach of the Atlanta Falcons. In seven years with the Falcons, he only did slightly better than he did with the Vikings, compiling a 37–49–3 record.

He never shied away from controversy. After losing a game in the final seconds on a field goal by a soccer-style European kicker, Van Brocklin said after the game, "They ought to change the goddamned immigration laws in this country."

When his coaching career was over and a brain tumor was found and removed, he later told the press, "It was a brain transplant. They gave me a sportswriter's brain to make sure I got one that hadn't been used."

Van Brocklin died of a heart attack in 1983 at the age of 57. He'll always be remembered for what he did for the Eagles in 1960.

"Best QB this team has ever had in a short period of time," Didinger said. "You can't compare the numbers because he was only here three years. He was a great passer. A true great passer, a great deep ball passer. And he was incredibly smart and a ferocious competitor and leader. Guys said all the time, they respected him but they also feared him."

17

THE PLAYERS' OWNER

There was a joke that made the rounds during the Philadelphia Eagles' 1980 Super Bowl run, after they lost a game to the San Diego Chargers 22–21. It went that Eagles owner Leonard Tose thought his team won because he thought the Chargers busted.

Funny, but sad. Because for all the good Tose did as owner of the Eagles from the time he bought the team in 1969 until he sold it to Norman Braman in 1985, he's mostly remembered for two things. First, he basically lost the Eagles, or was forced to sell the franchise, because of his Atlantic City gambling losses, particularly in blackjack. Second, people remember that he almost moved the team out of Philadelphia to Phoenix, Arizona.

While there is no denying Tose's bad luck at the A.C. tables (the obvious basis for the 22–21 joke), Tose should be given some credit for keeping the Eagles in Philadelphia when the team was up for sale at the end of the 1984 season. A year earlier Tose had almost come to a deal with local businessman and racehorse owner and enthusiast Lou Guida to sell the team. Guida actually thought the deal was finished and he had become the owner, but ultimately the deal fell through before completion.

Then in 1984, James Monaghan, a Phoenix real estate magnate, met with Tose. The two had a deal in place that would have moved the Eagles from Philadelphia to the Southwest desert. According to reports then, the deal would have kept Tose's daughter Susan Fletcher, who was then running the business side of the team, employed. Additionally, Tose would have also remained a minority owner.

It was a good deal for the Toses, if not Philadelphia. The local outcry that followed was as expected. And the Eagles owner became Public Enemy No. 1. And when the city, under then Mayor

Wilson Goode, stepped up and gave the team a new lease and an improved Veterans Stadium, the deal with Monaghan was off the table. Tose then sold the team to Braman in what was a lesser deal.

"People can say what they want about me," Tose said in interviews before he passed away in 2003, "but I turned down a much better deal to keep the team right here in Philadelphia. I never wanted the team to move."

Indeed, there was much more to Leonard Tose than hitting on 16, or trying to sell a football team out from under a city. It was under Tose that the Eagles Fly for Leukemia charity and the Ronald McDonald House program got their starts. Both are still going strong in 2016. "His generosity touched so many people," former Eagles general manager Jim Murray, the owner's right-hand man, said when Tose passed away in 2003. "Today there are people big and small, that he helped all throughout this city who are shedding a tear over Mr. Tose's passing. He was a man of great excesses, but especially in his generosity of spirit."

When financial troubles threatened to shut down football at several Philadelphia public high schools, Tose wrote a check to keep them afloat. He would read in the newspaper of a family having troubles and do the same. It didn't matter that he didn't know them.

He did get to know his players. Tose grew up an Eagles fan in the Bridgeport section of Montgomery County, just outside the city limits. He's the last Eagles owner to grow up locally and root for the team before he bought them.

"I loved the man," said Eagles Pro Bowl linebacker Bill Bergey. "He never got involved with the coaches. He let them coach. He was great to the players. He told us, 'If you ever have problems with anything football-related don't come to me, go to your coaches. Now, if any of you have any problems with girls, come to me. I can help you there.'"

While that might seem odd in today's game, it was just as rare in the 1980s. Then again, Leonard Tose was a rarity too.

"He was great," Pro Bowl wide receiver Mike Quick said. "As an owner he allowed the coaches to do whatever they needed to do and he supported them. He was around a lot. We always saw him. And he was very accommodating. And his generosity, that's all everyone talked about. He was so generous to everyone.

"Me personally, what I admired was how well he dressed. I was always into that myself, and you would see him he would have the cufflinked shirts with his initials on the sleeve. He was just immaculately dressed. I liked that."

Eagles Pro Bowl tackle Stan Walters says sometimes that generosity became embarrassing. "I remember going to A.C. once with my wife, and we see Mr. Tose," Walters said. "He hands my wife a handful of black chips and says 'You're Irish. You're lucky.' That's just how he was. Sometimes you wanted to avoid him because he was always doing stuff like that. You didn't know how to react.

"When my wife graduated from the Wharton School [of Business at the University of Pennsylvania], her parents came down and my parents came down and we all went out to Bookbinders [a well-known restaurant]. All of a sudden Leonard walks in and sees us and comes over. He meets our parents and asks if we're celebrating something. I tell him Kathy just graduated from Wharton. Next thing I know we have a bottle of expensive champagne sent over. And then he takes care of the bill. He did things like that all the time."

It wasn't just about buying the players expensive dinners. Tose showed he cared about what happened to them on the field as well. Wide receiver Harold Carmichael, a seventh-round pick out of Southern University, got hurt in his rookie year. In the 1970s players who got hurt, especially rookie seventh-rounders, didn't have to get paid their regular pay. They were, however, if they were Eagles.

"He was terrific to me," Carmichael said. "He really took care of me. There were times when we had to go home in the off-season to get jobs, because we didn't make a lot of money back then. He worked it out for us to be able to stay here and get paid. Then during my rookie year I got hurt, blew my knee out, and he came to me right after the game and said, 'Don't worry. You're going to get paid.' That was my rookie year, too. That just didn't happen."

Tose's generosity stretched way beyond expectation. This was an owner who spent lavishly on meals for the media. "They would serve lobster thermidor at the Monday press conference," longtime Eagles radio voice Merrill Reese said. "We used to joke and call it Le Bec Wing [in reference to the famous five-star Philadelphia restaurant Le Bec Fin]. Leonard was a great character. Kind of a Damon Runyon story. It was let the good times roll. He was passionate. He loved the football team. He gave the coaches anything they wanted and did anything for the players. He was terrific like that."

Tose would frequently show up for games at Veterans Stadium in a leased helicopter. He would also fly it to training camp some days as well. He was known for having a drink in one hand and a cigarette between his lips, accompanied by one of the five women he married and later divorced. Celebrities such as Don Rickles and Bob Newhart, two comedians with whom he once shared a yachting vacation, were regulars at the games. And when the Eagles won the NFC Championship in 1980, he sent a team jacket to Frank Sinatra.

That win over Dallas that sent the Eagles to Super Bowl XV was the highlight of Tose's ownership. The coach he hired and grew to love as a son, Dick Vermeil, had made the Eagles a winner and that was really all the owner ever wanted.

That friendship between coach and owner lasted right until Tose's death. "I've lost a very close friend," Vermeil told Philadelphia newspapers the day Tose died. "I think the National Football League has lost one of its most unique characters in a position of ownership [who] ever existed. He was not ordinary. He lived life to its fullest. He tested it and, for the most part, got the most out of it."

Bergey and Murray were with Tose the day he passed away. "He's the only person I ever saw die in front of my eyes," the linebacker said. "I was there with Jim Murray and his driver, Don Fitch. We were there in the hospice. He'd take a breath, let it out, another one, and finally he stopped breathing. I ran and got the nurse, she came in and said, 'He's gone.' We cried a little bit and that was it."

18

COMING HOME

There were other options for Troy Vincent in 1996. The Detroit Lions, a playoff team in each of the past three seasons, were one. The Cincinnati Bengals were another. Vincent's current team, the Miami Dolphins, had placed the transition tag on him as an unrestricted free agent, meaning the Dolphins could match any free agent offer the cornerback received.

"It was an interesting time in my young professional career," Vincent said 20 years later. "I was Miami's transition player, and as a team the Dolphins were transitioning from [Don] Shula to Jimmy [Johnson]. Marco Coleman and Bryan Cox were free agents, too. They had a lot of decisions to make."

So did Vincent. He had heard from both the Lions and Bengals and both teams were preparing offer sheets for him to sign and force the Dolphins to match if they wanted to keep their first-round pick of the 1992 Draft.

Then another team got involved. "The Eagles actually came on a little later," Vincent recalled. "I remember hearing from [defensive coordinator] Emmitt [Thomas] and then [head coach] Ray [Rhodes]. They felt they were close. They had made the playoffs the year before. They thought they were a couple pieces away from being right there with the Cowboys."

Vincent mulled his options and ultimately signed the Eagles' offer sheet: a five-year, $16.5 million deal that included clauses that made it tough for the Dolphins to match. "I didn't want Miami to be able to come to me and ask to restructure right away," Vincent said. "We did the contract as such, so that couldn't happen."

Still, Johnson and his front-office staff went right to the seven-day deadline before they let Vincent go. When they did he was an Eagle, playing professional football not far from where he grew up in

Trenton, New Jersey, or played his high school football at Pennsbury High School in Lower Bucks County, Pennsylvania.

"There are pros and cons in coming back home to play," Vincent said. "I won't say it was a dream come true, but it was out of a storybook to go from growing up in Trenton, playing high school ball in Lower Bucks County, to now playing pro ball at the Vet. How many kids get the opportunity to live that out? I was fortunate we were able to make it happen.

"The family dynamics, relative dynamics, in-law dynamics, I'm not saying they were all bad. It's just all part of playing at home. You're seeing the guys you played with in high school, the guys you played against in high school. And the expectations are high. The availability and the access to you, you have a job to do, but you have to be cordial too. There's a lot that goes into coming back home to play at the pro level.

"And there was more risk than reward. Because keep in mind, and even today, most free agents don't pan out. They don't live up to the expectations and to the money they get."

Vincent did. He had played well for the Dolphins in his first four years, but in an AFC loaded at cornerback including Pittsburgh's Rod Woodson and Oakland's Terry McDaniel, Vincent never made a Pro Bowl. With the Eagles, playing in front of his hometown fans, he took his game to another level. Vincent made five Pro Bowls as an Eagle, including his final year with the team, 2003.

For the Eagles the addition of Vincent was key to Rhodes and Thomas' remaking of the Eagles' secondary to take on the Cowboys and the rest of the NFC East. A year earlier a trade up in the second-round of the 1995 Draft netted cornerback Bobby Taylor of Notre Dame. Just after Vincent's signing, the team spent another second-round pick on safety Brian Dawkins of Clemson.

Vincent helped the Eagles get back to the playoffs in 1996 and was an integral part of a team that made it to three straight NFC Championship Games from 2001 to 2003.

"I really learned a lot. Not that I didn't learn from Shula's staff, but learning from Ray and Emmitt and that staff really helped me," Vincent said. "I learned football. I learned every position. Backside reads, front-side reads, the double, triple coverages, blocking schemes, the real intricacies of the game. I learned the entire makeup of professional football."

It was more than his play on the field, however, that separated Vincent from other great NFL players. There was his leadership in the locker room; his work off the field that led to becoming the only player in NFL history to win the Walter Payton Man of the Year Award, the Byron "Whizzer" White Man of the Year Award, the Athletes in Action Bart Starr Award and The Sporting News No. 1 Good Guy.

"Troy was obviously our rock behind the scenes," former Eagles linebacker Ike Reese said. "You see where he is now, and it's no surprise to any of us. He had that sort of view about life. A lot of what Troy was about was life after football. He was the first person who made me think about life after football. He was always preparing and using the game, instead of letting the game use you. I learned a lot from him."

Vincent thought nothing of taking a young player such as Reese under his wing and showing him the right way to do things on and off the field. Players listened because of who he was on the field and the presence he carried off it.

"Troy made an impact on all of us because of that," Reese said. "As great a teammate as he was and as great of a player as he was, and a leader by example, he had an even greater influence on all of us,

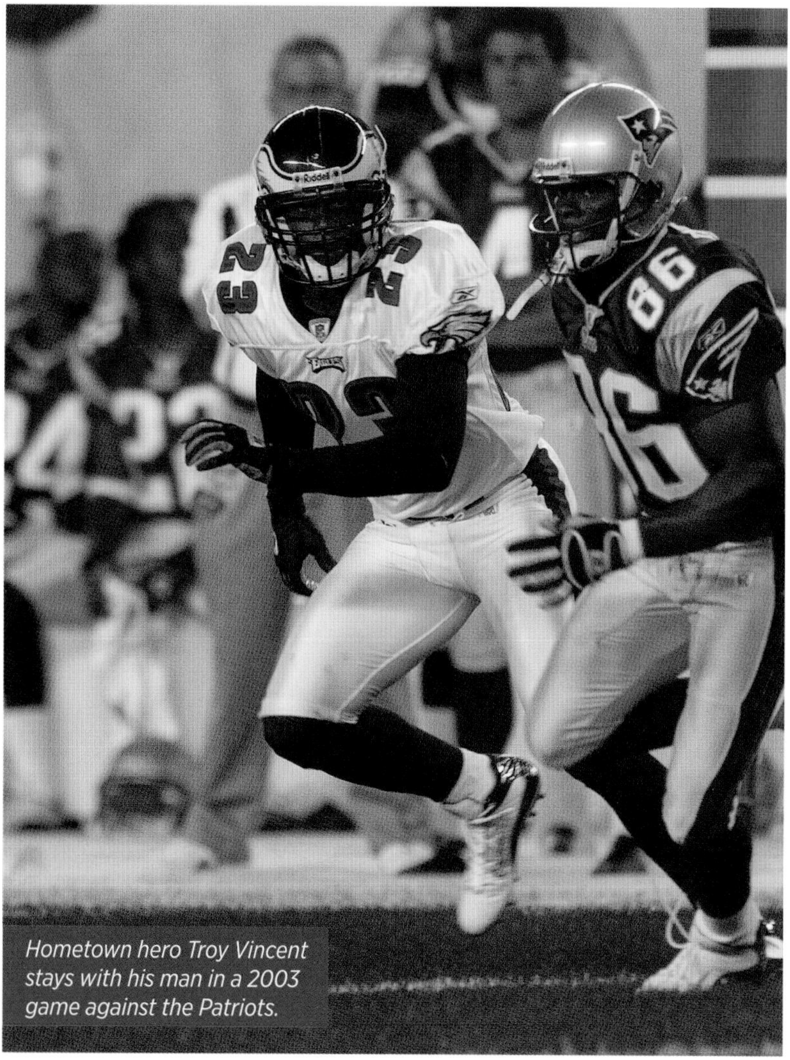

Hometown hero Troy Vincent stays with his man in a 2003 game against the Patriots.

not just me, but Dawk, Trot [Jeremiah Trotter], Bobby [Taylor], Hugh [Douglas], all of us.

"He was a great player, one of our greatest players, but when I think of Troy all of us think about how much he helped us off the field. He'll always be Big Bro. He's still Big Bro to all of us."

Vincent wonders what might have been, had he signed with the Lions or Bengals, or if the Dolphins would have matched the offer sheet and kept him for at least five more years. Chances are his game would have still been the same and he would have been just as much of a leader and as charitable off the field. It just wouldn't have happened at home.

"I don't know," he said. "Some of it might have still happened no matter where I was. I think there was a plan for me." Part of the plan was to bring him, his wife, Tommi, also from Trenton, and their family back home in 1996. "Being at home, the fan base was my neighbors," Vincent said. "I got it. I knew Philadelphia and the area. I was once a part of that culture. I understood how the fans think. Philly is a put-up or shut-up kind of town."

Vincent gave the fans what they wanted, great play on the field and a role model to follow in all of his off-the-field activities. Ask him what he appreciates more and the answer is easier than picking the Eagles over the Lions or Bengals. "The body of work off the field and maintaining a level of respect and integrity and care and empathy for people, while performing at the highest level on the field," Vincent said. "You don't do things for individual accolades. Caring about people that you saw every day, that were homeless, strung out on drugs. How do I make a difference?

"I mean, I saw it all the time. I would see things and knew I lived in that house. Now the question was, how do I become a part of the solution? Football was a byproduct of everything I did in life."

And that football was just enhanced a few levels when he came home. "Best decision I ever made, professionally," Vincent said. "Without a doubt, the best decision of my professional career."

19

HAROLD AND WILBERT

One was a 1971 seventh-round draft pick out of Southern University; the other was a 1977 sixth-round draft pick out of Abilene Christian. They went on to become two of the greatest players in Philadelphia Eagles history.

If you think you have to be a high draft pick or come from a big school to make it in the NFL, check the stories of Harold Carmichael and Wilbert Montgomery.

Carmichael, who last played for the Eagles in 1983, is still the team's all-time receiving yards leader with 8,798 yards, the team's all-time receptions leader with 589, and the team's all-time touchdown receptions leader with 79. He is more than 1,500 yards ahead of anyone else in yards, more than 130 receptions ahead of anyone else, and 13 touchdowns ahead of the field. He went to four Pro Bowls and was named to the NFL's All-Decade Team of the '70s. That's not bad for a seventh-round pick from the Southwestern Athletic Conference.

"Coming out of Southern University, there were guys from the SWAC that were getting drafted," Carmichael remembered. "The way I understood it from Pete Retzlaff [Philadelphia's general manager at the time and, coincidentally the Eagles player second to Carmichael in yards and receptions], they had me listed as a six foot eight defensive back who could also play wide receiver. I never even knew this until I saw Pete at a function in 2010. The last time I had played DB was my senior year in high school. I was a free safety. But I never attempted to play defense in college. My agent at the time told me I would go between the first and third round. I don't know what happened."

Montgomery was the Eagles' all-time leading rusher for 20 years until LeSean McCoy passed him in 2014. Montgomery's 6,538 yards still rank second all-time on the franchise's all-time list; and his 45 rushing touchdowns are second to Hall of Famer Steve Van Buren. From 1978 to 1981, when the Eagles went to the playoffs in four straight years after not making the postseason since 1960, Montgomery averaged over 1,200 yards rushing and 40 receptions per season. That's not bad either for a sixth-round pick who was thought to be just a kick returner.

"Wilbert ran a kickoff back against the Giants for a touchdown, and after that Dick [Vermeil] put him in there at running back," Eagles left tackle Stan Walters remembered. "After that he never lost the job."

Yet Carmichael and Montgomery shared more than being low-round picks turned stars. Although maybe it was because of it that they had the same character trait. "They were both very quiet guys, very shy, when they first got here," longtime Eagles radio broadcaster Merrill Reese said. "Harold, I remember I did an interview with him when he first got here. I asked him a question and he answered, 'Yes'. I asked him another one and he said, 'I think so.' It wasn't going very well. But by the end of his career, I would have him on and he would take over. I think he would have done the commercials too.

"When Wilbert was a rookie, whenever Dick Vermeil walked into the locker room, Wilbert would duck inside of his locker. He felt that if Vermeil saw him, there was a chance he would cut him. So he thought if he didn't see him he wouldn't cut him."

Their teammates saw something special in the two. "Harold really matured and became the ultimate team player," Pro Bowl linebacker Bill Bergey said. "I remember when I first saw him, I wasn't sure about him. But he really came into his own and became the great player he was. He was really a great player.

"Wilbert was so quiet and reserved. I remember Dick would want him on his TV show and he wouldn't show up. But on the field he gave everything he had every single play. I remember Dick saying, 'We have to start playing this guy. I want to see if he is as good as I think he is.' He was."

Montgomery got his chance at the end of his rookie year after that kickoff return against the Giants. "I had been returning kicks, but I hadn't played on offense," he remembered. "Coach told me to go into the game and I said, 'Coach, I haven't had a playbook since we were in training camp.'

"When Dick got to Philly in 1976, he weeded out the guys who didn't fit and looked for guys who put team before themselves. We became a family. There wasn't one player on that team that didn't get along with everyone else on that team. We all pulled for each other and cheered for each other. All we wanted to do was win."

That's all Carmichael wanted too. In his first six years the Eagles went 6–7–1, 2–11–1, 5–8–1, 7–7, 4–10, and 4–10.

"There was a little bit of light in the tunnel with Mike McCormack (the 7–7 season in 1974), but then that fizzled out," Carmichael said "It wasn't until Dick got there that we started to put it together and started to win. I don't think anyone had the feeling that I had when we won [the conference] in 1980. I had been there the longest. To be in the NFC Championship Game, I remembered back to 1971 when we were really bad. It's something I'll never forget. The Super Bowl, unfortunately, we lost, but to beat the Cowboys in that NFC Championship Game, that was the best."

That was Montgomery at his best as well. Bothered by a knee injury that kept him out of four regular-season games and reinjured during the week of practice before the title game, the Eagles' star running back wasn't even sure he would play against the Cowboys. "We were practicing in Tampa all week," Montgomery said. "I was running down the field, and my leg just gave out. It felt like somebody shot me. I was down for the count. [Trainer] Otho [Davis] worked on me the next few days. They packed it in ice and told me to rest. On Sunday I didn't even come out for the pregame warm-ups. I was still inside getting treatment. Louie Giammona was the starting running back."

However, it didn't take long for Montgomery to not just get in the game but make an impact with one of the greatest plays in Eagles' history. "I came down the tunnel, and I'm on the sideline," Montgomery said. "I told Coach Vermeil, 'I'm ready to go.' He looked at me and said, 'Get in there.'"

On second down, out of a three wide receiver set that usually meant pass, Montgomery broke a 42-yard run for a touchdown and in the process the Cowboys' backs.

Montgomery's bad knee came from the beatings he took week after week. It was yet another trait he shared with Carmichael. Let Pro Bowl takle Stan Walters tell it: "Wilbert was a quiet guy, but he was tough. He was real tough. As a player he took a beating too. I'd see him in the trainer's room after a game and I mean he was just beat up, welts all over his body. He just looked bad. I don't know how he did it week after week. I mean we all took beatings, but I didn't get beat up like that."

Carmichael did. "Harold used to get mugged," Walters continued. "I mean, he had these smaller defensive backs on him, so I guess the refs felt they would let them get away with anything. He really got mugged. Then when he would go across the middle, they would take his legs out. Back then they could hit you before the ball was thrown. In today's rules, without being able to touch receivers, he'd be unbelievable. In the end zone he'd be unstoppable. He'd either catch it or it would be pass interference. There would be no way to stop him."

Carmichael admits today that he sometimes wonders what it would be like to play with today's rules that favor receivers so heavily. "I tell people though I don't know if I would have gotten drafted, because of my speed. I ran a 4.6, maybe. That's slow today," he said with a laugh. "But I would have found some kind of way, just as I did [then].

"You would get hit when you weren't even involved in the play. You would be on the other side of the field and you would get clotheslined, just to take you out. I saw [former Green Bay linebacker] Dave Robinson at Super Bowl 50 and he told me they would [defend] me and they would call it the Sequoia Axe. They would chop me down at the line of scrimmage. I never knew where it was coming from—the defensive back, the linebacker, who would come and try to chop me down. There were times I thought I was the [girl] in *The Exorcist*, because my head had to be on a swivel. It makes me crazy now when I hear them [call a penalty] for a defenseless receiver. If that was the case then, I'd still be playing the game now at 100 years old."

20

T.O.

There may have never been a happier beginning and sadder ending then the Terrell Owens Saga that engulfed the Eagles through the 2004 and 2005 seasons. In reality it lasted just 20 months, but it seemed like 20 years.

Owens, one of the greatest wide receivers of his time, in those 20 months, managed to win a battle with the league that allowed him to become an Eagle; was on his way to breaking every single-season record with the team before breaking his leg; came back from the injury in six-and-a-half weeks to play in the Super Bowl; demanded a new contract; got suspended; did push-ups on his front lawn in front of TV cameras; got into a fight with a well known team employee; and was finally released. All in just 20 months.

Let's start at the beginning. On the first day of free agency in March 2004, a story broke that the San Francisco 49ers had traded Owens to the Baltimore Ravens. That came as a shock to the Eagles, who heard the news as they prepared a press conference for their newly signed free agent defensive end Jevon Kearse. The Eagles felt they had a deal in place with the 49ers in exchange for the talented wide receiver, a package of draft picks and players, and were just awaiting word from the league for approval.

Owens wasn't thrilled either. He didn't feel he should be traded anywhere. He felt he should be an unrestricted free agent and was fighting the fact that a clause in his contract voided the final year, 2004. He wanted to be able to choose where he would go. And he wanted to go to Philadelphia.

"I went out and got T.O.," said Eagles quarterback Donovan McNabb, who recruited Owens during the Pro Bowl that January.

"I talked to Andy [Reid] and said, 'Hey, we need to get this guy.' Because we needed something to get us over the hump on offense. Every top quarterback in the league always had a No. 1 receiver that teams had to focus on. I didn't have that. T.O. gave us that extra oomph.

"I got criticized, if you remember, when I said just after [the 2003 season] that we needed to go out and bring in some playmakers. They said I turned my back on our guys. Then we sign T.O. And that's all I was saying. Can we just get another guy in here to make plays, to change the game? That got us over the hump."

After a month-long battle, both the Eagles and Owens got their way. The league ruled that the Eagles could acquire Owens from the 49ers in exchange for defensive end Brandon Whiting and a mid-round draft pick; while the Ravens for their trouble were also given a mid-round pick.

Owens came into Philadelphia, where the fans were starved for a big-time wide receiver. They had tired of the Charles Johnson / Torrance Small combination of 2000; and the James Thrash / Todd Pinkston combination of 2001 to 2003. They were just as frustrated as McNabb was—maybe more.

Those fans lined the Lehigh University practice fields that summer, setting ridiculous weekend attendance records and averaging more than 20,000 fans per day. They went wild every time Owens caught a pass and chanted his nickname "T.O." over and over.

"There was some jealousy, no question," said Eagles Pro Bowl defensive end Hugh Douglas. "You come into the city and you immediately become the fans' favorite. That doesn't sit well [with other players]. I'm not saying it was all Donovan's fault. That's not what it was. But Donovan felt all along the city didn't love him. And then they fall in love with T.O."

Owens gave the fans plenty to cheer about right from the start. On the first play of his first home preseason game, McNabb and Owens hooked up for an 81-yard touchdown pass. "That's what the people came out to see," Owens said after the game—against, of all teams, the Ravens. "That's what the Eagles brought me here to do and that's why I wanted to come here and play with No. 5."

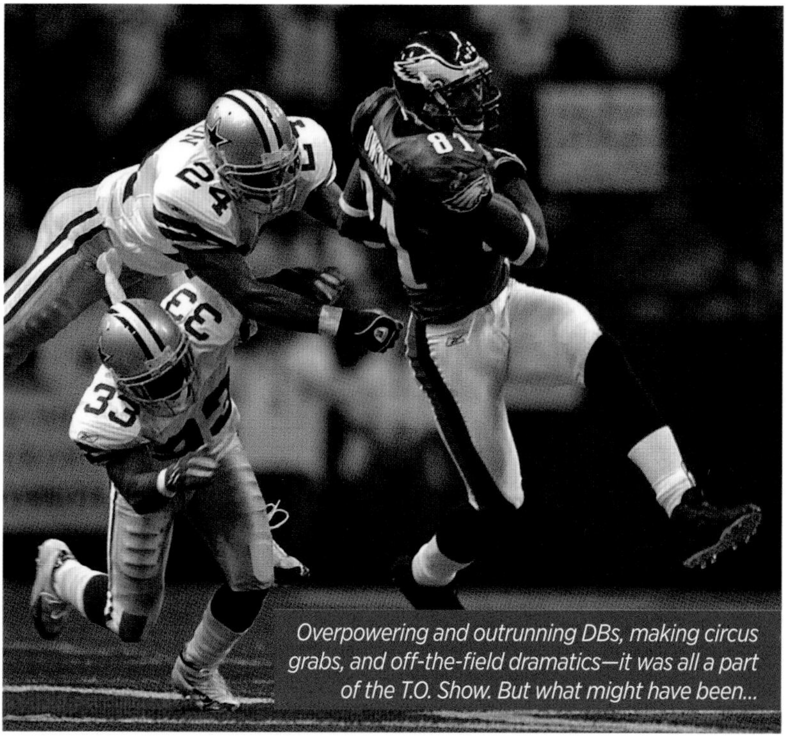

Overpowering and outrunning DBs, making circus grabs, and off-the-field dramatics—it was all a part of the T.O. Show. But what might have been...

Sure, it was just preseason, but it made a statement. "It was what we were going to be all about," McNabb said. "It was like we had arrived."

The Eagles won 12 of their first 13 games and Owens had 77 receptions for 1,200 yards and a team-record 14 touchdown catches. He needed 11 more receptions to break Irving Fryar's all-time mark at the time of 88. And he needed 209 yards to break Mike Quick's all-time mark of 1,409. He had three games to do it.

Except early in that 14th game, against the Dallas Cowboys, he suffered a broken leg. That was it. He missed the final two games of the regular season and was out for the postseason as well. He told people he would be back for the Super Bowl if the Eagles got there. But it seemed more of a wing and a prayer than reality.

When the Eagles beat the Atlanta Falcons in the NFC Championship Game, however, word started to spread that Owens would try to play in Super Bowl XXXIX. He not only played, he caught nine passes for 122 yards.

And that's where the happy part of the story ends.

Owens had signed a seven-year deal with the Eagles after the trade was finalized, a deal the NFL Player's Association advised him not to sign. Then, after what he did all season and in the Super Bowl he wanted a new contract. The Eagles and team President Joe Banner felt otherwise.

"This is what I think happened," Douglas said. "T.O. looked at his contract and realized he was underpaid. And after what he did you could make that argument. But he signed that contract. So there's that. But I do think it could have been handled better on both sides. T.O. felt strong on his position; and the Eagles felt strong on their position. Everyone was playing hardball. You can't deny what he brought to that team. The Eagles thought they could get by without him, and they didn't. And it was unfortunate the way it went down."

Owens became a distraction to the team. He didn't exactly follow in order during the 2004 season, but in the summer of 2005 it got to the point where Reid suspended him from training camp for a day.

When newspaper reporters and television cameras followed him to his home in Moorestown, New Jersey, they found him on his front lawn doing push-ups. And it just got crazier from there.

"The thing about Terrell is, on the field, [he has] outstanding talent. He's one of the best to have ever done it," McNabb said. "Andy was a very disciplined guy. He wanted things structured. People [started] to follow Terrell, and Terrell knew that. Terrell had these guys [thinking] his way is the way to do it, when, no, that's not how we did it in Philly. We're going to do it the way it's supposed to be done. So then there were people on Terrell's side and people who were on my side."

Owens, still unhappy about his contract situation, did everything he could to get out of Philadelphia. He was openly critical of things the team did and most of the wrath was aimed at McNabb, who did not back him in his quest for a new contract.

"That whole T.O. saga thing, when you're in the middle of it, it's just kind of surreal," safety Quintin Mikell remembered. "It's like, 'Man what the heck is going on?' We still felt we had enough good players to get back there, but that's when you realize it's not that easy. We knew he did a lot for the team. I don't know if we underestimated it or not, but that's when we learned how much chemistry means to a team and how much distractions can hurt it."

When the team was 4–2 in 2005, but coming off a loss to the Dallas Cowboys, Owens told ESPN the Eagles would be undefeated if they had Green Bay's Brett Favre at quarterback. He added later it wasn't him who got tired at the end of the Super Bowl, again pointing fingers at McNabb.

One of those people on McNabb's side was Douglas, who retired after the '04 Super Bowl but was hired by the team as an ambassador of sorts. After a 49–21 loss to Denver that dropped the Eagles to 4–3, and just two days before the next game at Washington, Owens and Douglas got into an actual fight in the team's training room.

"We're in the training room, and I'm talking to Hugh about some things and I'm like, 'I know where this is going to go,'" McNabb said. "So I go back to the locker room, I'm talking to [backup quarterback] A.J. [Feeley] and people are coming in telling me what's going on in the training room. T.O. came in like he was [wrestler] Junkyard Dog, taking on everyone."

Said Douglas, "I just had Don's back that day."

Reid suspended Owens indefinitely before that Redskins game—and he never played another down for the Eagles. In the 21 games he did play, he caught 124 passes for 1,963 yards with 20 touchdowns.

"I knew wholeheartedly what went on in that locker room," Owens said. "I did what I could. They brought me there to help get to the Super Bowl. I did everything I could, even playing on the ankle I did in the Super Bowl. I did it because I knew the city wanted me there. I wanted to be there, and everybody realizes that when I got there, I don't think [McNabb] expected the city to embrace me the way [it] did. And I think maybe there was some jealously and envy there."

Who knows what might have been? "If they would have played it right, we would have won a Super Bowl," Douglas said. "We might have won that Super Bowl. I'm just saying."

Other Eagles from that team say the same thing. "We win a Super Bowl," safety Brian Dawkins said. "There's no doubt in my mind. You could never say anything is certain. But if he would have come back and just played, and maybe something could have been done, but him and Donovan whatever they needed to handle, man, we would have won big."

Said Mikell, "I honestly feel we could have been a dynasty. We had stars on offense, stars on defense, our special teams were phenomenal. We had a team that could have really accomplished a lot. And that's the saddest thing about it."

Ten years later, just before Super Bowl 50, as he awaited his fate for the Hall of Fame for the first time, Owens reflected on his 20 months with the Eagles. "As the years progressed, I think everyone has seen it wasn't really my fault that I left," he said. "I tried to be as honest as I could with management. Obviously there were some situations going on there. Nothing really panned out since [me] leaving. Nothing. I think management could have changed that. I wanted to stay. Could I have done some things different with my teammates, coaches, and maybe management in terms of communications? That is something I've grown to be better with since I left."

McNabb, like everyone else, also wonders how things could have been different. "When I look back on that period, my year and a half with T.O., we finally brought out everything we had," McNabb said. "We finally got to display all the talent we had. We could have broken records like Peyton [Manning] and Marvin [Harrison]. That would have been easy for us. When you get that success, you get cocky, though. I'm not just saying T.O. You had Freddie Mitchell, L.J. Smith—they all thought it was their time to shine too. It turned into individualism instead of team. All of a sudden we get over the hump and guys are doing their own websites, having their own shows, talking about being on *SportsCenter*. It was what breaks up relationships. If you compare it to music, it was like breaking up the band."

21

WHO IS PERRY TUTTLE?

Mike Quick has told the story so often, even he sometimes wonders what might have been. What if he would have been drafted by the New Orleans Saints instead of the Philadelphia Eagles? What if the Buffalo Bills hadn't traded up ahead of the Eagles and taken Perry Tuttle? Where would Quick have played his career then?

There are almost as many what-ifs as the 61 touchdown passes Quick caught in his brilliant Eagles career, which began when the Eagles took him in the first round of the 1982 NFL Draft. And that's where it all starts.

The Eagles clearly wanted a wide receiver in the first round of that draft. Harold Carmichael, their star receiver, was turning 33 that September, and there wasn't a whole lot opposite him. A wide receiver was definitely a priority. The question was, which one?

Head coach Dick Vermeil and his staff liked Tuttle, the gifted but slender, six foot, 178-pound receiver out of Clemson, who upon his graduation ranked second in school history in touchdown receptions (17) and first in receiving yards (2,534) and receptions (150). And when Tuttle caught the winning touchdown pass against Nebraska in the Orange Bowl to secure the national championship for the Tigers, that was all the Eagles needed to convince them he was their guy.

As legend has it, Vermeil, talking with his friend Chuck Knox, who was then the head coach of the Buffalo Bills, mentioned his desire for Tuttle in passing. No harm in that. Knox and the Bills owned the 21st pick in the draft and the Eagles had the 20th. Until the actual day of the draft.

With the Denver Broncos on the clock at No. 19, one pick in front of the Eagles, the Bills traded with the Broncos and selected Tuttle.

Vermeil and his people were stunned. What to do now? They still wanted a wide receiver. They even stayed in the Atlantic Coast Conference and took Quick, out of North Carolina State. While his college stats (116 receptions, 1,934 yards, 10 touchdowns) weren't as impressive as Tuttle's, he was bigger at 6'2", 190 and was known as a very good route runner.

Still, the marriage of Quick and the Eagles came as a surprise to both parties. "I had gotten a lot of conversation from the New Orleans Saints coaching staff at the combines," Quick recalled. "They

A QUICK SIX

It's a record that will never be broken. It's been matched 12 other times, but it will never be broken.

When Mike Quick and Ron Jaworski teamed up for a 99-yard touchdown pass to beat the Atlanta Falcons 23–17 in overtime during the 1985 season, it put them in the record books to stay.

"It's second-and-10 and we're at the 1," Quick said. "We didn't get anything on first down and we're in the huddle and it's like, 'Let's just get something. Let's run a quick hitch and get out of the end zone and get some breathing room.'"

Quick ran a hitch and Jaworski hit him in stride just shy of the 20-yard line. Eighty yards later they had a 99-yard touchdown pass.

"We knew if we could get the corner to play outside, Mike would have a chance to split the zone," Jaworski said. "That's exactly what happened. He split the zone and he was gone."

It was the Eagles' first-ever overtime win as well.

"I knew they couldn't catch me," Quick said. "I just ran until I got to the end zone. As I was running, it was like, 'This isn't actually happening.' It was the kind of stuff you usually dream about."

actually had two combines then, and at both of them the Saints were talking to me a lot. I really thought that's where I was going to go. Cleveland was involved as well, a little bit anyway. I really thought I was going to New Orleans, with Cleveland as a possibility. The Eagles? I did meet with Vermeil once, but I didn't think they were that interested."

Because they weren't. They wanted Tuttle.

As the draft unfolded, the Kansas City Chiefs, with the 11th overall pick selected the first wide receiver, Anthony Hancock, out of Tennessee. New Orleans, at No. 13, took another wide receiver, just not Quick. Instead, they went for Lindsay Scott out of Georgia. The Bills made Tuttle the third wide receiver taken at No. 19; and the Eagles took Quick at No. 20, the final receiver taken in the first round.

"I remembered all of those guys," Quick said. "Lindsay Scott, Anthony Hancock, Tuttle. I watched what all of them did. It wasn't out of vengeance or anything like that, I just liked to pay attention to see how they did. Listen, I was happy when the Eagles drafted me. I was a first-round pick in the NFL Draft. I was thrilled. I didn't find out until later on about Buffalo moving up ahead of the Eagles because of Dick wanting Perry Tuttle.

"Funny thing is I knew Perry pretty well from playing against him in the ACC. He was OK. But I knew I had something burning in me that other players didn't have."

Here's how those first-round picks actually played out over time.

Hancock played five years, all with the Chiefs, and started just eight games. In those five years he caught 73 passes for 1,266 yards with five touchdowns. Yes, he was a first-round bust.

Scott, who the Saints chose over Quick, was even worse. He played four years in the league, all with the Saints, and caught a total of 69 passes for 864 yards with all of one touchdown. Yes, he was a bigger first-round bust.

Tuttle, however, the guy the Eagles really wanted was the worst of all. He played just three years, two of them with the Bills and then he split his final season between the Atlanta Falcons and Tampa Bay Buccaneers. In total he caught 24 passes for 375 yards with three touchdowns.

And then there was Quick. In his nine years, all with the Eagles, and despite nagging knee problems from playing on the Veterans Stadium turf, he caught 363 passes (sixth most in franchise history) for 6,464 yards (third most in team history) and the 61 touchdowns (second most in team history).

From 1983 to 1987 Quick was one of the best wide receivers in the game, going to five straight Pro Bowls for an Eagles team that failed to post a winning record. Then, when the Eagles got good in 1988, Quick's knees began to give out.

"That's the shame of it," said linebacker Garry Cobb, Quick's former teammate. "He missed his chance for true greatness. As bad as some of those Eagles teams were, Quick was still one of the marquee receivers of his era. But could you imagine if he [had been] on a better team? He was making great catches, great plays, but nobody outside of Philadelphia knew it. If he could have stayed healthy a few more years, when the team got good, he'd be in the Hall of Fame."

In those five Pro Bowl years, Quick caught 309 passes for 5,437 yards and 53 touchdowns. Then the knee injuries and a broken leg limited him to just 18 games over the next three years on playoff-bound teams. His only playoff appearance came in the 1988 Fog Bowl, a game in which passing became next to impossible in the second half.

"The guy was unbelievable," said teammate and cornerback Eric Allen. "He was uncoverable. You look at great receivers, [Quick] was more physical than [Randy] Moss, a little bigger than Marvin Harrison, and you couldn't jam him because he would beat that and be gone. If he would have stayed healthy? I can't even imagine the numbers he would have had."

Quick, just as he did the 1982 Draft, takes it all in stride.

"I was blessed," he said. "I made it to the NFL. But timing is everything. I came around at the right time to make it. But I caught Ron [Jaworski] at the end of his career and Randall [Cunningham] when he was just starting."

22

TOMMY

Tommy McDonald had a ritual of sorts that he performed before every home game he played for the Eagles at Franklin Field. As McDonald walked through the tunnel and onto the field he would pause at the brick wall that sat just outside the one end zone and scrape his hands—or more precisely, his fingers—over the bricks. He did it over and over again.

"I wanted my fingers to be smooth," McDonald said years later. "I wanted to be able to feel the pebbles on the ball. That was important to me, having a good feel for the ball."

It's a ritual that has often been compared to a safecracker using sandpaper on his fingers before opening a safe. So what did McDonald do on road games, when the Franklin Field brick wall wasn't unavailable?

"I used sandpaper," he said. Of course.

Whatever he did, it worked. McDonald, the Eagles' third-round draft pick out of the University of Oklahoma in 1957, had perhaps the greatest hands in the history of the game. According to Eagles historian Ray Didinger, who also gave McDonald's induction speech into the Hall of Fame, McDonald did the unthinkable. "I've said this a number of times," Didinger said. "But I never saw him drop a pass. Never."

And he wasn't the only one who said so. When Didinger, once a Hall of Fame voter, was making his case for McDonald's induction into Canton, he sent letters to some of his former teammates as well as opponents, asking them to write letters of recommendation. Sonny Jurgensen, McDonald's quarterback for a couple of years with the Eagles, echoed the opinion. As Didinger recalled, "Sonny wrote back, '[McDonald] had the best hands I ever saw. He never dropped a pass in a game or in practice.'"

McDonald smiles when he hears that. He gives credit to helping his father when he was growing up in Roy, New Mexico. "My dad was an electrician," he said. "When I was growing up in New Mexico, I used to help him. I would put in the receptacles for him and I would have to screw them in with a screwdriver. It made my wrists and fingers so strong. I always say that's what's helped me have such good, strong hands. It was actually a blessing in disguise.

"I had a method. Everybody has a method, right? I would never reach out to catch a pass. I would always kind of cradle it into my body and trap it between my forearm and elbow. I never wanted to let a defensive back be able to slap it away. And no one ever did.

When San Francisco 49ers cornerback Jimmy Johnson was voted into the Hall of Fame, he was asked upon his induction who was the most difficult receiver he ever faced. Without hesitation he responded, "Tommy McDonald."

Another of the great cornerbacks of the 1960s and '70s, Johnny Sample—who played for the Baltimore Colts and the Super Bowl III–champion New York Jets and once wrote a book titled *Confessions of a Dirty Player*—said McDonald was the one receiver he feared. "Because he never quit," Sample said. "He never, ever gave up. It didn't matter what you did, the guy came to play every down."

McDonald went to six Pro Bowls in his Hall of Fame career, five of them during seven-year career with the Eagles. When he retired after the 1968 season, McDonald's 84 touchdown receptions ranked second in NFL history to only the Green Bay Packers' Don Huston (99). After the 2015 season, he was tied for 18th on the all-time list. He also ranked sixth all time in receptions with 495 and fourth all-time in yards with 8,410 when he left the league.

"You put his numbers against any receiver of his time and he blows them away," Didinger said. "He was just an amazing player in terms of the big plays he made."

During the Eagles 1960 NFL Championship season, McDonald caught just 39 passes—but a third of them, 13, went for touchdowns. He caught a 14th, a 35-yarder, in the biggest game of the year and probably his career, the 17–13 win over the Green Bay Packers for the title. The following year, with Jurgensen as his quarterback, he had his best season with 64 receptions for a league-leading 1,144 yards and another 13 touchdowns. From 1958 to 1962, McDonald scored 56 touchdowns, second only to the Cleveland Browns' Jim Brown during that time span.

"I would study [a defensive back] on film," McDonald said, "and I would know him better then he knew himself sometimes. Whenever I went out on that field to play I knew whether I could double-fake him or single-fake him or anything else I could try to do to try to score a touchdown.

"I think catching passes is judgment, mostly. I had good vision, good peripheral vision. I think sometimes I saw things the defensive back couldn't see. I'd watch for him to make his move and if he's a fraction late compensating for mine, then I've got him beat. Sometimes there were guys I could just run by. But I always did what I could do to get in the end zone. That was my job: to get into the end zone, score points."

Didinger remembers as a child going with his parents to Hershey, Pennsylvania, to watch Eagles training camp. McDonald was his favorite player, and as kids did with their favorite player back then, he would walk with him to the field, carrying his helmet. Sometimes he did it twice a day. "He was every little kid's favorite player," Didinger said. "He was the smallest guy on the team. He was only five foot nine.

He didn't wear a facemask. He wore short sleeves. And he had that air of defiance about him—that he was this little guy playing against the big guys, but he was going to show them he was as tough as they were and he belonged with them. And he was a great player. He played with this high energy that as a kid you watched him and said, 'That's how I would play if I had the opportunity.' He played like a kid in a man's game."

23

TIME RAN OUT

Maybe it was just too easy. Or maybe that year the power was just in the AFC. Whatever the case, the Eagles barely broke a sweat during the 2004 regular season and playoffs on the way to Super Bowl XXXIX.

They were 13–1 and had clinched home-field advantage in the playoffs for the third straight season when head coach Andy Reid shut it down for the final two weeks of the season and saw his team lose to the St. Louis Rams and Cincinnati Bengals.

Reid's decision, which was a good one, came after wide receiver Terrell Owens suffered a broken leg against the Dallas Cowboys on December 19. The game clinched home-field advantage for the Eagles, so there was no reason to risk injuries to other players in two games that were now essentially meaningless.

"Andy got a little cautious, but that was OK," defensive end Hugh Douglas said. "We did what we needed to do. Now, it was time to get ready for the playoffs."

The gambit worked out fine. As they had done all season against NFC competition (the Eagles only "meaningful" regular-season loss was to the Pittsburgh Steelers; and they struggled past the Cleveland Browns, 34–31 in overtime; as well as against the Baltimore Ravens, winning 15–10) they rolled in the playoffs as well.

"We had a running joke," said safety Brian Dawkins. "It wasn't were we going to win. It was how much are we going to win by and when were the starters coming out of the game? We would try to guess when the coaches would take us out."

One of those guys replacing the starters was special teams stalwart and safety Quintin Mikell. He recalled that same feeling. "All I remember is we were blowing teams out," Mikell said. "The young guys, like myself, we got to play a lot at the end of games. That was fun. But that's how naive I was. Being that young, I thought this was easy. We just blow everybody out. We're going to do this every year and go to multiple Super Bowls. Little did I know. But really it felt like being back in Pop Warner Football, where you put the scrubs in at the end of the game. And I was one of the scrubs."

Right tackle Jon Runyan, who had been to a Super Bowl five years earlier with the Tennessee Titans, saw a stark contrast between the two teams' runs through the season. "It was one of those years everything just clicked for us," Runyan said. "It was almost easy. There was no stress. The only stress was the Pittsburgh game. That was it. We just went out did what we did, we had a smile on our face, and we won.

"It was a lot different from the Super Bowl I went to with Tennessee a few years before that. We're getting blown out the first game of the year at Cincinnati, had to come back from like 21 down to win. Then in the playoffs, we had the 'Music City Miracle' against Buffalo. We go down to Indy and there's one touchdown in the game, Eddie George scored on like a 60-yard run. Then we had to go to Jacksonville and beat them for the third time. That year [with Philadelphia], 2004, was easy. Even the playoffs were easy."

In the playoffs the Eagles would be without Owens, who was the missing piece the offense had needed after the team had come close the past three seasons. The former 49ers star receiver caught 77 passes for 1,200 yards with 14 touchdowns before his season was cut short. "That was the big question going into the playoffs," Douglas said. "Would the other receivers step up with T.O. hurt? And they did."

After a bye week, the Eagles beat the Minnesota Vikings 27–14. Quarterback Donovan McNabb, even without Owens, passed for 286 yards and two touchdowns. Brian Westbrook ran for 70 yards on just 12 carries and caught five passes for another 47 yards. And wide receiver Freddie Mitchell caught five passes for 65 yards, scored two touchdowns—one on a fumble recovery in the end zone—and after the game, as only he could, he thanked his hands.

Defensively, linebackers Jeremiah Trotter and Ike Reese each picked off Vikings quarterback Daunte Culpepper. McNabb threw an early touchdown pass to Mitchell and then one to Westbrook at the start of the second quarter. Just like that it was 14–0, and the Vikings never threatened.

That set up another NFC Championship Game, the fourth straight for the Eagles and the third straight against the winner of the NFC South. After losing to the Tampa Bay Buccaneers in 2002; and the Carolina Panthers in 2003; this time they were getting the Atlanta Falcons and quarterback Michael Vick.

"Playing Atlanta, it was almost a feeling of 'here we go again,'" Dawkins said. "It was snowing. They had beaten Green Bay in the snow. And then all we hear all week is about the past three years and how we lost those games. Then it was all T.O. Could we win without him? We were hearing all of that. It made us feel like we were the underdogs in that game."

The Eagles beat the Falcons 27–10, pulling away from a 14–10 halftime score to win going away. McNabb threw two touchdown passes, both to tight end Chad Lewis. Westbrook ran for 96 yards on 16 carries and caught five passes for 39 yards. And coordinator Jim Johnson's defense, led by Trotter and defensive end Derrick Burgess, did a great job against Vick. The mercurial quarterback was held to 136 yards passing and 26 yards rushing.

"To finally get over that hump, that's why we celebrated the way we did," Dawkins said. "It was a celebration of getting over all those losses we had before."

In the Super Bowl, their first since 1980, the Eagles faced the New England Patriots, who were looking for their third Super Bowl win in a four-year span. Las Vegas had the Pats as a seven-point favorite.

"We felt we could win that game. No question we felt we could win that game," Dawkins said. "And we had our chances too. You look back at all the what-ifs in that game. Man, we had our chances."

Owens, six-and-a-half weeks after having surgery to repair the broken leg and torn ligaments in his ankle, returned. He actually played 63 of the 72 offensive plays the Eagles ran and caught nine passes for 122 yards—but he was denied the end zone.

Two first-half turnovers killed the Eagles, but the game was still tied 7–7 at the half and 14–14 after three quarters.

"What it really came down to was in the biggest games we didn't play very well," Runyan said. "We had played so well all year and we played great the week before. Then we got to the Super Bowl and we didn't play well. Turnovers killed us, or we would have blown them out of the water."

And if the beginning of the game hadn't killed the Eagles, the end surely did. New England led 24–14, and the Eagles had the ball at the 21-yard line with just 5:40 left in the fourth quarter. On 11 of the first 12 plays of what turned into a 13-play drive, the Eagles had McNabb under center instead of in the shotgun, and huddled after every play. Even the Patriots defenders were perplexed.

"I remember looking right at McNabb and just seeing the seconds ticking away and wondering what they were doing,"

HUGH DOUGLAS

Hugh Douglas, in 1998, was traded from a New York Jets team that had just gone 1–15 to a Philadelphia Eagles team that was about to go 3–13. "Two-game improvement, right?" Douglas said with a laugh. "Man, those times were tough. That's what made winning for me feel so good."

Douglas was a key part of the Eagles teams that got to the NFC Championship Games in 2001 and 2002. He parlayed that success into a big free agent contract with the Jacksonville Jaguars. Then when it didn't work out there, the Jaguars released him and he was back with the Eagles. It was just a part-time role for the former Pro Bowl defensive end, but it came in time for the 2004 Super Bowl run—where, ironically, the game was played in Jacksonville.

"Getting to the Super Bowl, that was the greatest feeling in the world, especially for me," Douglas said. "My body had started to give out. I knew this was it for me. So I just enjoyed the ride. That's what I did, I enjoyed the ride. And I thank Andy [Reid] for bringing me back and letting me be a part of it, even though we didn't win the game. I know a lot of guys out there who wish they could have just gotten to the game. I was one of them."

When he left the Eagles, did he ever think he would be back? "Never ever," Douglas said. "But playing in Philly the way I did, and then had they gone [to the Super Bowl] and I wasn't there, that would have really hurt."

New England linebacker Tedy Bruschi told author Bob McGinn in *The Ultimate Super Bowl Book*. "Why didn't they have a sense of urgency? Maybe they knew something I didn't know. But what I knew was the fourth quarter of the Super Bowl was winding down and they don't have more points than we do."

The Eagles scored on a 30-yard touchdown pass from McNabb to Greg Lewis to make it 24–21, but just 1:48 was left on the clock. The Eagles tried an onside kick, but the Pats recovered.

Two years later, for McGinn's book, Eagles head coach Andy Reid admitted he probably should have shown a little more urgency on that final drive. "Yeah, I probably should have done that [no-huddle] a little bit more," the coach said. "When your quarterback is getting hit [McNabb was hit four times on the first five plays of the drive], it's hard to get that no-huddle going. The end result, which I think people overlook, is we did score a touchdown on that drive. And we had time to get another. We just didn't get it done."

24

RAIDED

As the Eagles rolled through the 1980 regular season and into the playoffs, where the roll continued, there were two words never spoken. "That entire season, before the season or during the season, we never mentioned the Super Bowl," Pro Bowl linebacker Bill Bergey said. "Never."

The Eagles, who got progressively better in each of head coach Dick Vermeil's first four years, saw it all coming together. And 1980 was the year it finally happened. The Eagles, who had posted two winning records from their last title in 1960 until 1978, had gotten to the Super Bowl.

"I never felt we looked at our record," Pro Bowl left tackle Stan Walters said. "We just went game to game. That's just how it was. That's how Dick wanted it. When we were bad, during those bad years, he said keep working to get better. So even now when we were winning, we knew we could still get better."

That 1980 season saw the Eagles win 11 of their first 12 games, the only blemish a 24–14 loss in St. Louis to the Cardinals. And most of the games weren't that close. Seven of the 11 wins were by double digits, and six were by at least two touchdowns.

"There were a lot of good teams that year," wide receiver Harold Carmichael said. "We were good and we were winning, but there were so many other good teams we didn't take anything for granted." Vermeil wouldn't allow it. It was the ultimate "one game at a time" approach. After each win the focus was on the next opponent, with one exception.

"What we did talk about was the Dallas Cowboys and how we had to get past the Dallas Cowboys," Bergey said. Dallas was the dominant team in the NFC, and especially the NFC East in the '70s. The Cowboys made the playoffs nine of the 10 years in the decade, went to five Super Bowls, and won two. They won the division seven times, including four straight from 1976 to 1979.

That was then. And this was the '80s—a new decade and a new team to challenge Tom Landry's group. And that team was the Eagles.

Roger Staubach, Dallas' Hall of Fame quarterback, had retired. His replacement, Danny White, wasn't bad—but he certainly wasn't Staubach. Whereas Vermeil's team had a balanced offense, with Wilbert Montgomery running and catching the ball out of the backfield and quarterback Ron Jaworski enjoying his finest season (3,529 yards and 27 touchdown passes to earn the NFC Player of the Year Award).

"Ronnie had a great year," Carmichael said. "We had a good line. We had Wilbert. It was a good team."

Bergey, who came back from a serious knee injury he had suffered in 1979, led a defense that forced 36 turnovers (25 interceptions, 11 fumble recoveries) and sent nose tackle Charlie Johnson and safety Randy Logan to the Pro Bowl.

"That wasn't the most talented team, especially on defense, but we played together. We didn't care who got credit," Bergey said. "It was as much of a team defense as I've ever seen. We just knew each other. We knew what we were going to do on the field. We just meshed together."

The Eagles beat the Cowboys 17–10 in week seven, and faced them again the final week of the regular season. Close losses to San Diego (22–21) and Atlanta (20–17) followed by a revenge win over St. Louis (17–3) left the Eagles at 12–3 as they headed to Texas Stadium. The Cowboys were 11–4. If the Eagles won, they won the division. If the Cowboys won, they had to win by 26 to win the tiebreaker of net points in the division.

"We're 12–3 playing in Dallas. We win the division as long as we don't lose by more than 26 points. And at one point we're losing by

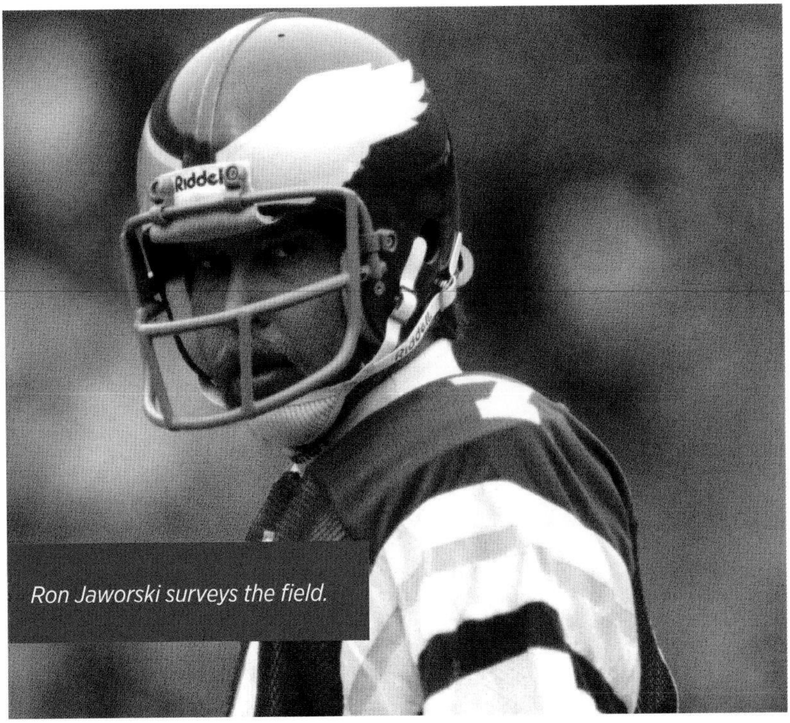

Ron Jaworski surveys the field.

more than that," Bergey said. "We came back, we lost, but we still won the division. Now we're celebrating in a losing cause in Texas Stadium. It was the craziest thing you've ever seen."

It wouldn't be the last time the Eagles saw the Cowboys that year.

After a bye week, the Eagles blew out the Minnesota Vikings 31–16. Meanwhile the Cowboys, the NFC's No. 4 seed, blew out the Los Angeles Rams 34–13 in the wild-card round and then went on the road and beat the No. 2 seed Atlanta Falcons 30–27.

There it was: the Cowboys, trying to get to their sixth Super Bowl vs. the Eagles, trying to get to their first, playing at Veterans Stadium for the NFC title.

"JAWS"

From the time the Eagles traded away Sonny Jurgensen to the Washington Redskins after the 1963 season, they searched for a quarterback. Norm Snead, acquired in the Jurgensen trade, wasn't the answer. Neither was Pete Liske nor Rick Arrington, a couple of unheralded players who started in 1971. First-round draft pick John Reaves and a past-his-prime Roman Gabriel didn't get it done, either. Dick Vermeil, in his second season as Eagles head coach, knew he was going nowhere fast without a quarterback. So he sent Charle Young, a three-time Pro Bowl tight end, to the Los Angeles Rams for Ron Jaworski. It worked.

Jaworski, after a shaky first season with the Eagles, took the team to the playoffs in four straight seasons and was named the NFC Player of the Year in 1980 when the Eagles reached the Super Bowl.

In his Eagles career (1977–86), Jaworski ranks second all-time in completions (2,088), yards (26,963), and touchdown passes (175).

"Before we played Dallas, we went down to Tampa to practice because the weather was so bad in Philly," Bergey said. "Dick Vermeil pulled out everything he had for that Cowboys game. I never saw anyone so prepared for a team or a game. We were overprepared, if that's such a thing. He even went right down to us wearing white jerseys. He said, 'We're going to make them wear those putrid ugly blue jerseys.' I have to stress this to you, walking down that tunnel, in my 13 years of football, never ever have I been so close to saying, 'We're going to win this game and go to the Super Bowl.' There was no doubt about it whatsoever. We were going to win."

That confidence spread throughout the team. "I don't know if I was as confident as Bergey was," Carmichael said. "But we did think we could beat anybody at that point. And we were fired up in that tunnel as we were getting ready to get introduced. You could feel it. I remember Randy Logan coming up to me and saying, 'Man, you're ready to go. I better buckle up my chinstrap.' We were ready."

Montgomery, who had battled a hyperextended knee all season, ran 42 yards for a touchdown in the first quarter. Dallas would come back to make it 7–7 at the half, but the Eagles pulled away in the third quarter and won going away, 20–7. They were going to the Super Bowl.

"We kicked their ass," Bergey said. "Wilbert ran for almost 200 yards. It was 20–7, but the score wasn't indicative of how we won. It wasn't really that close.

"So we're whooping and hollering and having a good old time after the game. We have overtaken the Dallas Cowboys. We were NFC champions. It was actually an afterthought, 'Oh yeah, we have the Super Bowl and the Oakland Raiders next.'"

The Eagles' real Super Bowl may have come in beating the Cowboys, a team against which they were 1–10 against in the 11 games prior to 1980. As prepared as they had been for that NFC Championship Game, they looked equally as unprepared for the Raiders in Super Bowl XV.

Oakland jumped ahead early; linebacker Rod Martin intercepted Jaworski three times; the Raiders defense held Montgomery to 44 yards; and Oakland quarterback Jim Plunkett threw three touchdown passes, including an 80-yarder to Kenny King, in a 27–10 rout.

"If you can't get ready for the world championship game, what good is it?" Bergey said. "We just couldn't get back to that same level: the mental approach, the physical approach, the emotional approach. And we had a couple things happen early in the game that went against us. It's fourth-and-6 and they're going to punt. 'Don't jump offsides!' [Joe] Turkey Jones jumps. Now it's fourth-and-1, they go for it, and get it.

"Then there's the 80-yard pass to Kenny King and it's 14–0. We get back out there and I look in the huddle and I could just tell it was over. We weren't winning that game. The sad part is getting to just one Super Bowl, coming up short, and never getting back. That just sucks really bad."

The Eagles wouldn't get back to a Super Bowl until 2004—and they would lose that one, too, to the New England Patriots. As of 2016, they have still not won a Super Bowl since 1960.

"You know," Walters said. "I do remember Dick saying things like 'We have to beat Dallas. We have to win our division. We have to get home-field advantage.' He might have even said we have to win the NFC Championship Game. He never said, 'We have to win the Super Bowl.' That was never mentioned. Maybe it should have been."

25

TRIUMPH AND TRAGEDY

Andy Reid's two finest decisions in his 14 years as head coach of the Philadelphia Eagles came in his first four months on the job. Reid, hired by the Eagles January 11, 1999, took 11 days to hire Jim Johnson as his defensive coordinator. Three months or so later he made quarterback Donovan McNabb his first-ever draft pick with the No. 2 overall selection of the 1999 NFL Draft.

With Johnson running the defense and McNabb guiding the offense, Reid became the winningest coach in Eagles history. He took the team to the playoffs five straight years from 2000 to 2004 and then again in 2006 and 2008. The Eagles' record with Reid, Johnson, and McNabb from 1999 to 2008 was 97–62–1. They won 10 playoff games, went to the NFC Championship Game five times, and the Super Bowl once.

After Johnson died from melanoma cancer in July 2009, Reid's Eagles were never the same. During the four years Reid continued to coach the team after Johnson's passing, the Eagles went just 33–31 and never won another playoff game.

McNabb was traded to the Washington Redskins on Easter Sunday night 2010; and in the three years Reid coached without him, the team was 22–26, and without a postseason win.

Oh, but from 1999 to 2008 that Eagles trio had it going. They never won it all, but they won quite a bit. "It was a good team, a good time," McNabb said. "We did a lot of things right. We won a lot of games. We just didn't win a Super Bowl."

Just as it had been when Reid was hired as the former Green Bay Packers' tight ends coach in 1999, Johnson came in as defensive coordinator without much fanfare. He was an assistant coach at Notre Dame under Dan Devine, coached in the USFL, and was a position coach for the Cardinals, Colts, and Seahawks. His only experience as a coordinator came with the Colts in 1996 and 1997, a 9–7 and a 3–13 team, respectively.

"I remember Jim coming from Seattle, and Seattle blew us out the year before, like 38–0," defensive end Hugh Douglas said. "So I was like, 'All right, well his defense blew us out. I'll respect that. I'll give him a chance.'

"Jim's defense was really kind of simple, at least for me. But we blitzed every play, so it was complicated from that standpoint. The linebackers and the guys in back had to learn a lot. For me as an end it was kind of easy. But there was one time where I kept screwing up this one play. It was a wing stunt. So we're in a meeting and Jim says we're going to change the wing stunt. And [defensive end] Brandon Whiting says, 'Yeah, because 53 keeps f——ng up the defense and doing what he wants to do.' Jim laughed. But Jim just let me play football, and that's all I wanted to do. He did that with everyone. He got the most out of all his players."

Johnson took safety Brian Dawkins, a quick but undersized player who was good in coverage his first two years with the Eagles, and turned him into a superstar, if not a superhero. It was Johnson's defensive schemes, after all, that gave birth to Weapon X.

Johnson did the same with middle linebacker Jeremiah Trotter, getting the most of the athletic, big-time hitter. "Jim made Trott a center killer," Douglas said. "You see the way Trot played middle linebacker like he was a nose tackle. That was Jim. He let him play downhill and let him do his thing."

Johnson's blitzing, attacking defense was the perfect complement to Reid's West Coast offense. And his media-friendly personality also complemented the head coach's stoic style.

"Andy comes from Green Bay as a quarterback coach and really nobody knows much about him," Douglas remembered. "We're in camp and we're going through those three days where we would hit three straight days. It's the second day and we're bitching and moaning. I remember being in the huddle and I was like 'Man, this cat don't know what the f—— he's doing' And he heard me. And he looks over and says, 'Quit your bitching. Can't you see you're getting better?' I looked at him and I figured it out. He was breaking us down to build us back up.

"Yeah, I think I drove him crazy a little bit at first. Then Andy would use me to get the team up sometimes. He'd say to me 'I need your juice,' and that was the relationship Andy and I had."

It was a strange, unique relationship Douglas shared with Reid. "Andy would tell jokes and I would never get them," Douglas said, "I'd laugh because he was laughing. But I would say, 'What the hell is he talking about?' And I would say stuff and Andy would shake his head and say, 'What is it with this guy?' After a while he just let me be who I was."

As a head coach, Reid was always in control. He wanted to know what everyone around the team, including the media, was doing at all times. The one exception was Johnson and his defense. "I'll give that to Andy," Douglas said. "He and Jim talked, but for the most part he let Jim run his defense. Andy was too busy with the offense anyway. But he never really questioned Jim... He trusted him."

Reid needed the trust and love of the organization when his family life began to deteriorate in 2007. On January 30 of that year, just more than two weeks after the team lost in the playoffs to the New Orleans Saints, both of his sons, Garrett and Britt, were arrested in separate incidents. Garrett Reid tested positive for heroin and admitted having used it that day he ran a red light in Plymouth Township, a suburb of Philadelphia, and hit another car. Authorities found syringes with heroin and testosterone in his SUV.

He was sentenced to two to 23 months in the county prison, plus one year of probation.

In a separate incident that same day, Britt Reid pointed a handgun at another driver following a dispute. He pleaded guilty to a string of charges, including carrying a firearm without a license. He was sentenced to eight to 23 months in jail plus five years' probation on gun and drug charges.

Montgomery County Judge Steven O'Neill, before sentencing both 22-year-old Britt and 23-year-old Garrett, was not kind to the Reid family. "There isn't any structure there that this court can depend upon," Judge O'Neill said. "I'm saying this is a family in crisis."

The Judge also noted that searches of the Reid home found illegal and prescription drugs throughout the house. "It sounds more or less like a drug emporium there, with the drugs all over the house, and you're an addict," O'Neill told Britt Reid in court. Andy Reid took a five-week leave of absence from the team during the crisis that off-season, but returned for the team's minicamps and training camp.

Unfortunately, tragedy stuck again on August 5, 2012, when Garrett Reid was found dead from an overdose of heroin in his dorm room at Lehigh University in Bethlehem, Pennsylvania, where he was assisting the team's strength and conditioning coach Barry Rubin during the Eagles' training camp. Investigators found 47 syringes and 65 needles in the younger Reid's gym bag, along with 19 vials of steroids.

"Today is one of life's tough days," Eagles owner Jeffrey Lurie said that day. "Andy is a rock-solid man. I think what makes him a great coach is his combination of compassion, feeling, and strength. And today he exhibited it all. It's unimaginable. We've all suffered. Most of us have suffered tragedy in our lives. Losing a son is unimaginable. Losing a child is unimaginable—the pain. Again, he is rock solid."

26

SNOWBALLS AND SANTA

Philadelphia Eagles fans are the worst. They booed Santa Claus. Donovan McNabb. And Michael Irvin, as he was knocked out on the Veterans Stadium carpet. It got so bad at the Vet they even put a courtroom and jail cell on the premises. One time a fan even shot off a flare gun in the middle of the game.

Yup, they're the worst all right.

"Far worse things have happened in stadiums around the country, but we're always the punch line," longtime Eagles fan Rocco Riccio (and part of the bunch that booed McNabb's selection in the 1999 NFL Draft) said. "We're the national joke when something like that happens. Wait a minute, what about all the other things that have happened? People running on the field and getting tackled by players. I've never seen that happen here. But we booed Santa Claus."

Indeed, that's where the legend was born. It was December 15, 1968, and an Eagles team that was about to finish the season 2–12 hosted the Minnesota Vikings. If it wasn't bad enough the Eagles were bad, it was worse that they weren't worse. By winning two straight games to get to 2–11 they blew the chance at the first pick of the 1969 NFL Draft and the opportunity to select USC running back Orenthal James Simpson—you might know him better as O.J.

So on that cold, snowy day at Franklin Field, 54,000 people showed up to watch the Eagles play the Vikings. At least they were going to get a good halftime show, or so they thought. One week before Christmas, the Eagles planned a holiday extravaganza, except the weather kept Santa Claus from getting to the game. So much for those reindeer, huh? An Eagles official found a fan in the stands with a Santa suit named Frank Olivo, and asked if he would fill in for Saint Nick. All he would have to do is walk across the field surrounded by the lovely Eagles cheerleaders, who were dressed as elves, and wave to the crowd.

"The fans were in such a bad mood, none of us wanted to see Santa Claus to begin with," former Philadelphia mayor and Pennsylvania governor Ed Rendell, who was at the game, said years later. "I actually remember feeling a twinge of anxiety that they might really hurt Santa."

Olivo, at five foot seven, 160 pounds, wasn't the ideal Santa. Other fans said he was drunk too, although Olivo denied it several times in interviews before his death in 2015. As he crossed the field, the boos started and became increasingly louder. Then the snowballs began to fly from the stands. Some of them actually hit Olivo—which, according to jokes, meant neither Eagles quarterback Norm Snead nor King Hill, was throwing them.

Yes, Eagles fans really did boo Santa Claus, albeit a poor facsimile on a bad day that ended a really bad season.

And a fan really did shoot a flare gun during the second half of a lopsided loss to the San Francisco 49ers on *Monday Night Football* in 1997. "I was there," Riccio said. "The guy just walked down to the lower tier and shot off the flare. Then he slowly stepped back, lit up a cigarette, and waited for the cops to come get him. It was incredible.' Did that just happen? Did he shoot that flare gun and then light up a cigarette?'"

Irvin and McNabb were not that bad, at least not as bad as they appeared. Irvin, whose career ended that 1999 day after a hit from Eagles safety Tim Hauck, lay motionless on the field. The crowd was quiet. When Cowboys teammate Deion Sanders began to do what he called a "healing dance" around Irvin, then the fans booed. They didn't like Irvin, but they *really* didn't like Sanders or his dance.

McNabb was another story. The fans, fueled by some in the media, especially sports-talk radio 610 WIP, and then-mayor Rendell, convinced themselves that with the No. 2 pick in the draft the team should select Texas running back Ricky Williams. It didn't matter that the team had a good running back in Duce Staley and was desperate for a quarterback in a draft that would produce five first-round quarterbacks. They wanted Williams and that was that.

So the radio station brought 30 fans, nicknamed "the Dirty 30" to New York for the draft and poised themselves to boo any name the commissioner announced that wasn't Williams. The clip lives on in infamy.

"I don't know much about that story, I've heard about it," laughed Eagles fan Shawn Young, the man dressed in full Eagles gear with eye black and all and in the middle of the booing. "I'm kidding, of course. Actually, now it is laughable. There was a lot that led up to that. There was a lot of verbal stuff going on before that between us and some Giants fans. A security guy called me over and wanted to talk to me. And then they moved me down 10 rows, front and center. I was kind of set up. If it bothered me, I would have hid. I wouldn't do what I do now. I would have stopped."

Since then, Young has parlayed his role as "Superfan" into helping several local and national charities and doing volunteer work to help area children in need. See? Eagles fans really aren't that bad.

ON THIS DATE

20 years after Eagles fans booed Santa Claus the Eagles beat the Dallas Cowboys 23–7 on the final day of the season to win the 1988 NFC East title. It was the Eagles' first division title in eight years and first playoff appearance in seven years.

"Philly gets a bad rap around the country, for sure," said defensive end Hugh Douglas, who played for the New York Jets and Jacksonville Jaguars around two stints with the Eagles. "All people know about Philly is what they read about Philly. It's not like that at all. When people say bad things about Philly to me, I just tell them 'You don't know, you just don't know.'

"*I* didn't know. I didn't know anything about Philly when I got there in 1988. I land at the airport and the guy at the baggage area knows me, recognizes me at least, and says, 'Hey, welcome to Philly. Now go beat Dallas.' That's how it is there. They care. And they care year round, not just during the season like some places. Now, I get in a cab and it's the same thing from the cabdriver, 'Hey, you guys gonna beat Dallas?' It's crazy. Do the fans do some bonehead things? Sure, but they do that everywhere."

Eagles fans are loyal. The fact that 54,000 showed up to boo Santa back in 1968 tells you something. And consider the team hasn't won a championship for five-plus decades.

"Frustration," Riccio said, is the one word to describe what it's like to be an Eagles' fan. "Every other team in the division has won multiple Super Bowls. We have none. It's humbling. We talk big, but sometimes we just don't have enough to back it up. We're actually a fan base that acts like we've won championships, the way we talk and boast. And ownership and management know that and take advantage of it. They know there's always going be a long waiting list for season tickets. They know the kind of fan base they have, that we're always going to be coming back for more."

Especially if the Eagles ever win a Super Bowl. After all the bad years, all the close years, could you imagine what that day would be like? Young thinks about it all the time. "That parade would be unbelievable," he said. "I mean, take any parade you've ever seen and multiply it by 100. That's what it would be. One day wouldn't be enough for it. They might have to close the city for a week. People would talk about it for decades and decades and decades."

Just like they do booing and throwing snowballs at Santa, and booing McNabb. "There's a sense of pride, they're still talking about it," Riccio said. "That so many years later it's still a highlight of the draft, and it was us. Every single time they show the scene we become more legendary. A whole group of fans became infamous."

27

CUTTING DESEAN

When the rumors started shortly after the end of their division-winning season in 2013, they didn't make any sense. Why would the Eagles release wide receiver DeSean Jackson after his first year in head coach Chip Kelly's offense produced a career-best 82 receptions, a career-best 1,332 yards and a career-best nine touchdowns?

Jackson, the Eagles second-round draft pick out of the University of California in 2008, had shown flashes of brilliance during his first five years in the league. And his speed made him a big-play threat and a receiver that would always keep defenses honest. Then finally, in Kelly's up-tempo attack, it all came together for him. His 82 catches were 37 more than he had the year before and 20 more than his previous career high. And his 1,332 yards were more than 600 more than the previous year and almost 200 more than his previous high. Then the Eagles, coming off a 10–6 NFC East title season, were just going to let him go. Why?

His contract, which had three years remaining, but no guaranteed years, was to pay him $10.5 million. That was fair market value for a guy who caught 82 passes for 1,332 yards. Then on Friday, March 28, NJ.com released a story the two writers had been working on for weeks that tied Jackson to assorted Los Angeles gang members. A huge part of the story featured LAPD detective Eric Crosson, who told the website he had reached out to the Eagles to inform them of Jackson's connections to an alleged murderer.

Minutes—literally minutes—after the story appeared on the website the Eagles announced they had released Jackson. There were no quotes from Kelly, general manager Howie Roseman, or owner Jeffrey Lurie, just a generic statement from the team that read: "After careful consideration over this off-season, the

Philadelphia Eagles have decided to part ways with DeSean Jackson. The team informed him of his release today."

Months later, when Kelly finally commented on the subject, all he would say about Jackson's release is that it was a "football decision."

Less than a week after his release, Jackson signed with the NFC East rival Washington Redskins. In his first interview after the release he expressed how he felt.

"I was definitely hurt," Jackson said. "I [had] a relationship with teammates, the front office, the fans. Not just the things I have done on the field. The fans have embraced me like no other in Philadelphia. We all know about the Philadelphia fans. There was something about them that made me feel great every time I went out on the field.

"To be released was a humbling experience, but at the same time it hurt. It was at the peak of my career. I just came off the best year of my six years in the NFL. I can definitely say it hurt. But it's a business. It's the NFL."

According to the NJ.com report, Jackson was not involved when on December 29, 2010, 14-year-old Taburi Watson flashed a rival gang sign at two men as he rode his bike through south Los Angeles. The men, reportedly members of the Crips, responded to the sign by shooting him multiple times. The police found Watson dead at the scene.

Jackson was, however, associated with Theron Shakir, who, along with codefendant Marques Binns, is a purported member of the Crips. Shakir, known as "T-Ron," is a rapper who recorded for Jaccpot Records, a label owned by Jackson. The two were close enough that they appear together frequently in photographs.

Crosson told NJ.com he interviewed Jackson on the phone in late 2011 and said he was "cooperative at the time." The detective then went on to say he reached out to the Eagles in 2011, before the Jackson interview, to alert them to his connection with Shakir. The Eagles would not comment on Crosson's comments.

Shakir was acquitted of Watson's murder and a related gun charge in January 2013, though he spent more than a year in jail awaiting trial. Binns was convicted of the murder and sentenced to 15 years to life.

But that wasn't the end of the story. Jackson's name found its way across Detective Crosson's desk once again, according to the report. This time Jackson's name surfaced as part of an investigation into a 2012 gang-related murder that occurred outside a south Los Angeles business where a party had taken place. The building was owned or leased by a member of Jackson's family, the police said. During a search of the building, Crosson told the website investigators found several documents belonging to Jackson, including a car title, a gun permit issued in New Jersey, and credit card receipts. After discovering the documents, Crosson said he made multiple attempts to contact Jackson by phone but never was able to connect with him.

Crosson made it clear that Jackson was never considered a suspect in the crime. He added that there was no hard evidence that Jackson was a gang member, but said that he routinely flashed gang signs in photos and even during games. "You don't want to see anybody throwing up gang signs like he did in the Redskins game [in 2013], Crosson said. "Those were neighborhood Crip gang signs and he flashed them during a game. He may not be affiliated with the gang, but they don't take kindly to those not in the gang throwing up those gang signs."

The only known trouble Jackson ever incurred while with the Eagles came in 2009 when he was pulled over in New Jersey for having tinted windows and, during the course of the stop, police officers discovered marijuana in the vehicle. He was arrested for possession of marijuana and operating a car with materials that obstruct or reduce the driver's view. The chargers were dropped and Jackson pled guilty to a disturbing the peace charge.

"Do I know friends that are out there involved [in gang activities]? Yes," Jackson told ESPN just after his release. "I try to stay away from them.... I'm definitely aware and know certain gang members, but as far as me being affiliated and me being a gang member, never have not once been. Never have had any affiliation with going out and doing things that are against the law.

"With the article, and how I feel about NJ.com, I think it was, from my point of view, very disrespectful. I don't think it was right, straight up. The things, the allegations, the things that were said in the article, they were from a long time ago. I felt like the club and the organization knew about in previous years before that. To sit there come 2014, and hear all these crazy allegations and crazy stories, half of which weren't even true, or whatever the case may be, I was just very disturbed and didn't like that at all."

After he signed with the Redskins, Jackson got a reality television show on BET called *Home Team*. In the first episode he again talked about his shocking release: "When I was released by the Eagles, I feel they tried to paint a picture that definitely wasn't true. It was a slap in the face, coming off one of my best seasons in the NFL," Jackson said on the show. "The Eagles tried to blow me up. That's cold how they did it."

One of his friends on the show responded, "Like they tried to persecute you from where you come from, bro."

"That's why I think they fired me. Have I went to jail?... I ain't done none of that," Jackson said.

During his first year with the Redskins, in which Jackson caught 56 passes for 1,169 yards and helped his team eliminate the Eagles from playoff contention with a 27–24 win in Week 16, Jackson again talked about his release.

"I was at the top of the top. And then I got released," he said. "It was a smear campaign. Things media said about me, I bet you could say that about the majority of people in the NFL. I got a second chance to play in the NFL and I'm proving I'm one of the best receivers in the game.

"They made the decision, They moved on. I moved on. I'm blessed, like I said, to have a second opportunity to play here in Washington and, you know, it's not about them anymore."

28

FOURTH-AND-26

One of the most amazing plays in Eagles history would have never happened if it hadn't been for a few earlier plays that have long gone unnoticed.

Even causal Eagles fans have heard of fourth-and-26, the play that enabled the Eagles to beat the Green Bay Packers 20–17 in overtime of the 2003 NFC playoffs.

Fourth-and-26 might not have even happened, or wouldn't have been as critical if it hadn't been for two fourth-and-1 plays earlier in the game.

Just before the end of the first half, with Green Bay ahead 14–7, the Packers faced a fourth-and-goal from the Eagles 1-yard line. Packers head coach Mike Sherman opted to go for the two-touchdown lead instead of kicking the easy field goal for a 10-point lead.

Ahman Green, who ultimately ran for 156 yards on the day, got the call. Eagles defensive tackle Corey Simon got just enough of a push on Packers guard Mike Wahle that the guard went backwards just a step and tripped up Green. Simon cleaned up the tackle inches from the goal line and the half ended with the score 14–7.

"You're right," Simon said. "That was a huge play in the game. But then with everything else that happened, it kind of got forgotten."

The Eagles got even late but Green Bay went back ahead 17–14 and got the ball back with 7:58 left in the fourth quarter. The Packers ran off 10 plays, nine runs, and moved from their own 16-yard line to the Eagles 40, facing fourth-and-1 with 2:30 to go. Green Bay's offense stayed on the field and the Eagles used their second timeout.

This time Sherman elected not to go for it. Brett Favre stood under center and gave a hard count, trying to get the Eagles to jump offside. They didn't bite. As the play clock hit zero, Green Bay took a delay of game penalty.

"We couldn't jump," Simon said. "That's what we talked about during the timeout. 'Don't jump. Don't jump.' Favre had a good cadence, but we couldn't fall for it."

Green Bay punted, and that led to the now famous fourth-and-26. Duce Staley carried on the Eagles' first play from the 20 to the 42, just a few feet away from where the Packers had just faced their fourth-and-1. And then it all started to come apart. Donovan McNabb, under pressure from Green Bay defensive end Aaron Kampman, threw incomplete on first down. Packers nickel back Bhawoh Jue sacked McNabb for a 16-yard loss on second down, making it third-and-26.

"I'm watching, and I'm thinking, 'How in the hell did we just lose 16 yards?'" Eagles linebacker Ike Reese said. "I'll be honest, I thought the game was over."

When McNabb threw incomplete for tight end Chad Lewis on third down, everyone else did, too. It was fourth-and-26.

What do you call on fourth-and-26? "Usually," Eagles head coach Andy Reid said, "a punt."

McNabb, who threw for 248 yards and ran for another 107 on the day, was one of the few who didn't think it was over. "You don't want to think negative thoughts at a time like that," McNabb said. "You just have to have the mentality that we're going to get it done."

Freddie Mitchell, who didn't have a catch to that point of the game and who wasn't one of McNabb's favorite targets, was as confident as his quarterback. "I didn't say anything to Donovan, because he wasn't going to listen to me anyway," Mitchell said. "But I told [wide receivers coach] David Culley, 'The middle has been open the whole game. You tell him I'm going to be wide open on this play.' Donovan said to me, 'You ready.' Am *I* ready? I've been ready the whole f——ing game."

Donovan McNabb's fourth-and-26 pass to Freddie Mitchell will forever remain one of the most unforgettable plays in Eagles history.

Green Bay defensive coordinator Ed Donatell (who was fired by the Packers a week later) had blitzed McNabb all game and sacked him eight times. This time, this play, the Packers decided to play coverage.

McNabb dropped straight back. He had time. He was looking for Lewis, but so were the Packers.

"I thought back to the NFC Championship Game two years earlier against St. Louis," Eagles running back and future running backs coach Duce Staley said. "We had a fourth down at the end of that game and Donovan threw to Freddie but the Rams brought the house and Donovan rushed his throw and got picked off. So I thought the Packers were going to blitz everybody, but they didn't bring anybody. Donovan had all day. He just had to find somebody."

He found Mitchell in between Jue and safety Darren Sharper in the middle of the field and just past the first down marker. "I saw him running down the middle and tried to put it in a position where he could at least compete for it," McNabb said.

Sharper, Green Bay's Pro Bowl safety, went too deep but came back and jarred Mitchell as he made the catch. But the receiver held onto the ball and fell forward for a gain of 28. "Freddie's problem was never holding onto the ball," then Eagles offensive coordinator Brad Childress said. "Freddie would hold on to the ball."

Mitchell, in a playoff win a year later, would thank his hands in a postgame press conference. This time he wasn't quite as cocky. "I was just like, 'I got to catch this,'" Mitchell said. "I stuck my hand out and it stuck to me. Then I just had to hold on to it. I hit the ground and started looking for the marker. It was going to be close."

Actually, while it appeared to be worth a measurement, a generous spot gave Mitchell and the Eagles the first down rather easily.

The Eagles went on to tie the game at the end of regulation on a David Akers field goal and then won it in overtime on another Akers field goal.

But it was fourth-and-26 that everyone remembers.

"I'm thinking as it happened, 'That did just not happen.' Maybe fourth-and-18, maybe fourth-and-20. Maybe even fourth-and-22," Staley said. "But fourth-and-26? I couldn't believe it."

What made it even more unbelievable was that Mitchell, the 2001 first-round pick who would play just four years for the Eagles before being out of football, was on the other end of the pass. "I didn't have the numbers and I didn't have the Pro Bowls," Mitchell said. "But the fans look for memories. The media called me a first-round bust, but fourth-and-26, that's a memory nobody can ever take away from me. Whenever anyone says 'fourth-and-26' they don't say 'Donovan McNabb threw that pass.' They say 'Freddie Mitchell caught that pass.'"

29

CLYDE AND SETH

They will be linked together in Eagles history forever. Whether it's Clyde and Seth or Seth and Clyde, you can't think of one without the other coming to mind.

Defensive end Clyde Simmons and linebacker Seth Joyner came to the Eagles together, left the Eagles together, and dominated at their respective positions the entire time they were together. And as much as their careers were similar, they couldn't have been more different off the field.

As his status grew in the Eagles locker room, Joyner became the team spokesman. Reporters flocked to his locker, especially after games and really especially after losses, because you had to hear what Seth would say and who he would rip. Usually it was head coach Rich Kotite, although there were a few moments reserved for an offensive lineman, like first-round pick Antone Davis, or the team's front office.

After one loss to the Washington Redskins, Joyner called the team's special teams "garbage" and said that all you had to do "was mention the words Washington Redskins and our offense falls apart."

During Kotite's first season as head coach, 1991, Joyner was quoted in the New York Times as calling his coach "a puppet."

Alternately, Simmons, once referred to by Cardinals Pro Bowl tackle Luis Sharpe as "a hungry, husky, man-child" was rarely in the center of media attention. He was friendly enough. It's just that he didn't have as much to say as his friend a few lockers down and to the left.

One time after a midweek Joyner rant about something or another, Simmons was approached for his view. He smiled and said, "Just put me down for whatever Seth said."

Simmons and Joyner came to the Eagles as afterthoughts in a crazy 1986 Draft, Simmons in the ninth round out of Western Carolina and Joyner in the eighth round out of Texas–El Paso. In today's NFL Draft, both would have gone undrafted.

"That's kind of amazing when you think about it," former Eagles teammate cornerback Eric Allen said. "I mean, Clyde was such a great player, a force on the line for all those years as both a guy who could stop the run and as a great pass rusher.

"Seth just had a great feel for the game. He had the instincts of a middle linebacker but was athletic like an outside linebacker. And he had the ability to rush the passer like a defensive end."

Joyner and Simmons, along with Reggie White, Jerome Brown, and Allen, made the Eagles defense one of the best in the game from the late '80s into the early '90s. In 1991 they ranked first in the league in run defense, pass defense, (obviously) total defense, and least points allowed.

"Sometimes people get caught up in the mystique," Simmons said. "They don't get motivated as much when they don't get the attention. I never let that get to me. I remember the one year [when] I was third in the league in sacks and didn't go to the Pro Bowl. That bothered me at first, but my teammates always supported me. That meant more to me than any outside attention."

Simmons, who played for the Eagles, as Joyner did, from 1986 to 1993 and then along with Joyner signed with the Arizona Cardinals in 1994, was overshadowed on a defensive line which also included White and Brown. There were those who thought Simmons' success was just a byproduct of playing opposite White, who drew constant double teams.

White wasn't one of them. "He doesn't need me on the other side," White said before the 1990 season. "[Simmons] is a great player in his own right. He's as good as any defensive end in this league. I'm happy that he's on the other side. He makes me better."

From 1989 to 1992, Simmons recorded 55 sacks, the second most in the NFL and one more than White, and finally got Pro Bowl recognition in 1991. He went again in 1992. When Simmons retired after the 1999 season, he had 121.5 sacks, the 10th most in NFL history.

"I never needed to be in the spotlight," said Simmons, who coached the defensive line with the Rams under his old defensive coordinator, Jeff Fisher. "We had enough great players on those teams. We kind of used that to challenge each other. Every time Reggie got a sack, I wanted to get a sack. Every time somebody made a big play, it made somebody else want to make a big play. I think that's what made our defense so great."

While Simmons never let being drafted in the ninth round get to him, Joyner used it as motivation throughout his star-studded career. And it worked—to the tune of 52 sacks, 24 interceptions, and 26 forced fumbles in his 13 NFL seasons. He's the only player in league history with more than 50 sacks and more than 20 interceptions.

"The thing is, when you talk about the draft, there are a lot of things you look at and a lot of things you can measure. But the one thing I believe, and I stand by this, you cannot measure what's in someone's heart and what's in someone's mind," Joyner said. "A player can go to the combine and train up and run all these numbers, but at the end of the day you can't measure those intangibles.

"For me, it was what, 30 teams back then? So 29 teams passed me over seven times. It was one of those things. I was always confident in myself, and I know Clyde was always confident in himself. It was just a matter of being in the right situation, being in the right system that allowed us to flourish.

"But every time I played against a team I had that extra incentive. It was 'This is what you could have had. You didn't think I was worthy of a pick. I'm going to make you suffer for not picking me.' That was the fire, absolutely, even to a fault.

"All of my time playing, I never got to the point where in the moment I could enjoy the success of what I had accomplished. It was always on to the next team. I was always driven to be the best. I was driven to win a Super Bowl. The losses were always more debilitating than the euphoria of the wins. And when we lost it was always 'What more could I have done so we could have won?' When you won, it was great we won, but it was 'Let's move onto the next one.'

"When I retired I finally, after 13 years of playing professionally, I asked myself how much time did I actually sit back and enjoy the blessing of being able to play for 13 years? And to be honest, it wasn't a lot."

Joyner after spending two season with head coach Buddy Ryan in Arizona after they both left the Eagles, found success his final two years in the league. He went to the Super Bowl with the Green Bay Packers in 1997 and then won a Super Bowl with the Denver Broncos in 1998.

It was poetic justice for a player who was never given quite the recognition he deserved and to this day isn't even in the conversation for the Hall of Fame—even when his numbers and play say he should.

"People always asked me, 'Why are you always so angry?' It wasn't that I was mad or angry, I was just driven," Joyner said. "Because I had people my whole life tell me 'You can't.' 'You can't play college ball.' 'Oh, you got drafted, but you're not going to make the team.' 'You're not going to stay on the team.' When you have that many naysayers, you just want to prove everyone wrong. Now, you make a Pro Bowl that's some validation, but you need to go again and keep going. Every year you have to prove your best. It's tough to live 13 years of your life like that."

30

THE MICHAEL VICK EXPERIENCE

If Michael Vick never thought he would end up in Philadelphia, then he would have never expected what happened next.

The Philadelphia Eagles signed Vick in August 2009, as the team prepared to play the New England Patriots in a preseason game. He was the team's third quarterback that season and the league's Comeback Player of the Year the next.

"I remember when it happened," former Eagles safety Quintin Mikell said. "It was funny, because it was during a preseason game. It's halftime, we're in the locker room and Sheldon [Brown] comes over to me and says, 'Guess who we just signed?' I said, 'Who?' He said, 'Michael Vick.' We just looked at each other."

Vick had been suspended by the NFL indefinitely in August of 2007 after he pleaded guilty to a federal charge of bankrolling a dogfighting operation at a home he owned in Virginia. He was freed from federal prison at Leavenworth, Kansas, on May 20, and returned to his home to serve the last two months of his 23-month sentence in home confinement.

"How I ended up in Philadelphia I really don't know," Vick said years later. "I thought my best options were Cincinnati and Buffalo. They looked to me like the best opportunities. At the end of the day, [NFL commissioner] Roger [Goodell] wanted me to go somewhere where it wouldn't be as much publicity bringing me in there. But still, the Eagles really came out of nowhere."

Donovan McNabb was still the Eagles' starting quarterback in 2009, and for that matter had taken them to his fifth NFC Championship Game the season before. On top of that, the Eagles had drafted Kevin Kolb to be McNabb's eventual replacement. Now they added Vick?

"I thought I'd go somewhere where the team needed a quarterback and I would at least compete for the job," Vick said. "When my agent called me and said Philadelphia wanted to sign me, I couldn't wrap my head around it. The one positive thing was my wife was from Philadelphia and her family was there. In terms of football, I didn't really get it, but in terms of family it was a blessing in disguise."

Of course there was the backlash that was going to come wherever Vick signed, and he was prepared as well as he could be. The Pennsylvania Society for the Prevention of Cruelty to Animals issued a statement immediately after the signing that it was "incredibly disappointed" at the news: "Philadelphia is a city of dog lovers and most particularly, pit bull lovers," Susan Cosby, the organization's CEO, said. "To root for someone who participated in the hanging, drowning, electrocution, and shooting of dogs will be impossible for many, no matter how much we would all like to see the Eagles go all the way."

Ed Sayres, president and CEO of the American Society for the Prevention of Cruelty to Animals, said in a statement that "Commissioner Roger Goodell and the Philadelphia Eagles have granted Michael Vick a second chance, and the ASPCA expects Mr. Vick to express remorse for his actions, as well as display more compassion and sound judgment this time around than he did during his previous tenure with the NFL."

The Eagles, particularly head coach Andy Reid, who saw both of his sons arrested and spend time in prison two years earlier, stood behind Vick. "There are going to be fans of ours who don't agree with this," Reid said. "I understand how that works. But there's enough of them that will, and then it's up to

Michael to prove that that change has taken place. I think he's there. That's what he wants to do."

Vick was reinstated to the league on a "conditional basis" at first. By Week 6 of the regular season, depending on the progression he made in his transition, he would either be fully reinstated or suspended again.

That was never a problem. "Mike was awesome. He really was," Mikell said. "At the time it was really crazy. He was a guy, tremendous athlete, tremendous player, and as a player all you care about is what he does on the field and can he help you win games. I didn't anticipate how much backlash he was going to get. I know there are a lot of dog lovers out there. But the guy went to jail, did his time, paid his dues. Let's give him another chance.

"It just wasn't that easy for some people. I was in his corner from the start. I believe, maybe not in every case, but that people can change. And he did change and he's a better person now. I believe that. He was a great teammate. Everyone said what a bad person he was. I never saw that. He was great to me and to everyone else."

Vick had to go through psychiatric evaluation, according to Goodell, before the league would even think about his reinstatement. He also worked closely with former Tampa Bay and Indianapolis head coach Tony Dungy, who became his mentor and advisor.

"I knew it was going to be tough anywhere I went. There would be obstacles and hurdles I would have to cross," Vick said recently. "Any team that was bringing me in was going to lend me their support and the Eagles were great helping me work my way back into the NFL. I mean, everyone there was great to me, Andy, [offensive coordinator] Marty [Mornhinweg], Mr. [Jeff] Lurie. They all helped me so much.

"Even though I know all my wounds were self-inflicted, but at some point in time when you're going through something so devastating, you start to point fingers at other people other than yourself. When I came to Philadelphia, so many people forgave me and gave me another chance and wanted me to succeed. I was able to change my ill feelings toward others. And it helped me to start making amends. That helped me get over the hump."

Vick didn't help the Eagles much in his first season, 2009, although he did rush for two touchdowns and pass for another in limited time. He also threw a touchdown pass in the team's wild-card playoff loss to the Dallas Cowboys.

It was the following season, 2010, when the Michael Vick Experience returned in full force. "I was hoping to get in a few plays, play a little bit and then maybe the next year find an organization that would see that and give me a shot and make that city my own," Vick said. "I didn't know it was going to happen the way it happened. Who knew all that would happen, that Kevin would go down the first game?"

In the off-season the Eagles traded McNabb to the Washington Redskins. That made Kolb the starter and Vick an experienced backup. But when Green Bay Packers linebacker Clay Matthews knocked out Kolb in the season opener, Vick took over. Boy, did he take over.

"There was pressure, because my future depended on how I played. But I had pressure before. I knew I had to go out there and win games. And then when Andy made me the starter, well, there were only two people who could have made that happen, God and Andy Reid, and I'm thankful for both of them."

Down 20–3 in that season opener to the Packers, Vick rallied the Eagles back only to fall short at 27–20. In the game he completed 16 of 24 passes and a touchdown and ran 11 times for 103 yards. He won his next two starts against the Detroit Lions and Jacksonville Jaguars, as Kolb remained out. Vick threw for a combined 575 yards with five touchdowns and no interceptions and ran for 67 yards and another touchdown in the two wins.

Vick's two best performances came on the road against the Eagles' NFC East rivals, the Redskins on *Monday Night Football* and the Giants in a game with critical playoff ramifications. Against Washington—and McNabb—he threw four touchdown passes and ran for two more in a 59–28 rout. Then against the Giants he brought the team back from a 21-point fourth-quarter deficit for a 38–31 win that sealed a playoff berth.

"That was the most fun I've had playing football," Vick said in 2010. "The guys on the team, the coaches, just the way I live my life now. It's been great. As a person and a player I learned a lot through my experiences on and off the field. Don't take anything for granted anymore. Certainly, back then [in Atlanta], I was just playing and having fun. I'm doing the same thing now, but I understand the importance of it and how hard it is to get to where we are today. I'm just thankful for the opportunity."

Vick was still disliked by some, but he won over a lot of his critics with his play and his work in the community as well. "He spends a tremendous amount of time in the public, in particular on his days off," Reid said in 2010. "Speaking at schools and in pubic, and doing the best he can to right the wrong. You can never erase that, but you can sure help change others from falling into that same problem."

There was no doubt that Vick became a different person off the field and remained the same exciting player he was when he debuted with the Atlanta Falcons in 2001 on the field.

"It was always a thought I might not play again," Vick said. "My agent, Joel Siegel, and I stayed in touch the whole time I was in prison and he kept encouraging me. He was confident. And I was confident in myself. I just needed that opportunity and I thank God the Eagles gave me that."

31

"YOUR NO. 1 PICK"

Bill Bergey knew he was headed out of Cincinnati, the only NFL home he had ever known, and didn't care where he went—as long as it wasn't Philadelphia. And then when he got there he never left.

It was 1974 and a new league, the World Football League, was threatening the NFL's monopoly and poaching some of its players. Bergey, one of the top linebackers in the game for the Cincinnati Bengals, was one of them. He signed a lucrative deal with the Washington Ambassadors of the WFL, and was promptly sued by the Bengals and owner Paul Brown.

"I was going to play my last year with the Bengals and then I was going to [go to] the World Football League," Bergey recalled. "It was strictly a money thing. I was making $37,000 with the Bengals and the World League offered me over $600,000. It was kind of a no-brainer."

Except the Bengals sued on grounds of signing with one team while being employed by another. Ultimately, the team lost. "After two weeks I won the court battle and Paul Brown challenged the ruling and I won the appeal," Bergey said. "Pretty much, I pissed off Paul Brown pretty good. [Meanwhile] the World League team I signed with is moving from Washington to Virginia to Orlando. I'm wondering, 'What the hell is going on there?'

"I went down to Orlando after the club had been sold twice and I meet with the new guy. I ask him, 'What's my situation?' He said, 'I have to honor your contract, but whoever gave you that contract was the dumbest son of a bitch I've ever seen in my life.' That pissed me off a little bit."

So with the WFL suddenly not looking so good, and his standing with the Bengals looking even worse after the lawsuits, what was next?

"Fast forward," Bergey said. "I go in and I talk to Paul Brown and his son, Mike, and I tell them, 'If you want to trade me somewhere, go ahead.' I knew there was no way I was playing for the Bengals again.

"I could have gone to Washington, New Orleans, Denver, Green Bay, or Philadelphia. I'm looking it over, and when it came to Philadelphia I'm thinking 'Why would I want to go there? They have the Liberty Bell, soft pretzels, and a losing football team.' I didn't want to go there."

But that's just where he went, on July 10, 1974. The Eagles, under Mike McCormack, had a good working relationship with Brown and the Bengals, since McCormack had played and coached under Brown. The teams had made several trades in the past, and this time the Eagles sent the Bengals two first-round picks and a second-round pick in exchange for the Pro Bowl linebacker who had been a second-round pick in 1969 out of Arkansas State.

"The Eagles owner, Leonard Tose, thought all he needed was a middle linebacker for Mike McCormack's team. And that's another thing—McCormack was one of the people who testified against me in the lawsuit," Bergey said

"But the Eagles were willing to pay me what I would have gotten from the WFL, so I was happy about that. I remember when I got to Philly they had a press conference and all of that and I leaned over to Leonard Tose and said, 'What did you give up for me?' He leaned back and said one word: 'Plenty.'"

The Eagles went 7–7 in Bergey's first year, an improvement over the 5–8–1 team of the year before. The following year they slipped back to 4–10.

"When I first got there, I have to say there were a lot of just flat-out dogs on that team," Bergey said. "I think they respected me, but a lot of them didn't like me either. I remember being down two, three touchdowns and I'm trying to get the team pumped up and they're looking at me like 'Here comes that crazy SOB again.'"

Bergey, who went to four Pro Bowls with the Eagles and helped them get to their first Super Bowl in 1980, had some fun with his new head coach, Dick Vermeil, who took over when McCormack was fired after the 1975 season. Apparently, he needed more than just a good middle linebacker.

"Bill would go into the draft room the day of the draft and say, 'Here's your No. 1 pick. How do you like me?'" longtime Eagles broadcaster Merrill Reese remembered. "It was funny. I'm not sure Dick thought it was funny, but that was Bill's personality. He had a great sense of humor."

Bergey confirms the prank. "Yeah, it's true. [Eagles GM] Jim Murray set me up," Bergey said. "It was his idea. 'Let's have some fun.' Dick, [defensive coordiator] Marion [Campbell], and the guys are in the draft room, and they're not doing anything, because they don't have any picks, and I walk in and say, "Hi, everyone, here's your No. 1 and No. 2 picks.' It didn't go over as well as we hoped."

The trade, as costly as it was, went over very well with the Eagles and their rabid fan base. Bergey became a popular figure immediately, and even though the team didn't win right away, they fell in love at first sight with No. 66.

"Now, I come there with a lot of pressure on me," Bergey said. "To give up that much for one player, I had better be good. And you know what? I never heard one person ever throw that back at me. That made me feel pretty good."

"He was great, a great player," sportswriter Ray Didinger said. "I thought when he first got here he was the best inside linebacker in football. It's a shame because the teams he was on were lousy, but he was a great player. And he got better. In my opinion, I've always thought he was better than [the New York Giants'] Harry Carson, and Carson is in the Hall of Fame. Carson deserves to be in the Hall of Fame. I just think Bergey should be too. You can certainly make a strong case for him."

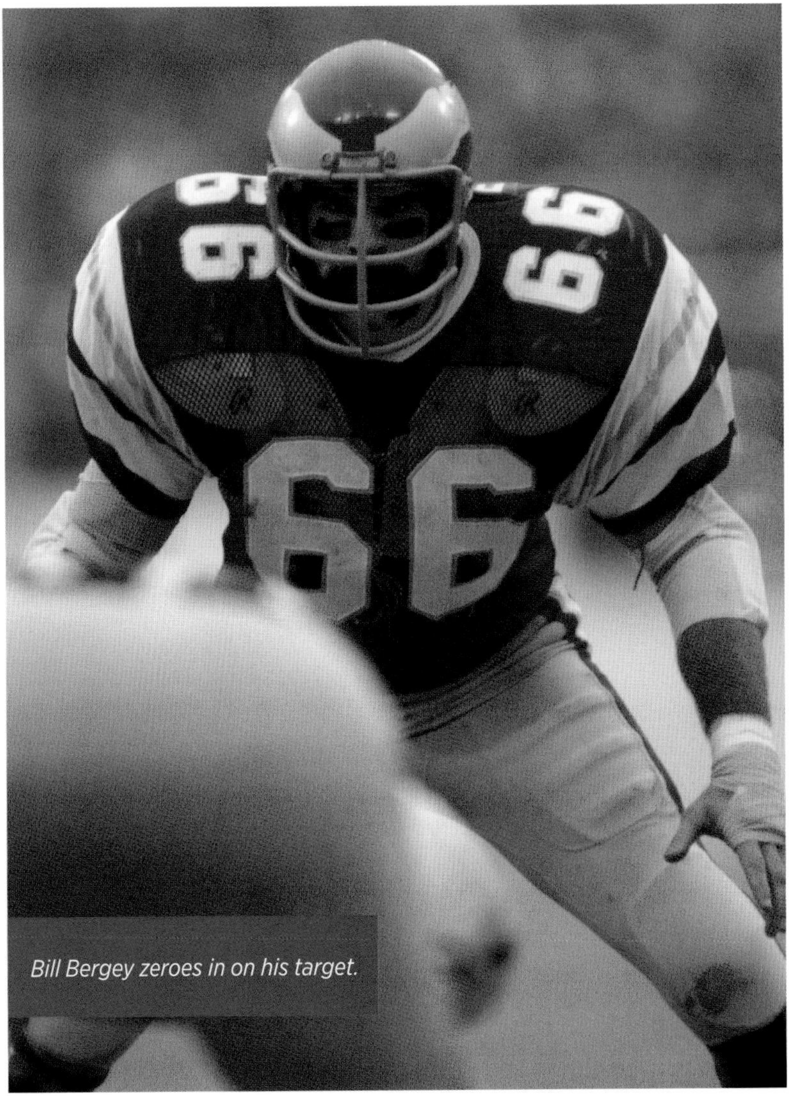

Bill Bergey zeroes in on his target.

THE INJURY

Merrill Reese, the Eagles' longtime radio voice, will never forget the phone calls, either of them. Or what transpired in between.

"It's 1979, and I'm watching a preseason game with the Cowboys," Reese said. "I'm watching the game and Dallas safety Charlie Waters gets hurt and is out. It looks pretty bad. Then they carry him off the field. My phone rings and it's Micky Bergey, Bill's wife.

"She says to me, 'Merrill,' and she's whispering, 'I just had a terrible thought. Bill has never been hurt, never. Not in his entire career. If I was Charlie Waters' wife, I would be so worried.' Then she says, 'Merrill, if Bill ever gets hurt, promise me you'll call me and let me know.' I told her I would."

Three weeks into the 1979 regular season the Eagles are in New Orleans when Bergey goes down with a torn ACL. "There it was," Reese said. "As soon as I could, as soon we had a break, I called Micky. She answered the phone—and remember this is before caller ID, or any of that—and she said, 'Merrill, how bad is it?'"

Bergey missed the rest of the '79 season, but came back to help the Eagles to the Super Bowl the following year.

"That was the story going into 1980: How was Bergey going to be?" Didinger remembered. "As it turned out, he was fine."

Bergey played 12 years in the NFL, seven with the Eagles. He finished with 27 career interceptions, and his 18 as an Eagle is still the second most by any linebacker. He also recovered 21 fumbles.

In a game against the Dallas Cowboys during the 1978 season he recorded 18 tackles, which led legendary Cowboys coach Tom Landry to heap praise on the Eagles linebacker. "It seemed to me like there was six of him out there today," Landry said. "Does he play like that against everybody?"

Just about everybody. “People think of Bill as being this big, punishing player,” Reese said. “And he was, but what impressed me most about him were his instincts. That, and how he played sideline to sideline. To me that’s what made him a great player.”

Didinger agreed. “He’s was 6′4″, 250, which was very big at the time,” he said. “But he was quick. He had the quickness and the agility of someone a lot smaller.”

Bergey’s last game as an Eagle was Super Bowl XV, a 27–10 loss to the Oakland Raiders. He stayed around the team and worked as a color analyst with Reese for a few years afterward. And he never left the Philadelphia area.

32

EVERYTHING BUT THE CHAMPIONSHIPS

When Jeffrey Lurie bought the Philadelphia Eagles from Norman Braman before the start of the 1994 football season, he made a list of promises to Eagles' fans who were somewhat skeptical of the Boston native turned Hollywood producer. Lurie told the fans in no specific order the team would build its own state-of-the-art practice facility; would in time move out of old, antiquated multipurpose Veterans Stadium and have its own football-only stadium; and the icing on top of it all was championships. Lurie promised fans the Eagles would win, in the plural, "championships."

Well, the team built the 110,000-square-foot NovaCare Complex, which houses the organization's offices and serves as the team's daily workout facility in 2001. The last game at the old Vet was the NFC Championship Game in 2002, as the team moved to spacious Lincoln Financial Field, one of the nicer stadiums in the league, in 2003.

Those championships, or even *one* championship, were still on hold as of the 2016 season. In 22 years as the owner of the Eagles, Lurie's teams have made the playoffs 12 times, advanced to the NFC Championship Game five times, and made it to the Super Bowl once (in which they lost to Lurie's hometown Patriots). Those same Patriots are the team Lurie wanted to buy back when he began to pursue NFL ownership in the early 1990s.

Growing up in Boston in the 1960s, Lurie's family members were Patriots season-ticket holders from the time the team (and the AFL) was founded in 1960. He and his friends, including the man he would name president of the Eagles, Joe Banner, attended Patriots games on a regular basis.

When the team went up for sale in 1993, Lurie was interested but dropped out of the bidding on the advice of his uncle Richard Smith. Lurie's name had also been connected to a proposed sale of the Los Angeles Rams as well as plans to bring an expansion team to Baltimore.

A year later he bought the Eagles for what was then a record $195 million. In 2016, the team was worth $2.4 billion according to *Forbes* magazine.

Lurie's family money came from his maternal grandfather, Phillip Smith, who founded the General Cinema movie theater chain. Jeffrey was one of three children to Nancy Smith and her husband, Morris Lurie. General Cinema continued to evolve throughout the 1960s and '70s and eventually became Harcourt General Inc., a $3.7 billion conglomerate based in Chestnut Hill, Massachusetts. At one point it was the fourth-largest chain of movie theaters in the country, owned several publishing houses, three insurance companies, and a leading global consulting firm.

Jeffrey earned his undergraduate degree from Clark University, his master's degree in psychology from Boston University, and a PhD in social policy from Brandeis University. He taught as an adjunct professor at Boston College before joining the family business. He was an executive in the company, basically working in conjunction with General Cinema Corporation and the production community in Hollywood. He was also an advisor in the General Cinema national film buying office. It was there he became a Hollywood producer.

In 1985 Lurie founded Chestnut Hill Productions, which produced three major motion pictures, *Sweet Hearts Dance* starring Don Johnson, Susan Sarandon, Jeff Daniels, and Elizabeth Perkins in 1988; *I Love You to Death* starring Kevin Kline, Tracey Ullman, River Phoenix, Keanu Reeves, and William Hurt in 1990; and *V.I. Warshawski,* with Kathleen Turner in the title role, in 1993.

Lurie put his movie career on hold when he bought the Eagles, opting instead to produce a winning football team. In his first season as owner, 1994, the team got out to a fast 7–2 start with lame-duck head coach Rich Kotite. It was no secret that the new owner wanted to bring in a new head coach, but with that kind of success it would be difficult. Then, when the Eagles lost their last seven games in what is the biggest collapse in NFL history (no team has ever started a season 7–2 and finished under .500), it made it a lot easier for him.

Kotite was fired the day after Christmas and two days after the end of the season. After an extensive coaching search, Ray Rhodes, the defensive coordinator of the Super Bowl. Champion San Francisco 49ers, was hired. Rhodes, who didn't seem (at least publicly) to have any problems with Lurie, clashed constantly with Banner. He was let go after four years, the final one a 3–13 disaster, the losingest season in Eagles history.

Lurie replaced Rhodes with Andy Reid, a relative unknown except inside football circles, who had been the Green Bay Packers quarterbacks coach and part of the ultra-successful Mike Holmgren coaching tree.

Reid lasted 14 years with Lurie. They went to the playoffs nine times together and formed a bond that eventually led to Lurie hiring Reid's right-hand man, Doug Pederson, as his head coach in 2016. The day Lurie fired Reid, after a 4–12 season in 2012, he mentioned how he couldn't wait to have him inducted into the team's Hall of Fame.

Firing Reid, which Lurie has said was one of the most difficult decisions he's had to make as owner of the team, came at the end of a whirlwind year for him. Earlier that year he had also come to a "mutual parting of the ways" with Banner, his boyhood friend and the man who had run the team for him from the time he bought it. And his 20-year marriage to Christina Weiss Lurie, who remains very involved in the team's charitable endeavors, came to an end as well.

Finding head coaches was never Lurie's problem either. Rhodes did great his first two years and was named Coach of the Year in 1995. Reid is the winningest head coach in Eagles history and was a two-time Coach of the Year. And Chip Kelly, who replaced Reid, won 20 games his first two years as head coach under Lurie.

No, the problem that has plagued Lurie throughout his ownership and perhaps why the team is still looking for those "championships" has been the team's structure and what, at least from the outside looking in, appears to be dysfunction in the front office.

With Rhodes as head coach, John Wooten, Dick Daniels, and Bob Ackles all made personnel decisions in one capacity or another. Even though Rhodes had a great first draft in 1995 and made several other good personnel moves, Lurie and Banner felt the need to bring in men over him... and then replace them.

Tom Modrak was brought in from the Pittsburgh Steelers in Rhodes' last year and got the opportunity to fire the head coach. Modrak, who it seemed would have worked well with Reid, and did for a few years, was out of a job by 2001 when Lurie handed total control to Reid.

From there, Tom Heckert, Jason Licht, Ryan Grigson, and eventually Howie Roseman all took turns in the personnel department. Roseman was actually removed as GM in 2015 only to return in 2016, when Lurie fired Kelly.

Back in Hollywood, Lurie's executive-produced *Inside Job*, a film about the nation's bank crisis in the late 2000s, won best documentary at the 2011 Academy Awards. It's hard to believe he won an Oscar before a Lombardi Trophy.

33

THE 2002 DRAFT

In the 2002 NFL Draft the Eagles had three of the first 59 picks and they knew what they wanted: defensive backs. But wasn't the team stocked in the secondary with Pro Bowl cornerbacks Troy Vincent and Bobby Taylor and a tough nickel back in Al Harris? All right, *maybe* they needed a safety to pair with All-Pro Brian Dawkins, but surely the team had greater needs at other positions.

"They knew what they were doing," Vincent said after that draft. "I told them to get our replacements on the roster and I'll start to groom them."

What the Eagles knew was Vincent and Taylor were both going to become free agents at the end of the 2003 season—and it was going to be very difficult to keep them both. "It was time," Vincent said. "They knew it. And it also gave the young guys time to work with us."

As it turned out both Vincent and Taylor left as free agents after the 2003 season. Vincent signed with the Buffalo Bills and Taylor signed with the Seattle Seahawks. The Eagles were also aware that Harris wanted a trade and a raise to become a starter sooner rather than later, and the team provided him with that when they sent him to the Green Bay Packers along with a fourth-round draft pick in exchange for a second-round draft pick in 2003.

So what left some scratching their heads in 2002 was actually forward-thinking. In order, the Eagles selected cornerback Lito Sheppard out of the University of Florida in the first round; safety Michael Lewis out of the University of Colorado in the second round; and cornerback Sheldon Brown out of the University of South Carolina, with the second of their two second-round picks. But it wasn't just DBs. In the third round, the Eagles hit the jackpot with running back Brian Westbrook out of nearby Division 1-AA Villanova.

The impact wasn't immediate, not for any of the four. The dividends, however, would start to pay off in the near future. In their rookie years none of the quartet of Sheppard, Lewis, Brown, and Westbrook—undoubtedly the best overall draft of the Andy Reid Era (1999–2012)—were starters.

Sheppard and Brown actually sat behind Vincent and Taylor for two years, playing sparingly as rookies and then working their way into different defensive packages in their second year, after Harris was traded. Lewis sat for a year behind veteran free agent addition Blaine Bishop before taking over as the starter in 2003.

Westbrook, the player who made the draft special, also did very little as a rookie. He carried the ball just 46 times for 193 yards and caught nine passes for 86 yards playing behind veterans Duce Staley and Dorsey Levens in the Eagles backfield. He didn't even get to show off his return skills, because the Eagles had a pretty good return guy in All-Pro Brian Mitchell.

"We didn't need immediate help that draft," Reid said a few years later. "Our roster was pretty good. We were looking toward the future and we got some pretty good guys there."

Westbrook, Sheppard, and Lewis would all become Pro Bowl players—and Brown should have been. Fans, perhaps upset in 2002 when none of the drafted players contributed much, started to take notice in 2003. And then they really tuned in by 2004, when all four were instrumental in the Eagles finally getting to the Super Bowl after 24 years.

Lewis, after becoming a starter in the 2003 season, took over as one of the team's leaders in 2004 when Dawkins missed half the season with a leg injury. Lewis also shared the team lead in interceptions with Vincent that year. And made it to the Pro Bowl when he led the team in tackles, with 129.

Sheppard also started half of the '03 season for first-stringer Taylor, who was bothered by a foot injury. Sheppard then became a full-time starter and Pro Bowl player in 2004 when he led the team with five interceptions and returned two for touchdowns. He went to a second Pro Bowl in 2006.

Brown also became a starter in '04, then led the team in interceptions in 2005 and 2007. Known as a very good cover corner, Brown could also deliver a punishing hit, as he did in the 2006 playoff game against New Orleans Saints running back Reggie Bush.

And Westbrook became the focal point of a running game dubbed "the Three-Headed Monster," also featuring Staley and Correll Buckhalter in 2003. The second-year back led the Eagles in rushing with 613 yards and a 5.2 average yards per carry to go with seven touchdowns. He was also second on the team in receptions with 37 for another 332 yards and four touchdowns and he led the NFC in punt return average at 15.3 yards. Two of the 20 punts he returned that year went for touchdowns. In 2004 he gained more than 1,500 total yards and scored nine touchdowns.

"I'd love to be able to tell you I knew, or we knew, how good he would be," Marc Ross, the Eagles director of college scouting during that 2002 Draft, said of Westbrook. "The truth is, he just kept getting better. We did know he could help us and that he would be a good return guy. But to say we knew he would be what he became, that would be a lie."

When the Eagles drafted Westbrook they thought they were getting a David Meggett–type player. (Meggett had been a very good return man and third-down back for the Giants in the '80s.) Instead they got another Marshall Faulk, a back who could put up more than 2,000 total yards in a season. And that's just what Westbrook did in 2007, when he gained 2,104 total yards.

"I was always being doubted," Westbrook said. "It was because I wasn't big enough. Or it was because I didn't go to a big enough school. All I wanted was a chance to show people what I could actually do."

Did he ever. In eight years with the Eagles he rushed for 5,995 yards, the third most in team history. His 37 rushing touchdowns are the fourth most. Add in the fact that he also caught

THE ONE THEY LET GET AWAY

Believe it or not, that 2002 Eagles draft could have even been better, if for a few dollars they would have signed their seventh-round pick. The Eagles—specifically director of college scouting Marc Ross—found a steal in the seventh round with defensive end Raheem Brock, a Philadelphia native and Temple University product.

Brock was thrilled to be drafted by his hometown team and couldn't wait to play for the Eagles. Except it never happened. Stuck in a contract impasse over a few thousand dollars, the Eagles released Brock before the start of training camp. He was claimed by the Indianapolis Colts and became a solid starter for eight years, going to two Super Bowls with the Colts and winning one.

He ended his career with the Seattle Seahawks, and finished with 347 tackles and 40.5 sacks in a 10-year career.

"The Eagles didn't manage their rookie pool right and now they're missing out on a good player," Brock's agent George Mavrikes said when he was cut. "I've never heard of a team doing this, just letting go of a player they drafted. Not unless the player got arrested or something. The Eagles will look bad if one of two things happen: If Raheem turns out to be a player at a position that's hard to find good players, or if one of the Eagles' defensive linemen gets injured."

Indeed, the Eagles ended up looking bad.

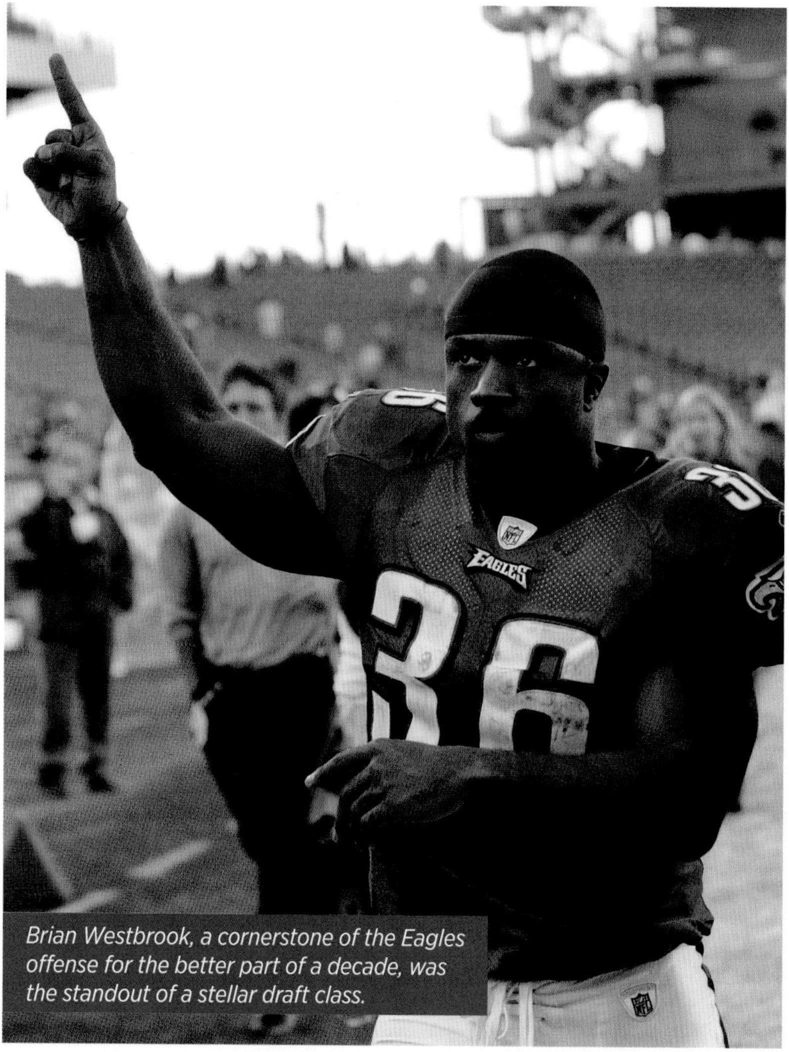

Brian Westbrook, a cornerstone of the Eagles offense for the better part of a decade, was the standout of a stellar draft class.

426 passes, again the third most in team history, for another 3,790 yards and caught 29 more touchdowns and the numbers start to jump off the page. Those 9,785 total yards are the most in team history, and his 66 total touchdowns are tied for third best with Hall of Famer Tommy McDonald and trail only Harold Carmichael (79) and Hall of Famer Steve Van Buren (72).

"I remember I scouted Brian Westbrook at Villanova, when I was [running backs coach] with the Rams," former Eagles running back Wilbert Montgomery said in 2010. "I wrote in my report, 'Brian Westbrook is the Marshall Faulk of college football.' I saved it, too, in case nobody believed me. People looked at Brian Westbrook's stature and said, 'He can't do this. He can't do that.' But you can't measure a man's heart."

34

FOR WHO? FOR WHAT?

Ricky Watters turned out to be right. After his first game as a Philadelphia Eagle in 1995, Watters uttered four words that would go down in both Philadelphia and Eagles history. Yet there was more to Watters' infamous "For who? For what?" quote than those four words, and that is where the truth was told.

The Eagles had lost that season opener in both Watters' and head coach Ray Rhodes' first game as Eagles. They fell 21–6 to the Tampa Bay Buccaneers in disappointing fashion. In the fourth quarter of the game Watters short-armed, or at least appeared to short-arm, a pass from quarterback Randall Cunningham. To see Watters, the team's big free-agent acquisition, shying away from contact in front of the Veterans Stadium crowd didn't sit well. The fact that he gained just 37 yards rushing on 17 carries didn't help his case either.

So after the game he was asked about his debut, and the one play in particular. Here's what he said: "You mean on that pass that was kind of high and away?" Watters began. "Hey, I'm not going to trip up there and get knocked out. For who? For what? I mean, there's another day. I'm going to make a whole lot of plays. I made a whole lot of plays where I was at before. And I'm going to make a whole lot of plays here. I've always made plays."

Watters started to make plays immediately after that opener. Over the next six weeks, Watters had five games of 100 total yards or more, including an incredible 139-yard rushing, 11-catch, 90-yard receiving game in a 37–34 win over the Washington Redskins. If it wasn't for a spectacular season by Green Bay Packers quarterback Brett Favre, Watters could have been the NFL's MVP in 1995.

Playing behind a patchwork offensive line of young players and veterans past their prime and without a viable passing game, Watters carried for 1,273 yards and 11 touchdowns. Indeed, he carried the Eagles all the way to the playoffs, where they won the wild-card game over the Detroit Lions 58–37. He was also second on the team in receptions with 62.

Watters followed his initial campaign in Philadelphia with an even better second year. In 1996, with the line and the passing game both slightly improved, Watters rushed for 1,411 yards and 13 touchdowns. He also caught 51 passes for another 444 yards, and the Eagles made the playoffs for a second straight year.

There were wild moments in between as well, as Watters partnered with running back Charlie Garner in what offensive coordinator Jon Gruden called his "Jersey Shore" offense. "Ricky was something. He was a guy who could go out there and influence a game, take over a game," said Barrett Brooks, a rookie starting at left tackle for the Eagles in 1995. "I just didn't think that him and Charlie, even though they were friends, they didn't blend well together.

"It was a different situation. Even in the huddle sometimes, Ricky and Gruden would be getting into it. Ricky would cuss him out and look up toward the press box [where Gruden was] and grab his crotch. Then Gruden would look down and flash him the middle finger. It was comical at times"

All told, in his three seasons with the Eagles Watters gained 3,794 yards rushing, caught 161 passes, scored 32 touchdowns, and went to two Pro Bowls. Those four words, however, uttered after his first game, are how he'll always be remembered. It's even the title of his autobiography.

"I wish I hadn't said it," Watters said years later. "Obviously I don't want to be known as that, especially in a city that I grew to love, with great fans that are definitely not fair-weather fans. I can tell you that much."

Before those four words, Eagles fans loved Watters, and they would again after. His free agent signing was as high profile as any acquisition the Eagles had until they traded for Terrell Owens in 2004. And Watters, who didn't always talk to the press, ate up the fans' love. "People here love me," he said during his first training camp. "I can't go anywhere without people all over me. I get mauled at the mall."

Watters, much different in his post-playing days, smiles at his old self. "I was young, and [brash]," he says. "That was my nature more back then. It's really crazy for me to even try to explain it because I am so different than that now, but at that time when somebody was to come at [me] or say anything that I felt was threatening to me, my way was to lash back, and that was how I lashed back and it was wrong.

"When I go all around the world, and I mean around the world, I see Philadelphia fans. And I know that they are Philadelphia fans because they let me know. They come up and say, 'Hey, I'm a Philadelphia fan, dawg. I loved you,' or whatever the situation is and 'I wish you would had stayed there and I believe we would have gotten a Super Bowl' and stuff like that. That is everything to me. That means so much."

ON THIS DATE

Exactly five years after Watters' infamous declaration, on September 3, 2000, Eagles running back Duce Staley ran for 201 yards in an opening-day 41–14 win over the Dallas Cowboys at Texas Stadium. After that game Staley, who had been a rookie in 1997, Watters last one with the Eagles, managed not to say anything close to that.

Watters was a star for the San Francisco 49ers before he came to the Eagles and scored three touchdowns in Super Bowl XXIX, his final game as a 49er. After he left the Eagles as a free agent for the Seattle Seahawks, he ran for three straight 1,200-yard seasons there.

The Eagles honored Watters as a team captain before a game in 2012 against the Lions. He actually appeared humbled to be back where he had been so controversial for three years. "That's a big part of me, wanting to come back, is to be able to express that to the fans that man, I really appreciated all the letters, the e-mails, everything that you're saying about I should be in the Hall of Fame. And when I do get in there, you believe I'm going to get in there, that you're going to come out to see me and you're going to be in the stands," Watters said. "I really appreciate that stuff and I think that that goes a long way as to, I think, you understanding that I really wanted to bring a championship home, and feel like it is home. I live right down the turnpike. I grew up in Harrisburg, Pennsylvania, so I feel like that's home to me. That's a big feeling for me right now, and it's really why I am so excited about this time. I've gone back and had this happen in San Francisco and Seattle, but it's really special in Philadelphia.

"I don't want to go there and people still think, 'For who? For what?' I really loved playing there. I felt like wherever I went people were coming up to me, and everyone acted and they treated me like their native son. And I think that, that's what I am. And I love that feeling."

35

THE STEAGLES

With war escalating across the world in 1942, the NFL had a problem that almost forced the league to suspend its operations. Most of its players were going into the services to fight for their country. The only players left on the league's 10 teams were men with some type of deferment.

They were either unfit for military service for physical reasons, or age, or were active servicemen who had obtained leave to play. There were three types of deferments. The 3-As were men supporting families; they were not priorities of the draft board. The second type consisted of men who worked in the war industry, making and preparing ammunition, weapons, and material for the war. The third group, labeled 4-F, were those deemed physically unfit.

"There were guys with bad eyes, bad knees, bad backs, punctured eardrums—things that could get you out of the service but not an NFL game," NFL historian and executive director of the Pro Football Hall of Fame Joe Horrigan said in an interview with ESPN years later. "A manpower shortage caused teams to hire players who were old, overweight, not otherwise qualified to be professional athletes."

In 1943 the Cleveland Rams, whose roster was so decimated by players either being drafted or enlisting, ceased operations. The Pittsburgh Steelers, with just six men on the roster and the Philadelphia Eagles, with just 16, were headed in the same direction.

Down to nine teams and on the way to seven, Steelers owner and future Hall of Famer Art Rooney had an idea to merge his Steelers with the Eagles. There was actually talk of doing the same thing two years earlier and calling the team the Pennsylvania Keystoners, according to various reports. That never flew, but in a war-torn 1943, and by a narrow 5–4 vote by the league owners, "the Steagles" were born.

The team was supposed to be called the Eagles, since the Steelers brought just six players to the team, but with two home games in Pittsburgh and co-coaches in Philadelphia's Earl "Greasy" Neale and Pittsburgh's Walt Kiesing, the media—or more precisely *Pittsburgh Press* sports editor Chet Smith—came up with the moniker "Steagles," and it stuck.

The Steagles did wear the Eagles' Kelly green and white—the only time in Steelers history they did not wear black and gold—and training camp was held in Philadelphia at St. Joseph's College (now University).

Neale and Kiesling, who had a history of not exactly sending each other Christmas cards, served as co–head coaches. Neale got his way to run the T-formation offense that he modeled after the success it had on the college level at Notre Dame under Frank Leahy and at Army under Red Blaik. That left Kiesling to run the team's defense. Still, it wasn't an easy marriage. (Think Buddy Ryan and Mike Ditka.)

According to Ernie Steele, a running back / defensive back on the team who, despite his name, was an Eagle in 1942, it got really bad between the coaches. One Friday, just two days before a game, both coaches stormed off the field after a shouting match. The players had no idea what happened, and they didn't see either man again until game day.

When the 1943 season began the Steagles had a 25-man roster composed of the 22 players they had combined and three rookies added before the season. And all 25 players had full-time war jobs, as well. In 1943, playing football was seen as more of a hobby, or a side job. According to the book *Last Team Standing* by Matthew Algeo, Ted Doyle, one of the team's linemen and an original Steeler, worked at Westinghouse Electric, where he assisted on the Manhattan Project, which famously led to America building the first atomic bomb.

There had been fear among some of the other owners that the merger of these two teams would be unfair, which is why the vote had been so close. When the team jumped out to a 2–0 start to the season, some of those fears started to be realized. Maybe this Steagles team was going to be too good.

"Everyone thought we would be great, putting two teams together," Eagles great Al Wistert said. "All it meant was we had twice as many lousy players."

Wistert wasn't far off, since in the four years prior to the merger the two teams combined for a record of 17–65–6. Still the Steagles handled the Brooklyn Dodgers, 17–0, in front of 11,000 fans at Shibe Park and the following week handled the New York Giants, 28–14, in front of 15,000 again at Shibe Park.

Surprisingly enough, in that win over the Giants the Steagles fumbled the ball a record 10 times, a "high" that has never been topped. Three teams—the Detroit Lions in 1967, the Kansas City Chiefs in 1969, and the San Francisco 49ers in 1978—have matched it. But no team has ever fumbled more in one game.

The merged team lost its next two games, at Chicago to the Bears, 48–21, and in a rematch with the Giants in New York, 42–14. They won their first "home" game at Pittsburgh's Forbes Field, 34–13, over the Chicago Cardinals, then played the defending 1942 NFL champion Washington Redskins to a, 14–14, tie.

The Steagles lost a rematch with the Dodgers in Brooklyn 13–7, but beat the Detroit Lions in Pittsburgh 35–34 and the Redskins in Washington 27–14. With one game left they stood 5–3–1 and had a chance to win, or at least tie, for the Eastern Conference title.

Tony Bova, the team's leading receiver with 17 receptions, 419 yards, and five touchdowns, was blind in one eye. Guard Ed Michaels and center Ray Graves were both nearly deaf. Fullback John Butler started for the team one day after being ruled 4-F by the draft board for poor eyesight and bad knees.

"It was tough, I'll tell you," Graves told the *New York Times* in 2009. "But even the president [Franklin Roosevelt] gave us a vote of confidence, told us we were out there entertaining the people and the families of the men in the service."

That final night of the season, December 5, just two days shy of the two-year anniversary of the bombing of Pearl Harbor, the Steagles hosted the Green Bay Packers in front of close to 35,000 fans, and more than triple the opening-day crowd.

Green Bay, with star receiver Don Hutson, led 17–14 at the half and increased the lead to 31–14 after three quarters. The Steagles fought back and got to 31–28 with five minutes to play. But Hutson's one-handed 24-yard touchdown catch sealed the 38–28 win for the Packers. The Steagles finished the season 5–4–1, one game behind the Redskins and Giants, co-leaders in the East. The team held a farewell banquet at a Philadelphia hotel after the game. It was the last time they would be together as a team.

In 1944 the Eagles fielded a full team and went 7–1–2 but lost the East title to the 8–1–1 Giants. The Steelers merged with the Chicago Cardinals on a team dubbed "Card-Pitt" and went 0–10.

In 2003, 60 years after the Steagles' only season, six of the nine surviving members of the team were honored during a pregame ceremony prior to a preseason game between the Eagles and Steelers at Pittsburgh's Heinz Field.

36

BRAMANOMICS

The Philadelphia Eagles team that Norman Braman bought from Leonard Tose on April 29, 1985, and the one that took the field for that season opener a little over four months later were not the same. In those four months from the time Braman forked over a reported $65 million for the team he later sold for $185 million, there were changes—lots of changes.

This was 1985, pre–free agency. When a player's contract was up, or about to be up, he either re-signed with his team for what they offered him or he held out for a better deal. It happened all over the league.

In Philadelphia in 1985 it happened a different way. Players unhappy with their contracts were traded or released. To say Braman had his own way of handling contract situations is akin to saying Don King has his own way of hairstyling. The Eagles were a business for Braman, just as his ultra-successful car dealerships had been. He was going to close deals on his terms, or you could just go shop somewhere else.

To be fair, the Eagles made some very good personnel decisions under Braman's ownership. But the constant turnover, like the buying and selling of cars, hurt the overall operation. He hired Buddy Ryan as head coach, only to fire him. He signed Reggie White out of the USFL, only to let him go as a free agent.

So that first training camp in 1985 saw several familiar faces absent; some of them never to return. Defensive end Dennis Harrison, a Pro Bowl player in 1983, was sent to the Los Angeles Rams; starting linebacker Jerry Robinson, the former first-round pick and a Pro Bowl player in 1981, was traded to the Oakland Raiders.

Suddenly with a need for linebackers, the franchise's all-time leading rusher at the time, Wilbert Montgomery—the hero of the 1980

NFC Championship Game win over the Dallas Cowboys and a two-time Pro Bowl selection—was traded to the Detroit Lions for linebacker Garry Cobb.

Starting left tackle Dean Miraldi saw his holdout end when the team simply released him.

"I was holding out too, but I was always holding out," wide receiver Mike Quick said with a laugh. "My holdouts weren't always about a contract. I just didn't want to go to camp. But you could tell things were going to be different with new ownership. You could tell [Braman's] heart wasn't into the team the way Leonard's was into the team. Norman was a great businessman. There's no question about that. And that's how he ran the team: like one of his businesses. I also think a lot of what he did helped the league in general, how he went about the shield and selling everything. It was more of a business venture for him. And a lot of teams eventually copied that style."

Braman's plan made waves throughout the league in revealing a new way of how things could be done. It also scared some of the younger players on the roster. "My contract was up after that year, and I'm starting in '85 after signing as an undrafted rookie contract in '84," linebacker Mike Reichenbach said. "I'm the lowest paid starter in the league. I'm thinking about renegotiating and Mr. Braman comes in and says, 'This is how we're doing things. You have a contract. You're playing to it.' Mr. Tose was so different. Mr. Braman was a businessman, plain and simple."

Braman's first football decision during that 1985 season was to fire head coach Marion Campbell with one game left in the season. The plan was to wait until after Sunday's final game in Minnesota and make the announcement that Monday. When word leaked out early that Campbell was gone and the next coach was going to be David Shula, son of legendary Miami Dolphins head coach Don Shula, Campbell confronted team president Harry Gamble on the flight home from San Diego, the next-to-last game of the season.

Campbell had gone back a long way with Gamble. They were both assistant coaches to Dick Vermeil, and he wanted an honest answer from his friend about whether he was indeed being fired. If the answer was yes, he wanted them to do it now rather than later.

Shula, who at 26 years old at the time would have been the youngest head coach in NFL history, never did get the job. Braman wanted him to sign a 10-year deal at a less-than-market-value rate. On the advice of his father, among others, he declined and the deal died. Braman eventually hired Ryan, and as more players left Ryan was able to build a team that through good drafts would go to the playoffs three straight years from 1988 to 1990 and again in 1992.

Winning on the field was nice for the owner, but in the grand scheme of things secondary. He won as a businessman. And he won big. According to documents that came out in 1993, as the players union continued its fight for free agency and a bigger piece of the NFL pie, staggering numbers were revealed. During the antitrust lawsuit on behalf of eight players, it was revealed Braman made an operating profit of $34.3 million during the first five years he owned the Eagles—far and away the largest return of any of the NFL's 28 clubs at that time.

During those five seasons, Braman raised ticket prices three times. In 1990 Braman did not file a profit-loss sheet with the league, but in a separate document, he disclosed that he paid himself a salary of $7.5 million for that season. Over the four years from 1987 to 1990, no other NFL owner, executive, coach, or player was paid as high a single-season salary as Braman in 1990.

The documents, which were marked "highly confidential" or "for designated experts only" showed that most of the NFL teams made

Norman Braman made a lot of money for and with the Eagles during his tenure as owner.

money. But none made more than the Eagles. The reports also showed that the Eagles had the league's largest operation profits in 1986, 1987, and 1989; they were the second highest in 1988 and fourth in 1985.

This was the best of both worlds, a playoff team on the field and the league champion in terms of finances. The tide started to turn, however, when players were granted free agency and a player exodus ensued.

Tight end Keith Jackson, who once said Braman told him "he owned him" was the first Pro Bowl player to leave as a free agent, in

A METEORIC RISE

While Norman Braman was the businessman owner of the Eagles who lived in Florida and vacationed in France, somebody had to run the day-to-day operations of the team in Philadelphia from 1985 to 1994. That was Harry Gamble, a football man through and through, who took an incredible road to get to the top of the Eagles hierarchy.

Gamble played college football at Rider College and then became head coach of Lafayette College and then the University of Pennsylvania. In 1980 he left Penn and a year later surfaced as a volunteer coach on Dick Vermeil's Eagles' staff.

In 1985, Braman's first year as owner, Gamble became the general manager and was then promoted by the owner to president and CEO. During his time in the Eagles' front office, Gamble, who passed away in 2014, had to often play the role of buffer between Braman and head coach Buddy Ryan, who would openly criticize the owner's hard-line stand on players' contracts among other things.

Dallas Cowboys general manager Tex Schramm said of Gamble in a 1989 story in the *Philadelphia Inquirer*, "His rise was one of the damnedest things I've ever seen in this business. Meteoric is an understatement."

1991. White followed in 1992 along with Keith Byars, Clyde Simmons and Seth Joyner left in 1993, and Eric Allen left in 1994.

"Once free agency came about, as players we realized the organization wasn't committed to winning, not truly committed," Joyner said. "Guys just started to leave, and eventually it fell apart."

Braman sold the team in April 1994 to Jeffrey Lurie for a then-record-high $185 million. Again, the car dealer made a good business deal. Players saw it way back in 1985.

"We knew it was different, that there was a new sheriff in town when we went to the equipment window with Rusty [Sweeney]. 'I have a hole in my sock. I need a new pair of socks.' He'd say, 'Let me see them.' I'd have to show them to him and then I'd get one pair. If you wanted another pair you had to buy them," Reichenbach said. "It was cutback time. This was the NFL. That's when we knew it was changing. It was a culture shock.

"Hey, the Eagles were an investment for him. And it was a great investment for him. Actually, as a businessman/owner he was a little bit ahead of his time. You look at how the league is run now, and how it's become such a business. That's how he ran his team back in 1985."

37

THE 2015 OFF-SEASON

Chip Kelly took an axe to the Eagles roster after the conclusion of a 10-win-but-no-playoffs 2014 season and that's what might have eventually gotten him the axe.

Kelly, with control of the Eagles personnel department after a department overhaul done over the New Year's holiday, saw a team that was good—10 wins certainly isn't bad—but just not good enough.

"I didn't think we were close enough," Kelly said after making moves that reshaped the Eagles roster. "I didn't think that the year before, either [when the team also won 10 games and lost in the first round of the playoffs]. I thought some moves had to be made. Some were performance related, some were financially motivated."

In no particular order Kelly got rid of the franchise's all-time leading rusher, their second-all-time sack leader, their starting quarterback, both of their veteran starting guards, and three-quarters of the secondary. The bottom line was that the moves dropped the Eagles to a 7–9 team and, among other things, led to Kelly's firing on December 29, 2015.

Here's exactly what transpired that led to the off-season of 2015.

The Eagles held first place at 9–3 after beating the Dallas Cowboys 33–10 on Thanksgiving Day, 2014. They lost their next three games to the Seattle Seahawks, those same Cowboys, and the Washington Redskins and were eliminated from the NFC playoffs. That's when Kelly decided changes had to be made to the roster, if he hadn't known already.

The organization had "soured" on quarterback Nick Foles even before he suffered a broken collarbone in the middle of the 2014 season, causing him to miss the final eight games. They also knew running back LeSean McCoy's contract and salary-cap number were approaching eight figures, and that was going to be a problem. There were also age issues on the offensive line as well as on the defense.

Oh yeah, the secondary—which allowed 30 touchdown passes and led the league in passing plays of both 20 yards or more and 40 yards or more—needed to be rebuilt.

That's a lot of work for a team that had gone 20–12 in the past two years. Kelly took to fixing it with his new personnel man: 30-year-old whiz kid Ed Marynowitz.

Before free agency began, Kelly released two 10-year veterans, guard Todd Herremans and linebacker Trent Cole. Both players had more than made the most of their careers, but both were aging, high-priced players whose best years were behind them. Herremans, a 2005 fourth-round draft choice out of Saginaw Valley State, had proven to be a reliable starter on the offensive line for a decade, but in year 10 injuries began to take their toll. Cole, a fifth-round pick out of that same draft, built himself up into one of the league's top pass rushers. In his 10 years with the Eagles he recorded 85.5 sacks, second only to the great Hall of Famer Reggie White (124) on the Eagles' all-time list. He had never been a good fit in the defense's new 3-4 scheme under Kelly, and with an $8 million contract and going into year 11, the move was made to let him go.

Less than two weeks later the team released its No. 1 cornerback, such as he was, Cary Williams, who had openly complained during the season about Kelly's practice methods. But Williams, a free agent addition in 2013, hadn't backed up his words with good play on the field.

That was just the appetizer. On the first day of the league season the Eagles announced (word had gotten out a day earlier) they had traded McCoy to the Buffalo Bills for linebacker Kiko Alonso and had traded Foles, along with a 2015 fourth-round pick and a 2016 second-round draft pick, to the St. Louis Rams for quarterback Sam Bradford, the oft-injured former No. 1 overall pick of the 2010 Draft.

So How Did They Do?

Chip Kelly replaced nine starters and a key backup from his 2014 Eagles team; all 10 had jobs at least for part of the 2015 season. So how did they do?

Guard Todd Herremans started the first two games for the Indianapolis Colts, was then benched and later released.

Guard Evan Mathis took a pay cut to sign with the Denver Broncos, started most of the season, and earned a Super Bowl ring.

Wide receiver Jeremy Maclin caught 87 passes (tied for 12th in the league) for 1,088 yards (18th). That was better than any Eagles receiver, but not $11 million good.

Running back LeSean McCoy was nagged by the kind of injuries that veteran backs get and rushed for 895 yards and just three touchdowns in his least productive season since 2012.

Quarterback Nick Foles started 11 games for the Rams before being benched for journeyman Case Keenum. In his 11 starts, the Rams went 4–7 and Foles threw more interceptions (10) than touchdown passes (7).

Linebacker Trent Cole signed with the Colts, played all 16 games, and recorded 32 tackles and three sacks. They were the lowest totals of his career.

Cornerback Cary Williams was released midway through the season by the Seattle Seahawks, as was Bradley Fletcher by the New England Patriots.

Safety Nate Allen began the year on injured reserve, designated to return with the Oakland Raiders. He came back for the final five games and had one interception and seven tackles.

Linebacker Casey Mathews went on the Minnesota Vikings injured reserve before the season began.

Kelly still wasn't finished. He tried to keep the one free agent the Eagles had who needed to be kept, wide receiver Jeremy Maclin, but failed. The Eagles offered Maclin a contract reported to be worth up to $10 million per year, but when the Kansas City Chiefs and Maclin's former head coach Andy Reid offered him an $11 million a year deal and a chance to return home to Missouri, he took it. Other free agents who walked were starting cornerback Bradley Fletcher (to New England), starting safety Nate Allen (to Oakland), and top backup linebacker Casey Matthews (to Minnesota).

With holes to fill, Kelly began by reshaping the secondary. He signed cornerback Byron Maxwell, who was coming off two Super Bowl appearances with the Seattle Seahawks, to a six-year, $63 million deal. He then added another former Seahawk, by way of the New York Giants, cornerback Walter Thurmond.

Maxwell, in a new system, struggled early when asked to play more man-to-man coverage. He got better, but never lived up to his lucrative contract, especially in the eyes of Eagles fans. Thurmond moved from cornerback to safety and played surprisingly well starting opposite the one player who remained in the secondary from 2014, Malcolm Jenkins.

Offensively, the plan to replace McCoy was the tandem of Ryan Mathews, a free agent from the San Diego Chargers, and Frank Gore, the veteran free agent from the San Francisco 49ers. Mathews signed. Gore balked and went to the Indianapolis Colts instead. That led to the big-time, high-priced signing of DeMarco Murray, who had led the league in rushing in 2014 with the Dallas Cowboys.

From the start of training camp, Murray was a bit of an enigma. He never seemed to find his rhythm in the Eagles offense and ended up rushing for just 702 yards, more than 1,100 less than the previous season with the Cowboys.

The One Who Got Away

All of Chip Kelly's moves during the 2015 off-season were geared toward one goal—one that couldn't be attained. He wanted to draft Oregon quarterback Marcus Mariota, who he had recruited and coached in college. Trouble was the Eagles had the 20th overall pick in the 2015 Draft and Mariota was going to be gone within the first two picks. (He ended up going No. 2 overall to the Tennessee Titans.)

Still, Kelly tried. That we know. However, what offers were actually made to either the Titans or the Tampa Bay Buccaneers, who owned the No. 1 pick, we may never know for sure. There were all kinds of rumors of players and picks the Eagles had offered. Las Vegas even set odds on whether Kelly would get his man. The betting opened at 4–1, dropped to 2–1, and was finally taken off the board. Kelly himself admitted that he tried on the night of the draft, using a poorly crafted house-hunting analogy. "We drove through the neighborhood," Kelly said. "We drove by the house. It was just too expensive."

Or maybe it just wasn't for sale.

Another former Cowboy, by way of the Cleveland Browns, Miles Austin, was signed to be a veteran receiver surrounded by talented, young players at the position. That worked out so poorly that Austin was released even before the season ended.

Then there was Evan Mathis, a veteran Pro Bowl guard, who had been injured in 2014. He wanted a raise from the $5.5 million he was scheduled to earn in 2015. The Eagles weren't going to give it to him. He skipped the team's OTAs and asked for a trade. The team tried, but found no takers on draft day.

Just as he was ready to report to the first mandatory camp, the Eagles gave him his release.

Kelly said Mathis' agent asked for a new deal or a release, and the release was granted. Mathis denied it and later signed a one-year deal in 2015 with the eventual–Super Bowl–champion Denver Broncos for $4 million.

The Eagles never really adequately replaced either of their two guards and Kelly was replaced with a week to go in the season.

38

THE '87 STRIKE

What went a long way in changing the landscape of the NFL was also instrumental in the eventual success of the Buddy Ryan Era Philadelphia Eagles.

There had been NFL strikes before 1987, and there have been strikes in the other three major American sports as well. Yet none was like the NFL players' walk-off in 1987, and nowhere was it like it was in Philadelphia.

During the 1987 season only one game was canceled due to the strike, but three games were played with "replacement" players, guys signed off the street to take the place of the NFL players who were on the picket line. That has never happened before or since.

"It's the darkest chapter in NFL history," Eagles historian Ray Didinger said. "And that [commissioner] Pete Rozelle signed off on it was sad. Thank God no real records got broken. That was my biggest worry."

In some NFL cities, the games were treated the same as any others. Fans showed up in their team jerseys and cheered for the Star in Dallas, or the *G* in Green Bay. Not in Philadelphia. Only one home game was played at Veterans Stadium during the strike and the crowd was a laughable 4,074 for the Eagles' replacement game against the Chicago Bears on October 4. Three weeks later when regular play resumed, 61,630 came to see the Eagles play the Dallas Cowboys.

"With this being the strong union town that it is, there was stuff happening outside the stadium that wasn't happening in other cities," Didinger said. "In other places, the striking players were popular. They were cheered. They were romantic figures. They made a movie out of it: *The Replacements*. That wasn't the case in Philadelphia."

THE FAKE KNEELDOWN

During the 1987 NFL Players Strike, the Eagles played the Dallas Cowboys in a replacement game in Dallas. The Cowboys, who had several star players cross the picket line and play in the game, won easily, 41–22.

Head coach Buddy Ryan was furious that Cowboys head coach Tom Landry not only used his regular players—including running back Tony Dorsett and defensive tackle Randy White, two Hall of Famers, and starting quarterback Danny White—but that he reinserted them back into the game late in the fourth quarter, when the lead was well in hand. Ryan would have his revenge.

In the first game after the strike ended, the Eagles hosted the Cowboys in the rematch. The Eagles led 30–20 and got the ball back with a little over a minute to go and the Cowboys out of timeouts. Three snaps, three kneeldowns, and the game would be over.

So on first down quarterback Randall Cunningham took the snap and took a knee. Same on second down. The clock continued to run. On third down, Ryan called a play never seen before or since.

"I didn't know we were going to do that until we did it," Cunningham said. "That was Buddy being Buddy. He said, 'Do it.' And we did it."

What Cunningham and the Eagles did was fake the kneeldown and instead throw deep. Cunningham's pass for Mike Quick fell incomplete, but Dallas cornerback Everson Walls was called for pass interference. With the ball at the 1-yard line, Keith Byars scored the rub-it-in touchdown to make it 37–20.

"You remember what happened in that [strike] game," Ryan said. "He put his front four back in the game—Dorsett, White, all of them. They said I opened a can of worms. Hell, he opened the can of worms. I closed it."

It was a crazy time, to be sure. While the Eagles replacement players practiced at Veterans Stadium every day, a few miles away at various high schools the Eagles regulars kept up practice. And Eagles head coach Buddy Ryan, who got the game plan to his players through one of their agents, made one thing clear. "He told the guys, 'If one of you comes in, you all better come in,'" remembered linebacker Garry Cobb. "Whatever you do, do it together. And that led to the team coming together. He didn't want the team to be splintered. And then after that you saw the success the team had. A lot of that had to do with what happened during the strike."

The Eagles were coming off a 5–10–1 season in 1986, Ryan's first year as head coach, and hadn't had a winning season since 1981. They split the first two games of '87, losing 34–24 at Washington and then beating New Orleans 27–17 at home.

The Eagles lost all three replacement games. First, the players they brought in weren't very good. Second, Ryan cared more about what the regular players were doing and barely coached the replacement players.

"It was costly for us financially because we lost four games' pay," linebacker Mike Reichenbach said. "And then we lost all three games they played too. That killed us for the season."

The Eagles finished that year a combined 7–8, but 7–5 in the non-strike games. One more win would have had them tie the Minnesota Vikings for the NFC's second wild-card spot. Two more wins and they would have had the second wild-card spot outright. More important, that strong finish to the season, once the strike ended, led to three straight winning seasons and a division title for the Eagles beginning in 1988.

"There's no doubt that [the strike] brought us together as a team," wide receiver Mike Quick said. "And then with Buddy supporting us through it all, it turned a lot of guys around on him too. It turned out to be a pretty big deal. But it was scary at times too."

Especially the Sunday when the "Eagles" played their only home game. "The whole thing was crazy," Reichenbach said shaking his head. "That day of the game I saw things I never saw before. People getting really roughed up going into the game. A woman throwing punches at other women. It was really out of control. But even before that and after that it was crazy. We're practicing on our own at high school fields. I had to meet [my agent, Jim Solano] every week to get the game plan from Buddy. Because we didn't know when the strike might end and we would be back and Buddy wanted us ready to play whenever that was.

"Then there [were] all the union things. [John] Spagnola was our player rep. Me and Jody Schulz were his right-hand men. So he had us meet with the union guys. We go and meet this guy, John, who I think eventually got in trouble with the law. We went and met him and he says, 'I want you to go meet this other guy down at the docks.' It was like a movie. Jody and I go down to this little diner near the docks. This guy is at the counter. We go up and introduce ourselves and he says, 'Not here'. We go out in the parking lot. We get in his car. And I can see some dents in the car. He says, 'Yeah, that's a bullet hole over there.' We're in the car and he says, 'What do you want done?' We're like, 'What do you mean?' He says, 'You want the players intimidated? You want the game to be stopped? You want the cameras to be cut? You want the television to be cut? What do you want?' I look at Jody, and this is not what we were looking for, we just wanted support."

They got support. From the unions to the fans to their head coach. Still, there were times when the players didn't know what to think. Mainly because they didn't know what would happen next. "I was a rookie during the '82 strike. For me, '87 was scary," Quick said.

"In '82, I was a rookie. I got my bonus. I didn't care. I went back to NC State and watched the basketball team play. That was the year they beat Houston [in the NCAA Championship Game]. In '87 I was more involved [with the team]. I was the assistant player rep to Spags. I was in on a couple of the meetings. But I was really scared as hell. I didn't want to lose all of this. I wanted to play football. But I went along with everyone else because it was best for all of us. And it turned out to be one of the most important years for all of us. Because of that strike the NFL got free agency. It allowed players to negotiate freely with other teams when their contracts were up. That really changed the landscape of the game and increased players' salaries tremendously."

It also turned a mediocre Eagles team into a three-time playoff team and a division winner.

39

THE DREAM TEAM

When backup quarterback Vince Young made the proclamation during training camp at Lehigh University that summer of 2011, it should have sent cringes through the rest of the team. It didn't.

Young's now infamous quote that the 2011 Eagles were a "dream team" was never disclaimed by anyone else on the roster, the coaching staff, or even the front office. They actually wore it as a badge of honor—until it all came tumbling down.

Young's exact quote, remarking on the team he like so many other big-name players had joined, went as follows: "Dream team. From Nnamdi [Asomugha] to [Dominique Rodgers-] Cromartie to Jason [Babin] to myself. I know they are going to do some more things. It's just beautiful to see where we're going to go."

In reality, the 2011 Eagles went nowhere. And most of the group of free agents and newcomers to the roster didn't last long. (Neither did head coach Andy Reid, who was fired a year later, after 14 seasons at the helm.) Worse than any of the failed free agent signings was the head coach's decision to move his trusty offensive line coach, Juan Castillo, to defensive coordinator. It was one mistake after another for an Eagles team that had won the NFC East in 2010 and was looking for more but instead ended up starting a trend that would lead to the team missing the playoffs four of the next five years—and counting.

But that summer of 2011 in the hills of Bethlehem, Pennsylvania, there was hope, there was enthusiasm, there was the dream team.

"I feel like we're the Miami Heat of the NFL," said Babin, echoing Young.

Even team President Joe Banner, who oversaw the transition of the roster and the addition of Young, Babin, Asomugha, Rodgers-Cromartie, Cullen Jenkins, Ronnie Brown, Steve Smith (not the good one from the Carolina, the injured one from the New York Giants), and Evan Mathis, got into the act. "It's a scary term," Banner said of the dream team moniker. "But somebody wrote the words 'the Eagles are all in,' and that's how we look at it. We're doing anything and everything we can. We're being aggressive about it and our expectations are high."

When the Eagles opened the season with a 31–13 blowout of the St. Louis Rams on the road, it appeared they were on their way. Then they lost at Atlanta, at home to the New York Giants and San Francisco 49ers, and then at Buffalo.

Wins at Washington against the Redskins and at home against the Dallas Cowboys got them back to 3–4, but consecutive home losses to the Chicago Bears and Arizona Cardinals turned "the dream" into a nightmare.

The Eagles finished 8–8, winning four meaningless games at the of the season to get to that achievement of mediocrity.

"We let a lot of people down," quarterback Mike Vick said at the end of that season, "including ourselves."

So where did it all go wrong for the dream team? Everywhere.

The Eagles top three draft picks that year were guard Danny Watkins in the first round, safety Jaiquawn Jarrett in the second round, and cornerback Curtis Marsh in the third round. All three were busts.

Watkins, out of Baylor started for the dream team and then part of the next year before he was benched, released, and ultimately out of football.

Jarrett, a total reach in the second round out of nearby Temple University (most teams had him as a low-round pick and some didn't have him on their board at all) was never a full-time starter, was also cut. He signed with the Jets, where he became a decent backup and special teams player.

not-so-dreamy team: coach Andy Reid
d quarterback Vince Young in 2011.

Marsh, out of Utah State, was a backup for three years before he was released and out of the league.

So there's that.

Then there was the promotion of Castillo. A week before he fired defensive coordinator Sean McDermott, Reid said there "would be no changes to the coaching staff." Castillo, who began as an Eagles assistant in 1995 under Ray Rhodes, was kept on by Reid when he took over as head coach in 1999. The hardworking assistant had come up the ranks and had made himself into a well-respected offensive line coach. Making him the defensive coordinator made no sense at the time it happened—or any time during his tenure.

And that just went along with the rest of coaching staff. Reid coaxed longtime offensive line coach Howard Mudd out of retirement and also added veteran defensive line coach Jim Washburn and his famed "wide-9" look. Neither of those moves worked either. Mudd acted as if he was still retired most of the year and Washburn's defense, forced upon Castillo, was just never a fit. A secondary with Asomugha, Rodgers-Cromartie, and holdover Asante Samuel gave up 27 touchdown passes, more than 3,400 yards, and 6 of the team's first 12 opponents scored 29 points or more.

The rest of the high-priced free agents didn't help much, either. Asomugha, an All-Pro with Oakland, looked at the end of the line when he got to Philadelphia and played like it. He signed a five-year deal as the top free agent on the market, but played just two of those years before he was gone. He totaled four interceptions in those two years, but was beaten seemingly constantly.

Rodgers-Cromartie, obtained in a trade for quarterback Kevin Kolb from the Arizona Cardinals, was played out of position as a slot corner his first year and like Asomugha was gone after his second year. To his credit, he went on to play much better with both the Denver

Broncos and New York Giants after he left. Think it might have had something to do with the Eagles defense, or the coaching staff?

Defensive tackle Cullen Jenkins came fresh from winning a Super Bowl with the Green Bay Packers to win 12 of 32 games in his two years with the Eagles.

Babin, a pass-rushing end, who actually fit the wide-9, had 18 sacks for the dream team, but fell to 5.5 in 2012. He was cut in the middle of the season just after Washburn and Castillo were both fired.

Brown, once upon a time a very high first-round pick of the Miami Dolphins, carried 42 times for 136 yards, an average of 3.2 yards per carry. He also had one of the worst plays in franchise history when on an ill-advised halfback option play near the goal line he threw a jump pass that resulted in a fumble. He was gone at the end of 2011.

Smith, still not healthy, played in just nine games and caught 11 passes for 124 yards. He also did not see the 2012 season.

There were others who never even made the final roster, like oft-injured safety Marlin Jackson, tight end Donald Lee and wide receiver Johnnie Lee Higgins.

And then there was the creator of the nickname himself, Young. The University of Texas star and No. 3 overall draft pick of the Tennessee Titans was forced into service in six different games for an injured Vick. He completed 66 of 114 passes for 866 yards with four touchdowns and nine interceptions for a dismal quarterback rating of 60.8.

With time to reflect on his summertime declaration, as the team was spiraling toward one disappointment after another, Young showed regret. "I wish," he said. "I would have just shut up and played football."

40

JURGENSEN FOR SNEAD (AND OTHER BAD TRADES)

It might not just be the worst player-for-player trade in Philadelphia Eagles history; it could be the worst player-for-player trade in NFL history. On March 31, 1964, the Eagles and first-year head coach Joe Kuharich traded quarterback Sonny Jurgensen to the Washington Redskins for quarterback Norm Snead.

"A big part of it was, Kuharich wanted to get rid of any personality on the team," longtime Philadelphia sportswriter Ray Didinger said of the trade. "And Sonny had personality."

It didn't matter that Jurgensen, who took over for Norm Van Brocklin as the Eagles starting quarterback in 1961, had already gone to the Pro Bowl and had begun to rewrite the team's record book. The big-armed quarterback threw for more than 3,200 yards in both 1961 and 1962 and had 32 touchdown passes in '61.

"The worst part was Snead came in and got hurt right away," Eagles broadcaster Merrill Reese said. "And Jurgensen went on to a Hall of Fame career with the Redskins."

Maybe even worse was that Jurgensen threw more touchdown passes in the 1960s (207) than any other quarterback, while Snead threw more interceptions (175) in the '60s than any other quarterback.

"Snead was a big, strong QB with a good arm," Reese said. "He wasn't bad. He just wasn't Sonny. He wasn't a Hall of Famer."

Jurgensen, who is in the Eagles, Redskins, and Pro Football Hall of Fame, also made the Eagles pay. In his first game against his old team, he completed 22 of 33 passes for 385 yards and five touchdowns.

In his career with Washington, he went 13–3–2 against the Eagles. Snead went 28–49–3 as a starter for the Eagles.

"After they traded me, [playing the Eagles] was always a special game for me," Jurgensen has said. "Anybody who tells you differently is lying."

Here are five other trades over time the Eagles would like to have back.

Draft Day, 1986: Eagles trade a 1986 third-round pick and a 1987 second-round pick to the San Francisco 49ers for quarterback Matt Cavanaugh

Buddy Ryan's first draft was very eventful, but not every moved paid off. Cavanaugh was never more than a backup quarterback for the Eagles. He threw a total of just 79 passes in his four years with the team, completing 38, with four touchdowns and six interceptions.

San Francisco used the draft picks to select cornerback Tim McKyer of Texas-Arlington and guard Jeff Bregel of Southern Cal. While Bregel was never more than a backup lineman for the 49ers, McKyer started 45 games in four seasons with the 49ers and was part of three Super Bowl teams, two with the 49ers and one with the Denver Broncos. He ended his career with 33 interceptions.

October 4, 1988: Eagles trade a 1989 first- and a 1990 fourth-round pick to the Indianapolis Colts for guard Ron Solt

Ryan was desperate for offensive line help and really wanted tackle Jim Lachey, who was unhappy in Oakland and asking for a trade, preferably to an East Coast team. He got it and went to the Redskins, where he enjoyed an All-Pro career. And the Eagles got Solt, who became one of the first players ever suspended for steroid use. Solt came to the Eagles after making the Pro Bowl with the Colts and before the crackdown on steroid use began. He also had a bad knee when he arrived in the middle of the '88 season. After serving a four-game suspension to start the '89 season, he started at right guard, but never came close to going back to a Pro Bowl.

With the picks the Colts received from the Eagles, they selected a pretty good wide receiver in Andre Rison and a backup offensive lineman Patrick Cunningham. "It figures," Ryan said years later. "We get Solt, and then they enforce the steroid rule."

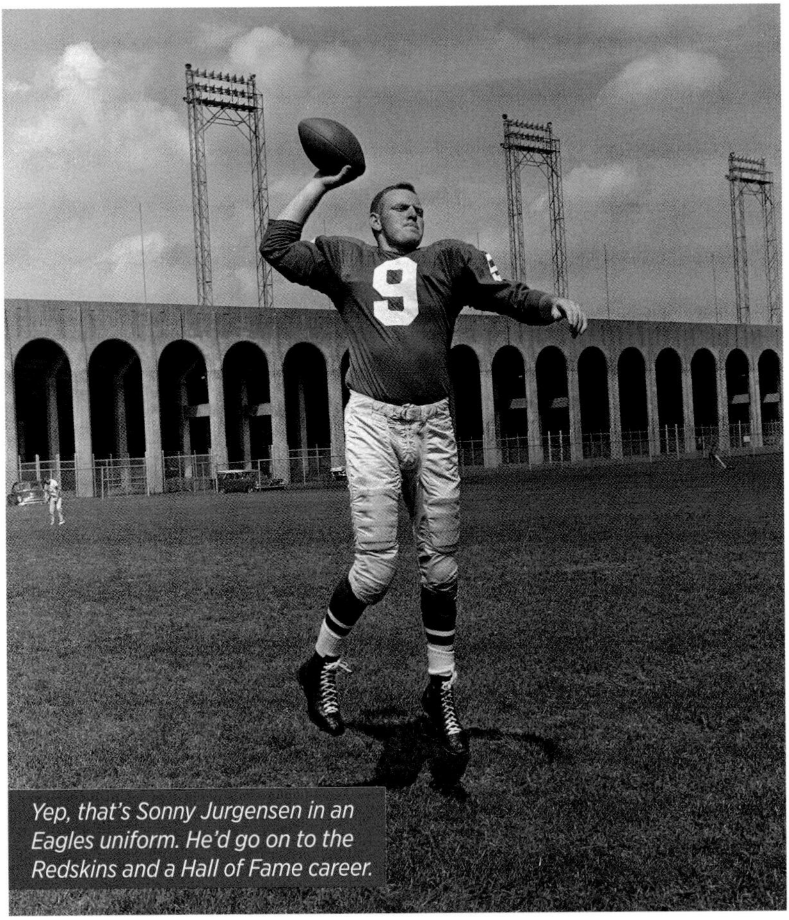

Yep, that's Sonny Jurgensen in an Eagles uniform. He'd go on to the Redskins and a Hall of Fame career.

Draft Day 1991: Eagles trade first-round picks (in '91 and '92) to Green Bay Packers for first-round pick (in '91).

Why does it always seem bad trades happen in a coach's first year? This was Rich Kotite's first draft, and he moved up from the

No. 19 overall pick in the first round to the No. 8 overall pick, selecting tackle Antone Davis of Tennessee.

The consensus was Davis and his Volunteers teammate Charles McRae were the two best tackles in the draft, but neither lived up to that billing. Davis started for the Eagles at right tackle, but mostly because he was a first-round pick.

Green Bay used the first of the picks on Ohio State cornerback Vinnie Clark, who, like Davis, never lived up to his first-round status.

In a rare off-the-cuff moment, Kotite talked about the trade before the start of a training camp practice the summer of 1991. "We got a steal," he said. "I'm not worried about next year's pick. What are they going to do with that pick?"

What the Packers did with that 1992 pick was trade it to the Atlanta Falcons for quarterback Brett Favre. You might have heard of him—three-time MVP, Super Bowl winner, 2016 Hall of Fame inductee.

Draft Day 2006: The Eagles trade defensive tackle Hollis Thomas and a fourth-round pick to the New Orleans Saints for a fourth-round pick.

One year removed from their Super Bowl run, Eagles head coach Andy Reid wanted to start to get his roster younger and shipped Thomas, a six-year starter and then a key backup, to the Saints. It was the picks that were made that rank this as one of the worst trades in Eagles history.

Moving up in the fourth round, the Eagles selected guard Max Jean-Gilles of Georgia. Jean-Gilles played in 42 games over the course of six uneventful seasons, five for the Eagles and one for the Carolina Panthers.

New Orleans, who added Thomas, also drafted a guard, Jahri Evans, out of Bloomsburg College. Evans went to six Pro Bowls and was still active as of 2016. What's worse, Evans is a Philadelphia native.

March 10, 2015: The Eagles trade running back LeSean McCoy to the Buffalo Bills for linebacker Kiko Alonso.

McCoy, in 2013, became the first Eagles back to lead the league in rushing since Steve Van Buren and set a franchise rushing record with 1,607 yards. He followed that in 2014 by rushing for another 1,319 and becoming the franchise's all-time leading rusher. His salary cap number was high, however, and head coach Chip Kelly felt he could get by without his best runner.

Alonso, whom Kelly coached at the University of Oregon, was coming off a torn ACL injury that had forced him to miss all of the 2014 season. He injured the same knee again the second week of the 2015 season, missed five weeks, and never looked right the rest of the year. He was traded to Miami in March of 2016.

McCoy, in Buffalo, battled nagging injuries himself and gained 895 yards in 12 games. It might not have been a mistake to trade away the running back; it's just that the Eagles should have gotten more than a linebacker with a bad knee in return.

41

THREE-BEAT

Jon Runyan did the math. The big right tackle-turned–New Jersey congressman had it figured out. All he needed in his 14-year NFL career was 10 more wins, not even a win per year.

"If I reverse-engineer the math over my career, if I would have won 10 more games I would have won six Super Bowls," Runyan said. "Can you imagine that? Six Super Bowls."

Runyan, much like the Eagles teams he played for, could be the King of Coming Close. He was part of the Tennessee Titans team that lost Super Bowl XXXIV to the St. Louis Rams by a yard. And there was his Eagles career.

The year after the Super Bowl loss, 2000, he signed a free agent contract with the Eagles and went to three consecutive NFC Championship Games. And lost all three. A popular joke during that 2001–03 run was that the winner of the Super Bowl gets the Vince Lombardi Trophy, the winner of the NFC gets the George Halas Trophy, and the loser of the NFC Championship Game gets the Andy Reid Trophy.

Jokes aside, the Eagles had built a good team—just one that wasn't good enough. They lost to the Rams in the '01 game, Tampa Bay in '02, and Carolina in '03.

"Each one had their own degree of difficulty and hurt in different ways," Eagles safety Brian Dawkins said. "The Rams game, that hurt, but we weren't even expected to be there. And quite frankly, we believed we could do it, but when we lost to the Rams—and we had a chance—that gave us fuel for the next year."

Going into the 2001 season, the Eagles were coming off a wild-card berth in 2000—where they won their playoff opener against Tampa Bay—before losing (for the third time that year) to the eventual NFC champion New York Giants in the second round of the playoffs.

Reid revamped his offense with two new starting wide receivers in Todd Pinkston and James Thrash, replacing Charles Johnson and Torrance Small, and a new center in Hank Fraley, taking over for Bubba Miller.

That team went 11–5 and unseated the Giants as NFC East champs. Another win over Tampa Bay in the first round of the playoffs sent them to Chicago to face the No. 2 seeded Bears in what would be the last game played at old Soldier Field. The Eagles breezed to a 33–19 win.

That set up Championship Game loss No. 1 against a Rams team then known as the "Greatest Show on Turf."

"I don't think anyone gave us a chance in that one," defensive end Hugh Douglas said. "The Rams had won the Super Bowl with basically that same team. We were the upstarts. But we gave them a hell of a game."

The Eagles led 17–13 at the half but then the Rams scored the next 16 points to take a 29–17 lead on the way to a 29–24 win. Running back Marshall Faulk took over the game for the Rams, running for 159 yards on 31 carries and scoring two second-half touchdowns.

"We had a chance. It came down to the final drive of the game," quarterback Donovan McNabb said. "We just came up short."

There were no major additions to the roster in 2002 (and in fact two starters on defense—middle linebacker Jeremiah Trotter and strong safety Damon Moore—were gone through free agency). A combination of playoff experience, the continued maturation of quarterback McNabb, another 1,000-yard season from running back Duce Staley, and a defense that held 11 of their 16 regular-season opponents to less than 20 points gave the Eagles the NFC's No. 1 seed and home-field advantage throughout the playoffs.

McNabb, who was injured during the season, returned in time for the playoffs and beat the Atlanta Falcons and Mike Vick 20–6 to get to their second NFC Championship Game, this one against a Tampa Bay team they knew so well.

"That second year, we thought we had the personnel and we had the experience of being there. Then we got home-field, and we felt that was key. We talked about that," Dawkins said. "We thought that was the team. Of all of our teams, even the one that eventually got to the Super Bowl [in 2004], I believed that team had it. We came up short and that hurt. That one really hurt."

On paper, Tampa Bay seemed to be the perfect opponent. The Eagles had beaten the Bucs the previous two years in the playoffs as well as during the 2002 regular season. The weather was going to be cold, and everyone knew the Bucs never won when the weather was cold. Tampa Bay was 1–21 when the temperature was under 40 degrees and the Bucs were 0–6 in road playoff games in their franchise history. It was also the last game at old Veterans Stadium before the Eagles were to move to the comparatively palatial Lincoln Financial Field in 2003. There was no way the Eagles could lose.

When Brian Mitchell returned the opening kickoff to the Bucs 26-yard line and two plays later Staley scored on a 20-yard run, it looked like the rout had begun. "I thought the game was over," Staley said years later. "There was no doubt in my mind we were going to the Super Bowl."

Bucs head coach Jon Gruden, the former Eagles offensive coordinator, came up with a great game plan. He kept the Eagles defense off balance with a good mix of pass and run, and the Bucs offense made enough plays to get an easy 27–10 win.

After Staley's touchdown run, the Eagles ran the ball just 17 more times; Staley got 12 carries, while Reid opted for 50 pass plays into the heart of the Bucs' defense.

One of the biggest plays of the game came late in the first quarter with the Eagles ahead 7–3. Tampa faced a third-and-2 from its own 24-yard line. Bucs quarterback Brad Johnson found wide receiver Joe Jurevicius on a crossing pattern that went for 71 yards to the Eagles 5. Mike Alstott scored on a one-yard run and Tampa Bay never trailed again.

"I still have nightmares about Joe Jurevicius." Douglas said 14 years later. "I still see him running."

The 2003 season began just as 2002 ended: with a loss to Tampa Bay.

"We closed their old stadium with a win, and we opened their new stadium with a win," Tampa Bay All-Pro defensive tackle Warren Sapp taunted the Eagles.

The Eagles were 0–2 and then 2–3 before a nine-game winning streak got them back in line for another No. 1 seed in the playoffs. This time it took a miraculous win over the Green Bay Packers. But there they were again in the NFC Championship Game, facing the Carolina Panthers. And that's where fourth-and-26 turned into third-and-none.

The Eagles had beaten the Panthers earlier in the season in Carolina, just as they had Tampa Bay the year before. But this day they did very little against their Southern foe. The Eagles offense managed just three points. The defense gave up a long touchdown pass from Jake Delhomme to Muhsin Muhammad, and running back DeShaun Foster broke six tackles on a one-yard touchdown run for a 14–3 Panthers victory.

Again, the Eagles were denied the Super Bowl.

"Then to pick yourself up, dust yourself off and go into that off-season after the Tampa loss wasn't easy," Dawkins said. "We knew we had a shot again. We had the coaches. We had the players. We had a shot. Then we face Carolina, and there was nothing about that game that I thought we would lose. We couldn't lose that game. And again we came up short."

Runyan knew the feeling. He had it with the Titans in the Super Bowl and, as it would turn out, five more times with the Eagles.

"The bigger thing is to put all that work in and come that close that many times and not win," Runyan said. "That's tough. That's real tough."

42

CHIP

His hiring created as much fanfare and hype as any coaching hire in Eagles history. Much more than that of Andy Reid, Ray Rhodes, or Rich Kotite, his three nearest predecessors, and on par with (maybe even more so) than Buddy Ryan. And when he was fired one game short of his third complete NFL season, it was as shocking as any firing of a coach in Eagles history.

Chip Kelly lasted just a little more than 35 months as head coach of the Eagles, but what a 35-month ride it was.

"Chip Kelly will be an outstanding head coach for the Eagles," owner Jeffrey Lurie said on the day he announced Kelly's hiring. "He has a brilliant football mind. He motivates his team with his actions as well as his words. He will be a great leader for us and will bring a fresh energetic approach to our team."

Kelly did all of that... and then he was gone.

So how did it all fall apart so quickly for a coach who took over a team that went 4–12 and was in total disarray the year before he got there and then won 20 games in the next two seasons?

You have to go back to New Year's Eve day 2014. That's when Eagles general manager Howie Roseman fired vice president of player personnel Tom Gamble. That set off a domino effect that resulted in Kelly with total control of the organization. It was something he never really wanted, but which he felt was necessary for success.

But wait, let's go back a little further. Roseman, who had said many times that his dream growing up was to be a NFL general manager, was instrumental in hiring Kelly in 2013. The coach, who had thrust the University of Oregon into the national limelight, had turned down the Eagles' initial offer to become their head coach—just as he had turned down the Cleveland Browns right before them and the Tampa Bay Buccaneers a year earlier.

Lurie and Roseman were moving on to the next choice, presumably Seattle Seahawks defensive coordinator Gus Bradley, when Kelly called back and changed his mind.

Roseman, who had worked his way up the Eagles' ladder on the business side but who was now in charge of personnel, had dreams of himself and Kelly becoming the decade's version of Giants tandem George Young / Bill Parcells or the Packers' Ron Wolf / Mike Holmgren. Kelly had other ideas. One of the coach's first decisions upon arriving in Philadelphia was to hire Gamble away from the San Francisco 49ers where he had a similar role. The two had gotten to know each other way back when Kelly had been the offensive coordinator at the University of New Hampshire and Gamble was a Northeast regional scout for the Indianapolis Colts and then the 49ers. They remained friendly through the years.

It wasn't hard to convince Gamble to come to the Eagles. He grew up in southern New Jersey, and his first NFL job was with the team when his father, Harry, was the team president in the mid-to-late 1980s. By 2013 his father's health had begun to fail, and a return home so his sons could be closer to their grandfather seemed like a good thing to do as well.

So Kelly had his man in the front office, but that never sat well with Roseman, who looked at Gamble as interference between him and the coach he hired instead of what he was: an experienced NFL personnel man. To say that Roseman and Gamble's relationship grew worse over time would be the understatement of the century. To this day, Gamble never mentions Roseman by name. And to hear Roseman tell it, it may as well have been Gamble who threw that first snowball at Santa Claus.

So after two 10–6 seasons, one that led to the NFC East title and one that missed the playoffs, Roseman got to owner Jeffrey Lurie and convinced him that Gamble had to go. On December 31, hours before the big ball dropped in Times Square, the Eagles dropped Gamble.

Two days later Kelly and Lurie had a sit-down, *Sopranos*-style. If Roseman whacked Gamble, then Kelly wanted Roseman whacked. He almost got his way. After a day-long meeting, with rumors flying on social media that had Kelly doing everything from quitting to getting fired to coming up with a new color scheme for the Eagles' uniforms, a decision had been made. Kelly would be in charge of the personnel department and would choose a personnel director. Roseman's lifelong dream of becoming GM had been stripped away, but he was reassigned—with a hefty raise, and would still work the team's salary cap. And Roseman's office in the team's NovaCare Complex was moved so far away from Kelly's that Gamble, who had gone back to San Francisco, might have been closer.

Suddenly, every move Kelly made as de facto general manager was scrutinized. And all the while he traded away popular players (who never won a playoff game and probably never would) and tried to build the team the way he wanted to, Roseman stayed in Lurie's ear. The two sat together in the owner's box at both home and road games. And as the team, with a whole new offensive look, struggled early in 2015 and were ultimately eliminated from playoff contention the next-to-last game of the season, Kelly was fired.

"It was a clear and important decision that had to be made," Lurie said the day he fired Kelly. "Nobody worked harder the last three years. A smart guy, it was a bold decision to hire him, and he had, certainly, some success. I wish him the very best. But the end result was mediocrity, and as the owner of the team I've got to look at the progress and the trajectory of where it's headed."

What a difference a few years make. Kelly and the Eagles appeared headed toward changing the way the game was played when he arrived in 2013. Everything was different under Kelly. The player's schedule now saw Monday as a day off and Tuesday as a work day. All around the league, for years, Tuesday had been the accepted off day. Nutrition became a major factor as players were given daily smoothies and their food intake and sleep habits were monitored. A sports science director, Shaun Huls, was hired.

> **ON THIS DATE**
>
> Two of the more polarizing figures in Eagles history, head coach Chip Kelly and quarterback Donovan McNabb, share the same birthday. Kelly was born November 25, 1963. McNabb was born November 25, 1976.

Music blared from several speakers during practice, which moved at a pace that hadn't been seen before either. This was Kelly's way, a new way, and it looked like it was going to work.

Kelly and his up-tempo, no huddle, fast-paced offense worked great for the Eagles, with Michael Vick and then Nick Foles at the controls in 2013. In Kelly's debut against the Washington Redskins on *Monday Night Football* the offense rolled up 443 yards in a 33–27 win. In that season the offense put up a franchise-record 6,676 yards, an average of 417.3 per game, and scored a franchise-record 442 points. The following year they topped the scoring mark with 474 points.

So Kelly's first two years produced the two highest scoring teams in Eagles history and he was gone before his third year ended. "I was surprised," Vick, who was with the Pittsburgh Steelers when Kelly was fired, said. "I was kind of shocked he didn't get at least another year, if not more."

The Chip Kelly/NFL story isn't over, because what he does—or doesn't do—as head coach of the San Francisco 49ers will define him. The 49ers hired Kelly just a few weeks after the Eagles fired him.

"Chip Kelly is a good coach. I know that. I have a feeling he's going to do really well there," Vick continued. "I think he'll learn from some of the mistakes he made, but I think his offense is still very good. I think it will work."

43

BOOKENDS

The similarities between them are obvious. And it's no coincidence that the Eagles didn't fare well during the span between the pairs' respective careers.

In 1975 the Eagles acquired left tackle Stan Walters in a trade with the Cincinnati Bengals, paired him with their 1973 first-round draft pick Jerry Sisemore, and watched as the two became bookend tackles in what ended with a 1980 Super Bowl run. Fast forward 25 years later to 2000, when the Eagles acquired right tackle Jon Runyan as a free agent from the Tennessee Titans, paired him with their 1998 first-round pick Tra Thomas, and watched as the two became bookend tackles in what ended with a 2004 Super Bowl run.

Déja vu?

History repeated itself for the Eagles in a good way, as Runyan & Thomas did for the Donovan McNabb Eagles' offense of the early 2000s what Walters & Sisemore did for the Ron Jaworski Eagles offense of the late '70s into '80.

In between it was a mess. Journeyman tackle after draft pick bust kept some good Eagles teams under Buddy Ryan and Ray Rhodes from achieving the ultimate success.

"If we could have put together a better offensive line, I think we would have won the Super Bowl, at least one," said linebacker Seth Joyner, who played for the Eagles between 1986 and 1993 and eventually went to Super Bowls with both Green Bay and Denver. "And then just before he got fired Buddy was looking to draft Eric Williams."

What might have been actually happened for the Eagles, first in 1975 when the team sent quarterback John Reaves, who was their first-round pick just three years earlier, and a second-round pick to the Bengals for Walters.

"I wanted to know if I did anything wrong, or what I did wrong," Walters said when he was told he was traded by the Bengals. "I went in and asked [Bengals GM and head coach] Paul Brown. He told me no, it was just a business deal. They got a backup quarterback that they needed, and a second-round pick.

"It still didn't sit right with me, then after I talked to Paul Brown, [Eagles head coach] Mike McCormack called me and I was still in shock."

Walters didn't react very well to the trade, not at first and not for a while. As a ninth-round pick out of Syracuse by the Bengals he had made himself, with the guidance of Brown and veteran offensive line coach Tiger Johnson, into a good left tackle. "There was just so much going on inside my head," Walters said. "First of all I grew up in North Jersey, right outside of the Meadowlands, so I was a Giants fan as a kid. The Eagles were a rival team. And everything I knew about Philadelphia was negative. Again, I'm from the New York area, even though it was close by, I had never even been to Philadelphia. And I didn't want to go there [then].

"And then I had Tiger Johnson as my coach with Cincinnati. To me, being drafted by the Bengals and being coached by Tiger was the greatest thing that had ever happened to me from a football standpoint. Tiger had just taught me so much about the game and how to play the game. I didn't want to leave that. And I didn't want to go to Philadelphia."

Runyan, as a free agent, had his choice of where to go in 2000, although it ultimately came down to staying with the Titans, who were coming off a Super Bowl season, or sign with the Eagles, who were coming off a 5–11 year.

The fact that the Eagles were offering to make him the highest paid right tackle in the game at the time with a six-year, $30 million deal that included a $10 million signing bonus made it a little easier to overlook the 5–11 record. And he also saw some promise in a team that was about to head to four straight NFC Championship Games.

"The business end of it was a big part of it," Runyan said. "Not only on the Eagles paying me, but the fact that they also had the cap room to sustain the contract. Tennessee had [Steve] McNair, [Eddie] George, [Brad] Hopkins, [Blaine] Bishop, [Frank] Wychek. Those guys were always having to redo their deals. And then they had guys walk because of the salary cap.

"Another thing was Brian Dawkins and I had the same agent, Ben Dogra. He had been watching Brian and told me he thought they had a pretty good defense. The only question we had was, 'Could Andy Reid run an offense?' And then the other was, 'Do they have a franchise quarterback?' And it turned out they had just drafted one."

It took Walters time to bond with his Eagles teammates and there were times when he just didn't want to be there. Finally Sisemore, the big Texan, became his roommate and a friend, and that made life in Philadelphia a little easier. "They were totally opposite kind of guys," longtime Eagles broadcaster Merrill Reese said of Walters and Sisemore. "Stan was outgoing, funny. It was what made him a good radio partner [he broadcast with Reese for 14 years]. Jerry was quiet, reserved. He didn't really say a lot. But together they formed a great pair of tackles."

By 1978 the Eagles were a playoff team, and in 1980 they were NFC champions, the two tackles were a large part of their success. Both went to two Pro Bowls in their careers with the Eagles.

"I had a hard time when I got there. I actually went into a form of depression," Walters said. "It took me a long time to get over the trade. I walked out of training camp my first year. I went home to New York. It wasn't just that I didn't like Philadelphia. I was just still very upset about the trade. I said some things I probably shouldn't have said. Keep in mind I had made the playoffs twice in three years

THE OTHER GUYS

From the time Jerry Sisemore and Stan Walters retired in 1984 until the team drafted Tra Thomas in 1998 and signed Jon Runyan in 2000, the Eagles went through nine left tackles and nine right tackles.
Here's a list of them:
Left tackles: Dean Miraldi (1984), Ken Reaves (1985), Tom Jelesky (1986), Matt Darwin (1987–89), Ron Heller (1990–92), Broderick Thompson (1993), Bernard Williams (1994), Barrett Brooks (1995–96), Jermane Mayberry (1997).
Right tackles: Leonard Mitchell (1984–86), Joe Conwell (1987), Ron Heller (1988–89), Reggie Singletary (1990), Antone Davis (1991–93, 95), Broderick Thompson (1994), Richard Cooper (1996, 98), Barrett Brooks (1997), Lonnie Palelei (1999).
And that's leaving out 1985 first-round pick Kevin Allen, who never became a full-time starter.

with the Bengals. There were guys on the Eagles at that time I don't know if they cared about winning at all. It was a bad situation. Sisemore and [Bill] Lueck took me aside, I started hanging out with them, and it made it a little better. That was a rough season though. Then Lueck got traded the next year and it was just me and Sise. We started rooming together and we got closer.

"Sise was very quiet, but every once in a while he would come out with a crazy statement that would have me rolling and laughing. He was a stabilizing force for me. He really was. I'm from North Jersey / New York. A coach says run through a wall, I say 'Why?' A guy from Texas, like Sise, just runs through it. He was the rock that kept me under control though, especially in those early years."

Thomas and Runyan weren't that much alike either. Thomas, a three-time Pro Bowl selection, was the Sisemore of his era. He was the quiet type, but when the big man from Florida State had something to say he said it with meaning. Runyan, while not as colorful perhaps as Walters, became a bit of a team spokesman. Then later, after his playing career ended, he became a New Jersey congressman.

Together with the Eagles they protected McNabb, opened holes for Duce Staley and Brian Westbrook, and allowed the Eagles to make it to the NFC Championship in 2001, 2002, 2003, and to the Super Bowl in 2004.

What Runyan also did was bring an attitude to the Eagles' offense that wasn't there when he arrived. His take-charge, take-no-prisoners attitude rubbed off not just on his linemates but the entire defense. "Oh, he made a difference," cornerback Troy Vincent said of Runyan. "All of a sudden the offense has the same kind of attitude we had on defense. That was good."

Runyan just played the game the only way he knew how. "You bring in a free agent and the guy makes his fortune in a two-minute signing, and he's going out there trying to take people's heads off. The accountability is there," Runyan said. "Coaches are saying 'If you want to get paid like him, do the same things he's doing.' It's not that complicated. But a big thing was getting guys who can play together. That's so important. We kind of worked together pretty well, me and Tra. It all kind of worked out."

Just as it did a quarter century earlier for Walters and Sisemore.

44

FROM KEVIN ALLEN TO MARCUS SMITH

There are several reasons, why Eagles fans have waited somewhat impatiently since 1960 for another NFL championship.

One of the more telling has been bad drafts—more specifically bad No. 1 draft picks. When you swing and miss in the first round of the draft year after year as the Eagles have done throughout their championship drought it comes back to haunt you. Sometimes you never catch up.

It also doesn't help when you go five straight years (1974–78) without a first-, or a second-round pick.

Here's a chronological list of the worst of those first-round misses.

1972: John Reeves, QB, Florida—Gator quarterbacks didn't make it in the NFL even back then. Reeves started seven games as a rookie, completed less than half of his pass attempts (108-for-224) and threw more interceptions (12) than touchdowns (7) for a team that went 2–11–1. It didn't take long for the team to give up on him. The Eagles traded for Roman Gabriel in 1973 and Reeves was traded, along with a second-round pick, to Cincinnati for left tackle Stan Walters in 1975.

1984: Kenny Jackson, WR, Penn State—Jackson was the No. 4 overall pick of the draft, which is why he makes the list. The Eagles drafted him primarily so he wouldn't go to the Philadelphia Stars of the USFL, who held his territorial rights. Jackson's best season was his second, 1985, when he caught 40 passes for 692 yards. You expect a lot more from a guy picked fourth overall in the draft.

1985: Kevin Allen, T, Indiana—This is the worst pick in team history when you consider all the factors. The Eagles needed a tackle in 1985, but the top three—Bill Fralic, Lomas Brown, and Ken Ruettgers—all came off the board within the first seven selections. That left the Eagles reeling and in panic mode. Instead of taking the best player, maybe a wide receiver named Jerry Rice or even trading down and getting more picks, they took Allen. He made the team as a rookie, but couldn't crack the starting lineup on an offensive line that allowed 55 sacks. In 1986, Buddy Ryan's first year as head coach, he was released. That same year he was arrested for sexual assault. As it turned out, Allen spent more time in prison than he did in the NFL.

1993: Leonard Renfro, DL, Colorado—What makes this pick especially bad, besides the fact Renfro couldn't play very well, is that he was selected with the compensatory pick the Eagles received from the league after losing future Hall of Famer Reggie White as a free agent. Trying to replace White was certainly a tough task, but Renfro lasted just two years, never recorded a sack, and was cut before the start of the 1995 season. That's a bad No. 1 pick.

1994: Bernard Williams, T, Georgia—This could have been a good pick, if Williams would have played. He actually started all 16 games his rookie season and showed promise as a tall, athletic left tackle with pass protecting skills. Then he tested positive for marijuana after the season, was suspended, and apparently never got clean because he never reapplied to the league or played again. What a shame; what a wasted pick.

1997: Jon Harris, DE, Virginia—Ray Rhodes didn't miss often, but when he did, he *really* did. You knew Harris was a bit of a reach in the first round when he said so himself. He was driving to his cousin's house to watch the second round on ESPN2 (he didn't get the channel at home) when he learned he was drafted. Harris lasted two years before he was traded to Green Bay for another first-round bust out of the same draft, tackle John Michaels.

2001: Freddie Mitchell, WR, UCLA—He'll always have the fourth-and-26 playoff catch against Green Bay, but that one play was just about all he did for the Eagles. Mitchell caught 90 passes in his four

THEY WEREN'T ALL BAD

Here's a list of the Eagles 10 best No. 1 picks.

1944: Steve Van Buren, RB, LSU—Went on to become the greatest back in team history and brought them two of their three NFL championships.

1949: Chuck Bednarik, LB/C, Pennsylvania—Played as a rookie on the second of back-to-back championship teams and then came out of retirement to help the 1960 team win another title.

1964: Bob Brown, T, Nebraska—Another Hall of Famer, who toiled on some bad Eagles teams in the '60s.

1973: Jerry Sisemore, T, Texas—Played his entire 12-year career with the Eagles and was a keystone of the 1980 NFC Championship team.

1982: Mike Quick, WR, North Carolina State—They got him by default—they wanted Perry Tuttle—but he turned out to be one of the greatest receivers in team history.

1987: Jerome Brown, DT, Miami—What could have been if he hadn't lost his life in a car accident during the prime of his career. Still a great defensive lineman.

1988: Keith Jackson, TE, Oklahoma—He started free agency and left for the Miami Dolphins as soon as he could, but he put up big numbers—242 receptions, 2,756 yards, 20 touchdowns—for the Eagles in just four years.

1998: Tra Thomas, T, Florida State—After missing early and often on the offensive line for years, the Eagles got it right with the three-time All Pro.

1999: Donovan McNabb, QB, Syracuse—Running back Ricky Williams was the people's choice in '99. Fortunately the Eagles chose McNabb, who became the most prolific quarterback in team history.

2012: Fletcher Cox, DT, Mississippi State—In 2016 Cox is just beginning to reach his potential, and a switch back to a 4-3 defense will only help that along.

years with the team and never landed anywhere else when he was released after the Super Bowl season of 2004. What's worse, wide receivers Reggie Wayne, Chad Johnson, and Chris Chambers were all on the board when Andy Reid selected Mitchell in the first round of 2001.

2003: Jerome McDougle, DE, Miami—Tom Heckert, who ran the Eagles personnel department at the time, never hid his affection for the Miami Hurricanes. So when the opportunity arose for the Eagles to move up in the draft in '03 and select McDougle they jumped at it. The defensive end cost a first and second round pick, which was a steep price for a guy who never started a game and recorded a total of three sacks in his uninspiring four NFL seasons.

2011: Danny Watkins, G, Baylor—Eagles fans knew this pick wasn't good the moment the team made the selection, as sighs of despair were heard throughout the Delaware Valley. They were right. Watkins, a hockey player from Canada and a volunteer firefighter, never really seemed to like football—and it showed in his play. He lasted just two years with the Eagles, was released and played another year, mostly on the inactive list, with the Miami Dolphins.

2014: Marcus Smith, LB, Louisville—As of this writing Smith still has time to prove his critics wrong, but it better happen soon. In two years with the Eagles, the pass rusher who in college finished second in the nation in sacks with 14.5, had 1.5 with the Eagles (and only three solo tackles as of this writing). With the Eagles changing to a 4-3 defense for the 2016 season his job could be in serious jeopardy.

45

THE 1986 DRAFT

It was Buddy Ryan's first draft as head coach of the Eagles, so it was nearly impossible to tell what was going to happen. And even if it had been possible, no one could have imagined what would transpire on those two days in April 1986.

In what was then a 12-round draft, the Eagles did the expected, the unpredictable, and made seven different trades along the way. They drafted one player Ryan said he never would, another he had said he would, and finally another who the Dallas Cowboys selected a year earlier. They drafted a punter in the fifth round who would never play a game for them and two of the greatest players in team history in the eighth and ninth rounds. When it finally shook out, the Eagles had their starting backfield for five years; a reliable, if seldom-used, backup quarterback; a starting left tackle; and two of the best defensive players in team history. All in all, that's one hell of a draft.

Let's go back and take a look at what was a whirlwind draft day in 1986.

First Round: Keith Byars, RB, Ohio State—After an outstanding career at Ohio State, the big Buckeyes running back was being talked about as a top 10 pick. There was one problem, however: a foot injury that concerned some teams.

Ryan, on his radio show the night before the draft, said about Byars, "He's a good back. But he's hurt. Our medical people call him a medical reject."

And then, with the 10th overall pick in the draft, Ryan selected him. "We were hoping that would get out and people would pick up on it," Ryan said of his comment the night before. "The clubs ahead of us ran a gut check on the Philadelphia Eagles and we passed. We're going to pass a lot of them this year."

As it turned out, Ryan was partially right about the injury concern. Foot problems throughout the early part of his career robbed

Byars of his speed and made him an ordinary runner. He did, however, develop into one of the best blocking/receiving backs in the league. As of 2016, he ranked fifth on the Eagles' all-time receiving list with 371 receptions, and later became a Pro Bowl player for the Miami Dolphins.

Second Round: Anthony Toney, RB, Texas A&M—After bashing Byars on the radio, Toney was the back Ryan praised. That led some to think the Aggies back might actually be the Eagles' first-round pick. "He's the best fullback in the country," Ryan said more than once leading up to the draft. "Sure, he's a first-round pick." And when he was still there in the second round, Ryan took him, saying, "I told you guys I liked him. Guess you didn't believe me."

Toney began his career as Byars' blocking back, and was also a good receiver out of the backfield. In their five seasons together, however, Toney outrushed Byars three times.

Second Round: Alonso Johnson, LB, Florida—After trading two of the team's starting linebackers from the year before, the position was a dire need. Johnson looked the part and had star potential. He just never realized it.

Expected to be a possible first-round selection, Johnson dropped to the second round mainly because of a failed drug test at the league's scouting combine. But that didn't deter the Eagles, who made him their selection. The big, athletic former Gator started nine games as a rookie, but off-the-field troubles, including more legal troubles with drugs, stymied his career. He played a total of just 18 games over two years, and after failing a drug test before the start of the 1988 training camp was out of the league for good.

Ryan admitted after Johnson was gone that the pick was a mistake. "I never knew anything about drugs," Ryan said. "I know too much about them now."

Third Round: Traded along with a 1987 pick to the San Francisco 49ers for quarterback Matt Cavanaugh—In a nonstop day of stories, Ryan traded for Joe Montana's backup. The Eagles already had veteran Ron Jaworski and second-year man Randall Cunningham on the roster. So something had to give.

"We're excited about him," Ryan said of Cavanaugh after the trade was made. "We think we got the best deal for the Philadelphia Eagles."

It led several to think one, or both, of two theories. Ryan didn't want Jaworski, or he didn't like Cunningham. The former was true. Jaworski, who had taken the Eagles to the Super Bowl six years earlier, started nine games in 1986 before being replaced by Cunningham. He was released the following off-season.

Cavanaugh, who threw just 79 passes in four years with the team, was never more than Cunningham's backup.

Fourth Round: Matt Darwin, T, Texas A&M—Darwin was taken by the Cowboys in the fifth round of the 1985 Draft, but never signed with his home-state team. He sat out of the entire season and reentered the '86 draft, when the Eagles took him a round earlier.

Darwin's NFL career was just as unpredictable as his draft status. He started 10 games at center his rookie season then moved out to left tackle where he started all of 1987, 1988, and most of 1989. He was a key to the playoff teams of both '88 and '89. Then, when his contract was up before the start of the 1991 season, and after battling a knee injury, he just walked away from the game.

Seventh Round: The Eagles traded starting linebacker Reggie Wilkes, also to the Atlanta Falcons, and drafted wide receiver Corn Redick, out of Cal-State Fullerton, who didn't make the team out of training camp.

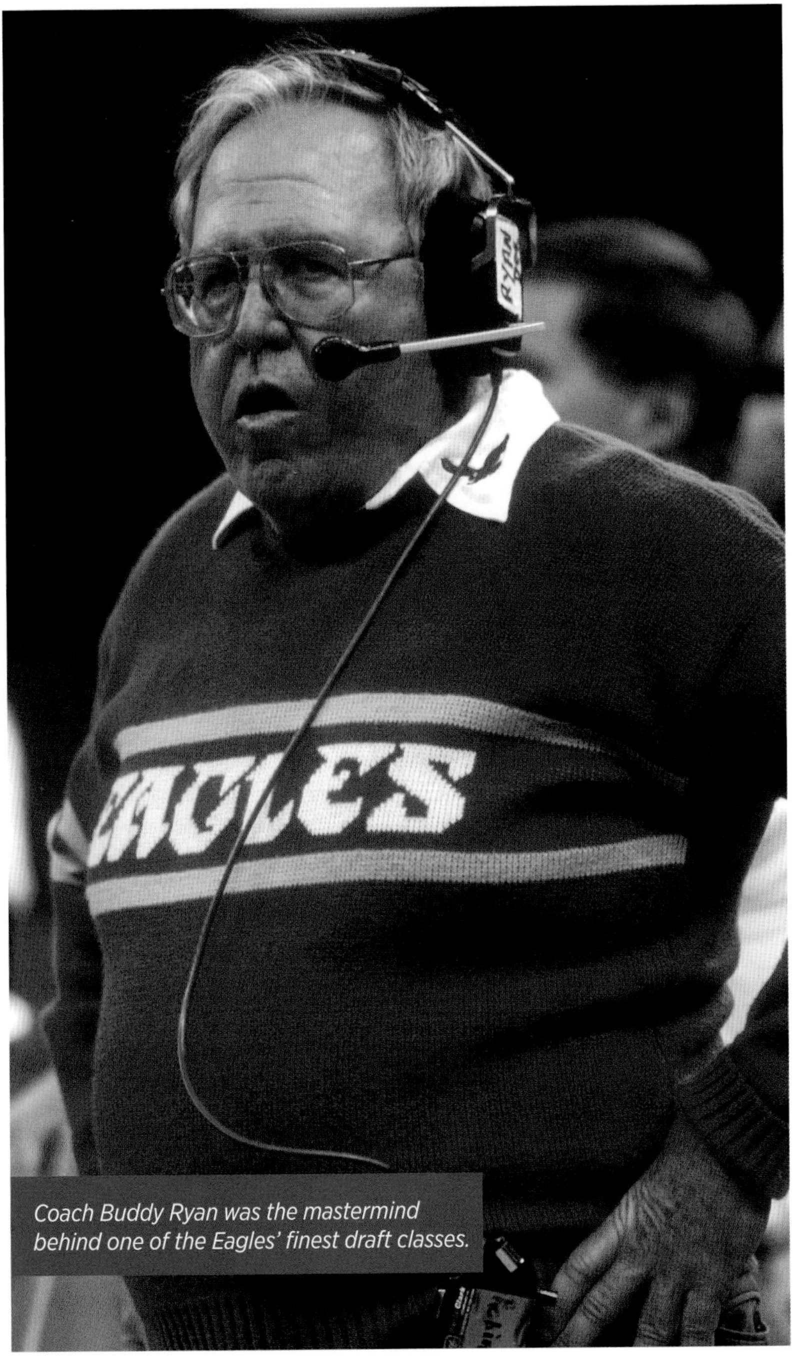

Coach Buddy Ryan was the mastermind behind one of the Eagles' finest draft classes.

Eighth Round: The Eagles traded another starting linebacker, Anthony Griggs, to the Cleveland Browns and drafted linebacker Seth Joyner out of Texas–El Paso.

"We would have liked to have gotten more for him, but it was the best we could do," Ryan said of trading Griggs.

He actually got more than he realized at the time. Joyner, who was actually among the final cuts but was re-signed after the second game of the season, became a starter by the 10th game of his rookie year. He would go on to become one of the greatest players in team history and one of the best linebackers of his time. Joyner played eight years with the Eagles (1986–93). His 37 sacks as an Eagle are seventh most in team history and the most by a linebacker. His 17 interceptions are fourth most by a linebacker, behind Bill Bergey, Williams Thomas, and Chuck Bednarik.

*Ninth Round: Clyde Simmons, DE, Western Carolin*a—At that point in his life, Simmons' claim to fame was being a Little League baseball teammate of Michael Jordan. He became much more. Simmons became a starter his second year and went on to record 76 sacks in his eight years as an Eagle, third most in team history. His 19 sacks in 1992 rank second to Reggie White's 21 sacks in 1987 for most sacks in a season by an Eagle. And his 4.5-sack game against the Dallas Cowboys in 1991 is tied with Hugh Douglas for most sacks in a game by an Eagle.

46

INVINCIBLE

Even if you never saw Vince Papale play for the Eagles, you probably saw the movie *Invincible,* which chronicled the unlikely story of a 30-year-old bartender-turned–NFL player.

"There's some Hollywood in it, but I would say 80 percent of it is accurate," Papale said of the film that starred Mark Wahlberg in the title role.

Papale's true-life story was made for the movies. "Back in 2001, NFL Films had done a piece on me to celebrate the 25th anniversary of *Rocky*," Papale said. "They did a little feature on the ESPN Sunday pregame show. The next thing I know, Disney is involved, and they wanted to know if I was OK with them making a movie of my life. Of course I said yes."

Rocky Balboa had become a Philadelphia hero, even if he wasn't real. Sylvester Stallone's 1976 Academy Award–winning Best Picture had won hearts across America, but especially those of people in Philadelphia and in particular South Philadelphia.

Meanwhile, across the street from the Spectrum, where Rocky Balboa fights Apollo Creed in the movie, a real-life *Rocky* story was happening at Veterans Stadium. "Dick [Vermeil] had just come in [as head coach] and he pulls this PR stunt," veteran safety Bill Bradley said. "He had over 150 guys come off the street and try out for the team. It seemed crazy, right? But then Vince comes out there and he really stood out. He wasn't just another guy off the street."

Papale was a college pole vault champion at St. Joseph's University, which did not have a football team. He did play briefly for the long-since-forgotten Philadelphia Bell of the World Football League. And was a star in the semipro leagues and rough-touch street games on the vacant lots of South Philadelphia.

Still, this was the NFL, and even in 1976 the NFL was the NFL. A 30-year-old man with no college football experience isn't expected to make a team. "You wouldn't think so," Bradley said. "But Vince came in that year and made the team. I mean, he made the team. They didn't hand it to him. He made it. He worked his tail off every day. And the guys certainly didn't take it easy on him. There were some guys who didn't want him to make it. But he was a good special teams player, real good. And as a back-up wide receiver, I'll tell you this, he made us work. All I know is, in practice he made us [defensive backs] work. He got us ready for Sunday."

Papale's story began in the summer of 1976 in training camp when, after the 150-man tryout, he was invited to join the team at Widener University, located in Chester, Pennsylvania, just south of the city. "We wrote stories about Vince every day in training camp," said Ray Didinger, Eagles beat writer for the *Philadelphia Bulletin* at the time. "He was a daily sidebar, but it was such a good story you had to write it."

The good story got better as the preseason began and Papale showed both his prowess on special teams and good hands on offense. That summer, as *Rocky* set box office records, Papale would lead the Eagles in receptions through their six preseason games.

"We would have been surprised if he didn't make it," Didinger said. "If you could get past the fact he was 30 years old, and a rookie, and had never played college ball, it wasn't that much of a surprise."

Vermeil, who gave Papale the chance and who was played remarkably by Greg Kinnear in the movie, says even today it wasn't just a stunt or an attempt to stir interest in a team that needed to be shaken up. In 1976, the Eagles were coming off nine straight losing seasons, and let's just say they were not the talk of the town. "It really wasn't a publicity stunt or anything like that, like people think,"

Vermeil said. "We brought him in because we thought he could help us, especially on special teams, and he did."

Papale made the final roster and opened the season with the team in Dallas where, of course, they lost to the Cowboys, 27–7. "I didn't play so well in that game," Papale said. "And Dick let me know it. I got knocked around pretty good in that one. On one play I got hit so hard I thought I had vertigo."

The following week was the home opener at Veterans Stadium, where just a year earlier Papale, his family, and friends sat in the stands and groaned as the Eagles went 4–10 in what would be Mike McCormack's final season as head coach. "There I was, on the same field where I grew up watching my heroes play for the past 10 years," Papale said. "In all reality, it doesn't get any better than that."

Then it did. In his first home game, Papale made the greatest play of his NFL career, one he will never forget. "We're playing at home and I'm really juiced up," Papale said. "All my boys are there in the stands, all the guys from the neighborhood. The same guys I used to sit and watch the game with were there and they're watching me, now. My dad was there. It was a pretty emotional day for me."

The Eagles led 13–0 early in the fourth quarter, but were forced to punt. The Giants were going to get the ball back, and then who knows. Remember, this was an Eagles team that invented new ways to lose every week. Papale was on the punt coverage team.

"They we're double-teaming me," he said. "Just as they had almost the entire game. The other team didn't want to get beat by this guy off the street. I had two guys over the top, and that's where the 'white knuckles' from the movie came into play. I always looked at the guy's hands in front of me. If his hands were in the ground to the point where his knuckles were white, I knew he was coming. I looked and I didn't see white knuckles, so I knew he wasn't charging. That gave me the advantage. I was able to split the double team and was the first man downfield."

Papale knocked the Giants blocker back into their return man Jimmy Robinson and the ball popped loose. "When he got knocked back, the ball just came right to me," Papale said. "It went right into my hands. It was crazy. I ran into the end zone, and that's the scene you see at the end of the movie. But, of course, you can't return a muffed punt. So we got the ball at the 9-yard line and eventually scored from there to put the game away."

The Eagles won that day, 20–7. It was one of just four wins on the season. But it is one Papale, who would play three seasons for the Eagles, still remembers years later. That game, that play, let him know he belonged. "That's when I was finally accepted," he said. "I went to my first team party after the game and there I was having beers with the guys I used to sit in the stands and cheer. Bill Bergey, Harold Carmichael, Frank LeMaster, Jerry Sisemore, those guys were my heroes. Now they were my teammates."

47

RAY-BOB

If a simple deal could have been completed, not just the future of the Philadelphia Eagles but the entire NFL could have been vastly changed. Ray Rhodes had been named head coach of the Eagles in February 1995, and brought in Jon Gruden from Green Bay to be his offensive coordinator. Quarterback Randall Cunningham was in the final year of his contract and did not seem like a fit for the West Coast offense that was going to be installed.

Rhodes and Gruden both knew Green Bay was looking to deal backup quarterback Mark Brunell, who was stuck behind Brett Favre and would become a free agent after the '95 season. A trade was made that sent a second-round pick and a fifth-round pick to the Packers in exchange for the quarterback.

Except it was never completed. The Eagles, more specifically president and contract negotiator Joe Banner, wanted Brunell to sign a long-term deal. The offer they made him was for five years. The quarterback, confident that he would prove himself to be one of the league's best, wanted no more than a three-year deal. The impasse was never settled.

As the draft grew nearer, the Packers tired of waiting for the Eagles to make something happen. And when the expansion Jacksonville Jaguars called and made Green Bay a similar offer, the Eagles' deal was dead.

"He wanted the chance to become a free agent after three years," Banner told the *Philadelphia Inquirer* in 1997. "That tells you something about his confidence. He knew he would be a good player and he wanted the chance to prove himself and become a free agent."

In his first year as a full-time starter for the Jaguars, 1996, Brunell took his team to the AFC Championship Game. They went back to the playoffs in 1997, 1998, and 1999. Meanwhile, the Eagles went through Rodney Peete, Ty Detmer, and Bobby Hoying at quarterback during that span and eventually Rhodes was fired after a 3–13 season in 1998.

To his credit, Rhodes never mentioned the Brunell deal publicly, or blamed anyone for failing to complete it. And even without a top-flight quarterback the Eagles still made the playoffs in 1995 and 1996. Rhodes was named NFL Coach of the Year after taking over a team that had lost its last seven games of the 1994 season and going 10–6 in 1995 with a wild-card playoff game win over the Detroit Lions.

Rhodes' strength was in his personnel decisions. His drafts, his free agent signings, and his ability to find players off the street not only helped him win in those first two years, but built the foundation for the Eagles teams that had success in the 2000s after he was gone.

"Look at the players he brought to the team who went on to have great success after he left," former Eagles linebacker Garry Cobb said. "Ray knew how to find good, tough football players. All those guys had one ingredient: toughness. They were great competitors. To be right on all those guys, that was the foundation of Andy [Reid]'s teams that went on to do so well."

Of Reid's first playoff team in 2000, three instrumental players on offense—left tackle Tra Thomas, left guard Jermane Mayberry, and running back Duce Staley—were all drafted by Rhodes. On defense, there were six starters—tackle Hollis Thomas, signed as an undrafted free agent; end Hugh Douglas, acquired in a trade; cornerback Troy Vincent, signed as a free agent; and linebacker Jeremiah Trotter, cornerback Bobby Taylor and safety Brian Dawkins, who were all drafted by Rhodes. The coach also added Pro Bowl special teams player Ike Reese through the draft and Pro Bowl kicker David Akers as a street free agent signed to a futures deal.

"I think his evaluation of talent was the best," said Eagles tackle Barrett Brooks, one of Rhodes' first draft picks. "He had a great eye for talent. Not just drafting guys either. He found guys everywhere. He doesn't get enough credit. A lot of people think Dawkins and Trotter were Andy's guys. They were Ray Rhodes' guys. And it wasn't just players. Ray knew good coaching too. Look at the guys on his staff when he was there and how well they have done."

Gruden, of course, went on to win a Super Bowl as the head coach of the Tampa Bay Buccaneers. The coach he beat in Super Bowl XXXVII, Bill Callahan of Oakland, was Rhodes' offensive line coach. Rhodes also hired another Super Bowl–winning coach in Baltimore's John Harbaugh, as his special teams coach. And highly successful college coach David Shaw of Stanford also spent a year with the Eagles as a defensive assistant under Rhodes.

"Ray left a good team behind, especially on defense," Douglas said. "He knew talent. He was an old-school, throwback coach that you loved to play for. Ray was the kind of coach, if he asked you to run through a brick wall, you would run through the brick wall because you loved him that much. I really loved him. We all did."

Rhodes was that classic players' coach. Even during that 3–13 season in 1998, the losingest season in Eagles history, his players stuck with him. Not one would blame him for what went wrong.

And years later the stars of that team still give him credit. "The belief," Dawkins said of what made Rhodes special to him. "[Rhodes and defensive coordinator Emmitt Thomas] believed what I could do. I remember Ray coming up to me one day and saying 'I see something inside of you. I coached an individual in San Francisco that you remind me a lot of, and he was talking about Ronnie Lott.' That was my hero growing up, so that meant a lot to me. I mean, I never saw that in me. But he did."

Vincent, who played for more successful coaches in Don Shula with the Miami Dolphins, Reid with the Eagles, and Joe Gibbs with the Washington Redskins, will always have a place in his heart for Rhodes. "I'll always be indebted to Ray, always will be," Vincent said. "His eye for talent, ability to scheme, and his care for his players. Ray was a joy to play for."

Rhodes did things his way. He was loyal to his players and expected the same in return. He told great stories, gave great pregame and postgame speeches—and most of the time they weren't rated PG. "When we got one of those speeches, the ones with the colorful language, we knew we were going to win the game," laughed Brooks.

Ray Rhodes is often overlooked in Eagles head coaching annals. He was an outstanding evaluator of talent and a true players' coach.

How many more games would Rhodes have won if the Eagles could have come to terms with Brunell? We'll never know, but the whole NFL landscape would have looked different. Rhodes, with a quarterback in place, would have likely stayed past 1998, which means Reid may have become a head coach somewhere other than Philadelphia. Certainly Jacksonville and head coach Tom Coughlin may not have had the success they enjoyed.

"That's right," Brooks agreed. "Who knows what would have happened? It would have been a different NFL, for sure."

48

FINAL DAYS

Two days, 20 years apart, rank as the most memorable in Eagles history. Not necessarily because of what they did on those days, but because of what was about to happen all around them. By the end of each of them, the Eagles somehow made it to the postseason when it hardly seemed possible.

Go back to the final day of the 1988 season, December 18. The Eagles took a 9–6 record into Dallas' Texas Stadium to face a 3–12 Cowboys team looking for the No. 1 pick in the 1989 draft. No problem, right? Except what the Eagles did in their game was only part of the scenario that would get them to the playoffs.

In fact, before the day's action began the Eagles could have lost to the Cowboys and still made the playoffs. Or they could have beaten the Cowboys and still missed out on the playoffs. That's how crazy it was.

"We had no idea what was going on," Eagles wide receiver Mike Quick said. "We just wanted to go out and win. Then somebody said that might not even matter. Yeah, it was kind of crazy. I'm just glad it all worked out our way."

The Eagles did win, 23–7, in what turned out to be Tom Landry's final game as the head coach of the Cowboys. He would be fired a week later and replaced by Jimmy Johnson, who would shrewdly turn that No. 1 pick into quarterback Troy Aikman.

The Eagles ended 10–6, their first winning season since 1981, but they had to wait for results from games around the country. At one point, it didn't look good. Had those scores held up, the Eagles would have been out of the postseason for the seventh straight year. Nobody broke a mirror, and the Eagles' luck turned when the New Orleans Saints came back to beat the Atlanta Falcons on a field goal in the final seconds. That meant that at least a wild-card berth was clinched. Now they hoped for more. It came down to a game at the Meadowlands between New York rivals, the Giants and Jets.

The Giants, just two years removed from their first Super Bowl title, led 21–20 late in the fourth quarter. If the Giants hung on they would win the NFC East. If the Jets, playing out the season but trying to climb over .500, could come back, the Eagles would have their first division title since 1980.

Eagles radio broadcaster Merrill Reese, instead of going to a postgame show, watched the end of the Giants game on a TV monitor in the Cowboys' press box and gave play-by-play to Eagles fans listening back in Philadelphia. Remember, this was 1988—there was no Internet and no scores popping up on your phone.

Eagles players also stayed on the Texas Stadium sideline huddled around public relations assistant Rich Burg, who was getting updates from the press box from Eagles director of public relations Jimmy Gallagher.

On the final drive of the game, the Jets moved into Giants territory and then got into field-goal range before quarterback Ken O'Brien (a future Eagle) found Al Toon for a touchdown pass with 37 seconds left to give the Jets a 27–21 win and hand the Eagles the NFC East title.

"I said 'Touchdown Jets.' and helmets went flying," Burg remembered. "Everybody started celebrating, hugging each other. It was quite a scene."

The Eagles are perhaps the only team in the history of the league to celebrate a division title on the sideline of an empty stadium. "We never did things the easy way," head coach Buddy Ryan said. "The tougher it was, the more we liked it."

It was as crazy, as it was tough. "Crazy is right," quarterback Randall Cunningham said. "That was one crazy day."

Not as crazy as the final day of the 2008 season, December 28.

The 2008 season was not a good one for the Eagles. Coming off an 8–8 season in 2007, it looked as if the Eagles were going to miss the playoffs for the third time in four years. In the middle of the season they played to a tie with a 4–11–1 Cincinnati Bengals team; and were blown out by the Baltimore Ravens 36–7. When they lost in Week 16 to the Washington Redskins 10–3, the playoffs seemed out of reach.

They were 8–6–1 going into the final game at home against Dallas and were given just an eight percent chance of making the playoffs. First they needed a few things to happen before they took on the Cowboys to even have a chance.

And those few things did.

The Houston Texans, 7–8 and playing out their schedule (but like the Jets 20 years earlier trying to get .500), came back from a 10–0 deficit and beat the Chicago Bears 31–24, dropping the Bears to 9–7. A Bears win would have kept alive their playoff chances and ended the Eagles' hopes.

One down, two to go.

With the Bears eliminated, the next team in the Eagles' way was the Tampa Bay Buccaneers. They were hosting the Oakland Raiders, who at 4–11 really had nothing to play for, except that Raiders pride. In an even more shocking upset, the Raiders went into Tampa, trailed by 10 in the fourth quarter and scored the final 17 points led by quarterback JaMarcus Russell, to beat the Bucs 31–24 (coincidentally the same score as the Texans-Bears game). The loss dropped Tampa Bay to 9–7 and out of the playoffs.

Two down, one to go.

Now it simply came down to the Eagles (8–6–1) vs. the Cowboys (9–6). The winner of the game would earn the final NFC wild-card spot.

"We turned off the TVs in the locker room because we needed the guys to forget everything else and just focus on the Cowboys," Eagles head coach Andy Reid said. "But we could all hear the roar of the crowd. We knew something pretty good was happening."

With everything that had just gone right for them, the Eagles couldn't blow their chance and lose to the Cowboys. Things started a little shaky when the teams traded field goals in the first quarter. The Eagles then put on a second-quarter blitz with 24 points on the way to a 44–6 rout, earning a playoff berth that eventually led to a trip to the NFC Championship Game.

"You just never know," quarterback Donovan McNabb said. "That's why you play it out. We needed to have a lot of things happen. Most people probably didn't think they would. But they did. Then, most important of all, we had to go beat the Cowboys."

McNabb threw for two touchdowns and ran for another and the Eagles defense sacked Cowboys quarterback Tony Romo three times, forced five turnovers, and scored two more touchdowns, one each by defensive end Chris Clemons and nickel cornerback Joselio Hanson.

"A lot had to go right for us that day," Hanson said. "Whatever happened, we wanted to beat the Cowboys. As it turned out, everything went our way. It felt like a miracle."

Just as it had 20 years earlier.

49

DOGS AND DOG BONES

There was optimism for the Eagles going into the 1975 NFL season. A three-game winning streak at the end of 1974 got the team to 7–7, their first non-losing season in eight years. But that optimism dissipated rather quickly.

The Eagles opened the 1975 season with a loss at home to the New York Giants (who were coming off a dismal 2–12 season) and then went to Chicago and lost to the Bears (who were in the midst of back-to-back 4–10 seasons).

Eagles head coach Mike McCormack wasn't happy, and he let it be known at his weekly Monday afternoon press conference the day after the Bears loss. As longtime Philadelphia sportswriter and Eagles historian Ray Didinger tells it, McCormack's anger that day led to one of the more interesting press exchanges in Eagles history, and as it would turn out, eventually led to the coach's firing. Tom Brookshier, one of the better players in Eagles history and now a television broadcaster, asked the question that got it all started. "Brookie just asked him flat out," Didinger recalled. "C'mon, Mike, just say it. How many dogs do you have on the roster?"

Questions such as that happen from time to time at press conferences around the country, but for the most part they go unanswered. Coaches will either refute the premise or ignore it and move on to the next question. That day Brookshier caught McCormack at either the right—or wrong—time.

"We're thinking he's not going to answer that," remembered Didinger, who was covering the team for the *Philadelphia Bulletin* at the time. "But I don't know if Mike was just that mad at how they played or what, but he thinks about it for a few seconds and says, 'You mean real mutts? Two.' Now the next question of course is who are they? He didn't go there. But that's the worst thing now because he's indicted everyone."

Maybe McCormack was trying to light a fire under his underachieving team. If that was the motive, it might have worked. The following Sunday they handled a decent Washington Redskins team 26–10. But that extra motivation didn't last long. The Eagles lost their next five games to drop to 1–7 on another season gone terribly wrong. The fourth of those five straight losses was a *Monday Night Football* game against the Los Angeles Rams. And it was the worst of them all. And Eagles fans were ready for it.

They chanted in unison "AL-PO, AL-PO", as in the brand of a popular dog food. Some creative fans brought a giant dog bone to the game that had the message, HEY, BEAGLES, HERE'S YOUR DINNER scripted across the front. The bone got passed around the lower level of the stands at Veterans Stadium, and when it got thrown onto the field it drew the loudest ovation of the night, according to those who were there.

Oh yeah, the Rams won the game 42–3.

"Yeah, I saw the bone," linebacker Bill Bergey recalled years later. "And there were other fans wearing dog masks. My first reaction was, 'Why?' Why would anyone go to that much trouble to humiliate us? I mean, it took time to make that [bone]. And how did they get it into the stadium? But the way we played that night, we probably deserved it."

Owner Leonard Tose, interviewed on national radio during halftime of the game, was furious. "In seven years, we haven't made any progress at all in my opinion," he said dating back to when he bought the team in 1969.

There were reports that Tose was going to fire McCormack the next day, but he waited and let him coach out the remainder of a season that would finish 4–10 and in last place in the NFC East. Tose fired him the day after a season-ending win against the Redskins.

Years earlier, when McCormack was hired in 1973 to replace the fired Ed Khyat, it was seen as sort of a coup for the Eagles. McCormack was a great player at the University of Kansas and then with the Cleveland Browns, under Paul Brown, where he was a part of back-to-back NFL Championships in 1954 and 1955. He was a Pro Bowl tackle on a line that blocked for Hall of Fame running back Jim Brown. McCormack retired as a player in 1962. After coaching in the College All-Star Game for four years, he was hired as an assistant coach with the Washington Redskins. He worked under his former Browns teammate and Hall of Fame quarterback Otto Graham and eventually for George Allen. In his final year with the Redskins, the team went to the Super Bowl and lost to the undefeated Miami Dolphins. So for the Eagles to get a coach who had been mentored by Brown, Graham, and Allen—well, there was a reason for optimism from a franchise that hadn't done much winning since 1960.

"I spent six weeks investigating coaching possibilities," Tose said after hiring McCormack. "Mike was No. 1 from the start. I wanted a man with class. I wanted a man associated with winning football. I wanted a knowledgeable man who could get along with his players. Mike is all of that and more."

McCormack brought Allen's "the future is now" approach to the Eagles. Draft picks were traded en masse for veterans, and unfortunately most of the trades failed.

In June 1973 the Eagles traded two future first-round picks to the Rams for 33-year-old quarterback Roman Gabriel, who had named his first son Ram. He never named any of his other children Eagle. Prior to the 1973 draft the Eagles also sent a second-round pick and future fourth-round pick to Baltimore for running back Norm Bulaich, who played one year for them and gained 152 yards on 50 carries.

In 1975 the Eagles didn't have a draft pick until the seventh round. Gabriel had cost them their first-rounder; the rest went for the lot of defensive tackle Jerry Patton, linebacker Dick Absher and running back John Tarver. None of those three played more than a year for the Eagles and only Patton ever started.

In 1976 their first-round pick was spent on quarterback Mike Boryla, who in his three seasons with the Eagles threw 29 interceptions and 20 touchdown passes. The second-round pick was dealt for left tackle Stan Walters, in one of the rare good moves.

And in 1977 the Eagles didn't pick until the fifth round after trading for linebacker Bill Bergey, another trade that worked.

It didn't work, however, for McCormack, in Philadelphia. He would go on to coach under Brown with the Bengals before becoming head coach of the Seattle Seahawks, and was then instrumental in getting the expansion Carolina Panthers into the league in 1995. He died of heart problems in 2013.

ALL-TIME TEAM

There are a lot of factors to be considered when picking a team that spans eight different decades.

It isn't easy to compare a player from the 1940s and '50s with one from the 2000s. Who knows how they would have competed in today's game, just as it's difficult to know how today's players would have fared years ago.

In selecting this all-time Eagles team factors such as how dominant was the player in his time; how important was he to his team; and how successful was he and the team were all weighed equally.

So here's the Eagles' All-Time Team.

Quarterback: Donovan McNabb (1999–2009)— If this were just for a single season an argument could be made for Norm Van Brocklin's 1960, the last time the Eagles were champions. All-time, however, McNabb is the easy choice. The six-time Pro Bowl selection, McNabb is the Eagles' all-time leader in completions, yards, and touchdowns. And the most telling stat of them all is his nine playoff wins, which is only one less than the organization has won without him.

Running Backs: Steve Van Buren (1944–51) and Brian Westbrook (2002–09)—Van Buren is without a doubt No. 1. He dominated during his era, became the Eagles first 1,000-yard rusher and won four league rushing crowns. He also led the Eagles to two of their three NFL titles. His 69 rushing touchdowns—accomplished in just 83 games—is still a team record.

Westbrook gets the slight edge over Wilbert Montgomery and LeSean McCoy because of his ability to change the course of a game and his success in the postseason. His 5,995 rushing yards are third all-time on the Eagles' list, as are his 426 receptions. His 9,785 total yards top the all-time list.

Wide Receivers: Tommy McDonald (1957–63), Harold Carmichael (1971–83), and Mike Quick (1982–90)—There's no doubt about this trio when it comes to Eagles history.

McDonald, a Hall of Famer, caught 66 touchdown passes in just 88 games and his 19.2 average yards per catch is also best in team history. He was also an instrumental part of that last championship team in 1960.

Carmichael is the team's all-time leader in receptions, yards, and touchdowns. And it's scary to think the kind of numbers the 6'8" Carmichael would have put up if today's rules had been in place.

Quick, whose career was cut short by knee injuries, is third all-time in yards, sixth in receptions, and third in touchdowns. But when it comes to pure receiving skills and talent, he may be No. 1.

Tight End: Pete Pihos (1947–55)—If Keith Jackson would have stuck around for more than four years, who knows? But he left as a free agent as soon as he could. They didn't call it tight end in Pihos' time, but that's what he was. And he was very good at it. He caught 373 passes, fourth on the all-time list, with 61 of them for touchdowns at a time when teams didn't throw the ball the way they do today. He was also a huge part of the back-to-back championship teams in 1948 and 1949.

Offensive Line: Al Wistert (1943–51), Chuck Bednarik (1949–62), Bob Brown (1964–68), Jerry Sisemore (1973–84), and Tra Thomas (1998–2008)—Instead of trying to pick two tackles, two guards and a center, I've chosen the five top offensive linemen.

Bednarik, who went to eight Pro Bowls and is considered perhaps the greatest Eagle ever, and Brown, who went to three Pro Bowls in five years, are both in the Pro Football Hall of Fame. Wistert probably should be; in his nine years with the Eagles, he was named All-Pro eight times.

Sisemore was considered a cornerstone on the Dick Vermeil–coached teams that continually improved and ultimately reached the pinnacle in Super Bowl XV. Thomas, drafted by Ray Rhodes, was a key to Andy Reid's teams that went to five NFC Championship Games and one Super Bowl.

Stan Walters, Jason Peters, and Jon Runyan were all highly considered here as well.

Defensive Ends: Reggie White (1985–92) and Clyde Simmons (1986–93)—White was the greatest defensive end of his time, and right alongside Lawrence Taylor as the greatest defensive player of his time. His 124 sacks in 121 games with the Eagles is just an incredible statistic.

Simmons is so often overlooked because he played opposite White. The low-round 1986 draft pick out of Western Carolina was a great player in his own right. He was as tough against the run as he was as a pass rusher, racking up 76 sacks for the Eagles. His 19 sacks in 1992 are the second most in a season in Eagles history.

Defensive Tackles: Jerome Brown (1987–91) and Charlie Johnson (1977–81)—Brown had emerged as one of the best defensive tackles in the game when his life was cut short in a tragic car accident in the summer of 1991. Who knows how great a player he would have become?

Johnson was a classic nose guard during the Dick Vermeil Era in Marion Campbell's 3-4 defense, tying up two blockers on almost every play. He went to three straight Pro Bowls from 1979 to 1981.

Linebackers: Bill Bergey (1974–80), Chuck Bednarik (1949–62), and Seth Joyner (1986–93)—Bergey was already a Pro Bowl player when the Eagles acquired him in a trade from Cincinnati. And he went to four more with the Eagles. A sideline-to-sideline player,

Bergey was the key in Dick Vermeil's rebuilding effort in the late 1970s that led to Super Bowl XV.

Bednarik makes the team on both sides of the ball. And it's impossible to argue with either selection, which should tell you just how good he was. The Eagles couldn't have won the 1960 Championship without him.

Joyner did it all for the Eagles in his eight years with the team. His 37 sacks and 17 interceptions as an Eagle and as a linebacker rank with the greatest players at his position.

Tommy McDonald routinely made great grabs like this one, although he typically did them wearing a helmet.

Cornerbacks: Eric Allen (1988–94) and Troy Vincent (1996–2003)—The Eagles have had several good cornerbacks in their history, but none better than these two.

Allen is the Eagles' co-leader all time in interceptions with 34 and did it in just seven years. He also returned five of them for touchdowns, which is the most in team history.

THE VOICE OF THE EAGLES

On the last page of his autobiography, *It's Gooooood*, Merrill Reese writes, "If you ever read that Merrill Reese has decided to retire from his job as play-by-play man for the Eagles, it is a boldfaced lie. They will have to take me kicking and screaming and clutching the microphone. Because I will never willingly retire... I want to do this forever."

Forever is a long time. And so is 40 years, which is how many years Reese has broadcasted the Eagles going into the 2016 season.

"Amazing isn't it?" marveled Stan Walters, Reese's broadcast partner for 14 years. "First of all, if it wasn't for Merrill I would have never lasted 14 years. I would have gotten fired long before that. He always made sure I was on time, didn't miss the bus, stuff like that.

"Somebody one time said he and I are good together because Merrill is a rabid Eagles supporter and I was more of the cynical guy. Merrill would say, 'What a great catch.' And I would say, 'It was kind of lousy defense by the defender.' But Merrill loves the Eagles. I think he takes winning and losing [harder] than the players. I've been gone a while now, and I wouldn't mind going back and doing one game for fun. But to do a whole season, I had enough. I don't know how he could do it for 40 years. Like I said, it's amazing."

Mike Quick took over for Walters in 1998 and has worked alongside Reese ever since. He echoes the same sentiments. "I don't think you could find a better voice for a team," Quick said. "He's going into his 40th season and is still as strong as ever. There is no one I'd rather be in the booth doing the game with than that guy. When you hear him doing a game you can tell how much he cares. You hear it in his voice, good and bad. Oh, there's a big difference when the team is doing well and when the team isn't doing well."

Good or bad, for 40 years Eagles fans have heard it all from the same voice, the only Voice of the Eagles.

Vincent had 28 interceptions as an Eagle, but was known as much for being an excellent run-support cornerback and also neutralizing wide receivers. He went an entire season (2002) without allowing a touchdown pass.

Safeties: Brian Dawkins (1996–2008) and Bill Bradley (1969–76)—This pick was rather easy as well.

Dawkins, the most popular player in Eagles history, was a safety like no other. He and Bradley share the interceptions mark with Allen, with 34 apiece. And he was just as well known for his crushing hits both in the running game and the passing game.

Bradley suffered through eight non-winning seasons with the Eagles, but that didn't stop him from being a great player and a three-time Pro Bowl selection.

Kicker: David Akers (1999–2010)—Throughout his career with the Eagles the team rarely had to worry about the kicking game. Akers is the team's all-time leading scorer by more than 400 points. He connected on 83 percent of his field goal attempts and has four of the team's eight longest field goals.

Punter: Donnie Jones (2013–present)—This might have been the toughest pick of them all. Joe Muha from the 1949–50 title teams was very good, as were Sean Landeta and Jeff Feagles.

It's Jones' numbers that jump off the page, however. In three years, going into the 2016 season, he's the team's all-time leader in gross average (45.29) and net average (40.4), with a good sample size of punts in 244. He's also put 96 of those 244 punts inside the 20-yard line—that's 39 percent. To put that in perspective, Landeta, who was also very good, put 96 of 376 punts inside the 20 (26 percent).

ACKNOWLEDGMENTS

There are so many people who were so helpful in making this project happen.

To former *Trenton Times* sports editor Jim Gauger, who took a big chance and gave me the chance to cover the Eagles way back in 1985.

To Gary Schnorbus, Harvey Yavener, and the late Harold "Bus" Saidt, you couldn't have been better mentors.

To Linda Hewitt and my other friends and family who understood when I said, "No, I can't. I have to get the book finished."

To Eagles public relations director Derek Boyko, whose help was instrumental and who went out of his way on more than one occasion.

To all the former players, along with Ray Didinger and Merrill Reese, who took the time to share their memories, which made this book possible.

To Eddie Martinez and Steve Dacey, without whose help the book would never have gotten finished on time.

To everyone at Triumph Books for presenting me with this opportunity.

And finally to my daughter, Erica, who makes it all worth it.